Opera Omnia

Volume VI

Cultures and Religions in Dialogue

Part Two

Intercultural and Interreligious Dialogue

Opera Omnia

I. Mysticism and Spirituality
Part 1: Mysticism, Fullness of Life
Part 2: Spirituality, the Way of Life

II. Religion and Religions

III. Christianity
Part 1: The Christian Tradition (1961–1967)
Part 2: A Christophany (1978–2002)

IV. Hinduism
Part 1: The Vedic Experience: Mantramanjari
Part 2: The Dharma of India

V. Buddhism

VI. Cultures and Religions in Dialogue
Part 1: Pluralism and Interculturality
Part 2: Intercultural and Interreligious Dialogue

VII. Hinduism and Christianity

VIII. Trinitarian and Cosmotheandric Vision

IX. Mystery and Hermeneutics
Part 1: Myth, Symbol, and Ritual
Part 2: Faith, Hermeneutics, and Word

X. Philosophy and Theology
Part 1: The Rhythm of Being
Part 2: Philosophical and Theological Thought

XI. Sacred Secularity

XII. Space, Time, and Science

Opera Omnia

Volume VI
Cultures and Religions in Dialogue

Part Two

Intercultural and Interreligious Dialogue

Raimon Panikkar

Edited by Milena Carrara Pavan

ORBIS BOOKS
Maryknoll, New York 10545

ORBIS BOOKS
Maryknoll, New York 10545

Fathers and Brothers MARYKNOLL

Founded in 1970, Orbis Books endeavors to publish works that enlighten the mind, nourish the spirit, and challenge the conscience. The publishing arm of the Maryknoll Fathers and Brothers, Orbis seeks to explore the global dimensions of the Christian faith and mission, to invite dialogue with diverse cultures and religious traditions, and to serve the cause of reconciliation and peace. The books published reflect the views of their authors and do not represent the official position of the Maryknoll Society. To learn more about Maryknoll and Orbis Books, please visit our website at www.maryknollsociety.org.

Library of Congress Cataloging-in-Publication Data

Names: Panikkar, Raimon, 1918–2010, author. | Carrara Pavan, Milena, editor.
Title: Cultures and religions in dialogue / Raimon Panikkar ; edited by Milena Carrara Pavan.
Description: English edition. | Maryknoll : Orbis Books, 2018– | Series:Opera omnia ; Volume VI | Includes bibliographical references and index.
Identifiers: LCCN 2017052757 (print) | LCCN 2018006405 (ebook)
ISBN 9781608337460 (part 1 : e-book) | ISBN 9781626982802 (part 1 : cloth)
ISBN 9781608337675 (part 2 : e-book) | ISBN 9781626983014 (part 2 : cloth)
Subjects: LCSH: Religions.
Classification: LCC BL80.3 (ebook) | LCC BL80.3 .P36 2018 (print) | DDC 201/.5—dc23
LC record available at https://lccn.loc.gov/2017052757

Series Foreword

All the writings it is my privilege and responsibility to present in this series are not the fruit of mere speculation but, rather, autobiographical—that is, they were first inspired by a life and praxis that have been only subsequently molded into writing.

This *Opera Omnia* ranges over a span of some seventy years, during which I dedicated myself to exploring further the meaning of a more justified and fulfilled human lifetime. I did not live for the sake of writing, but I wrote to live in a more conscious way so as to help my fellows with thoughts not only from my own mind but also springing from a superior Source, which may perhaps be called Spirit—although I do not claim that my writings are in any way inspired. However, I do not believe that we are isolated monads, but that each of us is a microcosm that mirrors and impacts the macrocosm of reality as a whole—as most cultures believed when they spoke of the Body of Śiva, the communion of the saints, the Mystical Body, *karman*, and so forth.

The decision to publish this collection of my writings has been somewhat trying, and more than once I have had to overcome the temptation to abandon the attempt, the reason being that, though I fully subscribe to the Latin saying *scripta manent*, I also firmly believe that what actually matters in the final analysis is to live out Life, as witnessed by the great masters who, as Thomas Aquinas remarks in the *Summa* about Pythagoras and Socrates (but not about Buddha, of whom he could not have known), did not write a single word.

In the twilight of life I found myself in a dark forest, for the straight path had been lost and I had shed all my certainties. It is undoubtedly to the merit of Sante Bagnoli, and of his publishing house Jaca Book, that I owe the initiative of bringing out this *Opera Omnia*, and all my gratitude goes to him. This work includes practically all that has appeared in book form, although some chapters have been inserted into different volumes as befitted their topics. Numerous articles have been added to present a more complete picture of my way of thinking, but occasional pieces and almost all my interviews have been left out.

I would like to make some practical comments which apply to all the volumes:

1. In quoting references, I have preferred to cite my previously published works following the general scheme of my publications.
2. Subject matter rather than chronology has been considered in the selection, and thus the style may sometimes appear uneven.

3. Even if each of these works aspires to be a self-sufficient whole, some ideas recur because they are functional to understanding the text, although the avoidance of unnecessary duplication has led to a number of omissions.

4. The publisher's preference for the *Opera Omnia* to be put into an organic whole by the author while still alive has many obvious positive features. Should the author outlive the printer's run, however, he will be hard put to help himself from introducing alterations, revisions, or merely adding to his original written works.

I thank my various translators, who have rendered the various languages I have happened to write in into the spirit of multiculturalism—which I believe is ever relevant in a world where cultures encounter each other in mutual enrichment, provided they do not mislay their specificity. I am particularly grateful to Milena Carrara Pavan, to whom I have entrusted the publication of all my written works, which she knows deeply, having been at my side in dedication and sensitivity during the last twenty years of my life.

R.P.

CONTENTS

SECTION I: INTERCULTURAL AND INTERRELIGIOUS DIALOGUE

Part One: The Intrareligious Dialogue

SECTION II: EXAMPLES OF DIALOGUE

Abbreviations

AV	*Atharva Veda*
BG	*Bhagavad-gītā*
BS	*Brahma Sūtra*
BU	*Bṛhadāraṇyaka Upaniṣad*
CU	*Chāndogya Upaniṣad*
JabU	*Jābāla Upaniṣad*
MB	*Mahābhārata*
MaitU	*Maitrī Upaniṣad*
P.G.	*Migne, J. P. Patrologia Cursus Completus, Series Graeca (Migne, Paris, 1857–66)*
P.L.	*Migne, J. P. Patrologia Cursus Completus, Series Latina (Migne, Paris, 1844–55)*
RV	*Ṛg Veda*
SB	*Śatapatha Brāhmaṇa*
SU	*Śvetāśvatara Upaniṣad*
TB	*Taittrīya Brāhmaṇa*

For the Bible the usual abbreviations are employed.

Introduction

The second book of the volume *Cultures and Religions in Dialogue* essentially concentrates on intercultural and interreligious dialogue as a path to survival, as we said in the introduction to the first book, where we developed the various aspects of pluralism, which is the basis of true dialogue, insofar as culture gives linguistic expression to religion and religion opens up the horizon to dialogue.

An Emerging Myth

One of the emerging myths of our time is that of the unity of the human family, seen from the global viewpoint of a culture of Man that embraces all civilizations and religions as many facets, mutually enriching and stimulating. This may be what Pierre Teilhard de Chardin, in his inimitable language, tried to express when he spoke of the need for "a field of sympathy on a planetary scale."

The truth is that we are still far from having accepted this myth. But since man cannot live without myths, there is a malaise among most of our contemporaries: they clearly sense the inadequacy of their own cultures and religions. And even if they discover, little by little, that no one has a monopoly on goodness and truth, they cannot yet work out what will emerge from the breakdown of their ways of life. We lack a universal horizon, a reference point that is accepted because it is acceptable, a unifying myth for our age. But it is in the process of being born; we can already see it dawning on the horizon.

It is quite curious and significant that this emerging myth presents itself as the reverse, so to speak, of the old myth of monogenism that put forward the unity of the human race by underlining its unique origin. The unity of mankind presents itself to us today much less in its beginning than in its end. We seem more inclined to think that we tend toward an omega point, that it is a spirit of convergence that draws us, rather than a physical (or metaphysical) force that propels us. Whatever may be the origin or causes of ethnic, cultural, and religious differentiation, we are as if drawn to believe that men are called to the sharing and integration of diverse human experiences in a harmonious whole, but without monochrony or monotony.

Some, perhaps, would rather lament the broken myths of our times and deplore the breakdown of ancient beliefs. It is no use denying this side of the coin while highlighting the other, more brilliant, more promising, or at least more interesting side.

My objective here will be to uncover this emerging myth.

We may study the history of the encounter between the religious traditions of mankind on the basis of the following typology. Of course, reality is much more complex and varied, and the bare-bones typology that I offer here may help us understand, but is generally not found in the pure state.

Isolation and Ignorance

Each culture has its own life and does not occupy itself with others. The cultures are so provincial and closed into themselves that, outside of the unavoidable contacts with neighbors, they hardly show any interest in each other. The *other* is not a problem. Theoretically speaking, we cannot say that each culture believes it is self-sufficient, since the question does not even arise. Basically, the other does not exist. Each culture considers itself de facto able to overcome its own difficulties. At best it may accept a certain learning, but not an expansion.

Indifference and Contempt

As the contact between cultures becomes an ongoing and inevitable thing, only a few rare, curious minds start admiring the outsider. Once one has overcome the shock of novelty with all that this implies—curiosity, interest, marvel, and even fear, suspicion, and self-defense—the reaction that follows is often guided by the conviction that our culture, our religion suits us more than any other; of course, we may want to perfect some of its aspects but only in order to better compete with the foreigner. The *other*, at best, is nothing more than a problem of rivalry.

Condemnation and Conquest

The moment contacts between civilizations take on a more stable character, the competition no longer is a question of rivalry but tends to actively challenge others, to justify converting them to our views by any honest means. The other almost becomes a threat we must do away with, a challenge to be faced. The maneuvers undertaken under this approach will vary according to the social and religious characteristics of each civilization.

Coexistence and Communication

It is not so necessary today to insist on the fact that, outside of a few exceptions, conquest and domination do not stand the test of time. Sooner or later, people realize that mutual tolerance and peaceful and sincere communication are the source of reciprocal and durable advantages. The *other* begins to intrigue us. We discover that he is capable, in his own way, of achieving what, until now, we thought possible only by means of which we thought ourselves to be sole possessors. This applies to all areas of culture: religious, political, economic, and so on. The balance between a progressive invasion by the *other* and loyalty to one's own culture is hard to maintain and constantly threatened. To learn from the other, to integrate without being alienated by him, depends on a personal equation whose historical and cultural coefficients are very precarious.

Convergence and Dialogue

In the long run, systems of thought seem to converge on all levels; cross-fertilization seems not only possible but desirable. The boundaries and limits of personal identity become less impenetrable; the incompatibilities vanish. Some misunderstandings and prejudices have yet to be overcome; techniques of *rapprochement* and of hermeneutics have yet to be created. True dialogue requires not only a welcoming and listening disposition, but also a capacity to understand, or even the possibility to do so. The *other* starts to become the other pole of ourselves. Comparison leads to complementarity. New ways of life appear, not without causing, often, victims on both sides: on the side of identity as on the side of otherness.

I would like to give an example of this encompassing dynamism that is found everywhere. It is an undeniable fact that some of today's Western youth are irresistibly attracted by Eastern spiritualities. There is no shortage of sociologists who have studied the problem and who have attempted to discover the causes of the attraction. But that is just a partial aspect of the phenomenon. In fact, Eastern youth are just as, if not more, fascinated by the lifestyle of the West as Western youth are by the spiritual message of the East. Certainly, in Asia there are more fervent students of Western technology than there are "practitioners" of Eastern meditation techniques in the West. Even allowing that a large number of Eastern people turn to Western technology first through vital necessity, in order to face the most elementary needs of life, nevertheless the interest in the technical ways of the West is also, for them, a road to liberation—just as much as the spiritual ways of their countries are a source of liberation for the young Westerners.

Moreover, a common trait seems to come out of these movements in both directions: it is an exogenous dynamism—one could almost say an exogamous law—that people try to marry outside their own tradition. Zealous preachers may well preach that "we" (Westerners, Christians, Hindūs, Japanese, Russians, etc.) also have in our own tradition what we are seeking elsewhere, but they are preaching in the desert because when people seek a solution, a complementarity, a way, a savior, a salvation, they seek it outside, elsewhere. A great wind is blowing, and it carries seeds, fertilization, germination.

One must understand the five moments more in a *kairological* than chronological sense, as interpenetrating and combining moments, thus giving birth to dynamisms and tensions in the life of people and peoples.

In our times, these five moments seem to be recognized, but we have not yet moved beyond them. As an example, how many average Europeans know Buddhism and consider it as a matter of personal interest at the existential level, to the point of believing that the Buddha's message might possibly contribute to real solutions of their personal and collective problems?

We could propose five other words to outline the present encounter between the religious traditions. Here is a brief summary. The encounter among religions is today:

Inevitable. Peoples and world religions can no longer live in isolation and mutual indifference. The expression "our pluralistic society" has almost become a cliché. In spite of the technical supremacy of the West, they impact each other, and nothing can escape the omnipresent action of the various worldviews.

Important. Religious encounter has always been at the very heart of cultures and of their fertilization. Religions, in their deepest, broadest, and undoubtedly most exact sense, are the soul of every culture, and because of this, they play an essential role in this world, which is becoming more and more uniform. By religion we mean not only traditional religions but all the ways that inspire people to an ideal of a full and free 1ife.

Urgent. Some things are important, but they can wait. It is not so here. For better or worse, today's world is in a simmering state, if not indeed at boiling point. To do nothing is to be a decisive factor in the mutation taking place. If mankind's true traditions do not contribute in forging a new mentality, it will be formed without their direct input. This fact may be seen either positively or negatively, but we cannot ignore the urgency of the situation.

Disturbing. The meeting of religions is certainly a challenging thing: it troubles one's peace of mind, disrupts the most deeply held beliefs of entire peoples, and creates confusion that can lead to internal and external strife. It questions what was hitherto undisputed, even undisputable. Often negative criticism wins over positive criticism, because it is almost impossible to build before having cleared the site.

Purifying. It is humiliating to lose assurance and confidence in oneself, but it is a great lesson to discover that none of us is self-sufficient. Nobody can lay claim to universality when the very way of expressing it is only partial. This awareness has a purifying effect. Human traditions discover that other systems and other beliefs, other habits and ways of life, can not only compare with our own but also purify, complement, correct, enhance, and even change what, until then, were considered definitive, and hence untouchable, acquisitions of mankind.

*

All these factors and more could be cited to contribute to defining the question of encounter between cultures and religions, an encounter that, in any case, constitutes a crossroads of our times.

One of the evils of our age is hasty and shortsighted synthesis. Before coming to any kind of overall view, we must study doctrines, know the facts, and discover the spirit of another tradition. The reader is invited to concentrate and reflect on precisely this preliminary phase of the study.

The real problems start when we fall into that schizophrenic outlook where all traditions are indiscriminately equivalent and all the colors of the spectrum tend to be lost in the "white light." This kind of agnostic indifference is no more satisfying than the sectarian and monolithic monopoly of our own particular kind of human experience to the exclusion of others. Is it possible to be concrete without losing one's own identity, and universal without losing one's sense of what is human? There is no point in saying that we often fall into the temptation of confusing the concrete with an excessive singularity, and universality with an abstract generalization. The question here is the following: how do we arrive at a true growth of awareness, to a personal synthesis that spontaneously informs all our life and translates into a new style that is expressive of that synthesis?

There are, of course, problems of method: how, from a given perspective, can one come to understand another viewpoint? Conflicts of loyalties and commitment must be resolved if there is to be real assimilation, without either interference or superimposition. That is an enormous task. Be that as it may, the first stage to cover is to know our own tradition as best we can, to develop empathy and understanding, to be aware that to discover another religion is at the same time to deepen and purify our own, and that to enter into another tradition can only enrich us. That is the spirit in which I would suggest this study be read.

*

The book is divided into two sections: the first is dedicated to intercultural dialogue and the second to religious dialogue in view of the fact that that the two subjects are intrinsically linked. The second section gives some significant examples of religious dialogue: a Buddhist-Christian dialogue; a Hindū-Christian dialogue on the possible presence of love, in an a-dualistic attitude, between the author and a follower of Viṣṇu who considers himself a monist; and a brief intercultural study on love as seen by the Hindū, Buddhist, and Christian traditions: *Bhakti–Karuṇā–Agapē*.

SECTION I

INTERCULTURAL AND INTERRELIGIOUS DIALOGUE

Part One

The Intrareligious Dialogue

Accidit ut post dies aliquot, forte ex diuturna continuata meditatione, visio quaedam eidem zeloso manifestaretur, ex qua elicuit quod paucorum sapientium omnium talium diversitatum quae in religionibus per orbem observantur peritia pollentium unam posse facilem quandam concordantiam reperiri, ac per eam in religione perpetuam pacem convenienti ac veraci medio constitui.

It happened after some days, perhaps as the fruit of an intense and sustained meditation, that a vision appeared to this ardently devoted Man. In this vision it was manifested that by means of a few sages versed in the variety of religions that exist throughout the world it could be possible to reach a certain peaceful concord. And it is through this concord that a lasting peace in religion may be attained and established by convenient and truthful means.

—*Nicola de Cusa*
De Pace seu concordantia fidei I.1[1]

Original edition: *The Intrareligious Dialogue* (New York: Paulist Press, 1999).

[1] See R. Llull, *Liber de quinque sapientibus*, expressing the same idea almost two centuries before.

A Note to the Reader

The author of this book can boast of centuries of matriarchal pedigree still alive in Kerala. This is another reason for not allowing males to usurp the monopoly on the words *Adam*, *puruṣa*, *anthrōpos*, *homo*, *Mensch* . . . thus splitting the human race into the dialectical dichotomy of divisive language: male/fe-male, man/wo-man, *ish/isshah*. . . . Furthermore, to use the word "person" instead of "Man" would not do for most non-Western cultures, which react negatively to this loaded and artificial word; nor will the expression "human being" convince those cultures that do not have the genius (or the obsession) of the Western mind for the classifying of everything. For many, the expression "human being" denies the uniqueness of every one of us; that would in fact mean that, among the many beings that exist in this world, humans are just a species, and among them the individual just a unit in the series. This attitude is felt to be contrary to human dignity, for we are not replaceable beings; each one of us is not a means for something else, but an end in himself—and thus nonclassifiable.

For this and many other reasons, the author will avoid the divisive language and employ the word "Man" as standing for that unique Being incarnated in any one of us between heaven and Earth, as the immense majority of human traditions understand the mystery of Man.

Preface

ουκ εμού,
αλλά τού λόγου ακούσαντας

not to me,
but listening to the logos . . .
Heraclitus, Fragm. 50

Dialogue as a human and humane act has never been so indispensable in all fields of life as in our age of endemic individualism. All our glib talk of "global village" takes place on artificial screens under lock and key, and the copyrights of "privileged" individuals jealous of their privacy moving around at high speed in bunkers called cars that cause over 1 million casualties per year. Either we discover again and anew the neighbor in flesh and blood, or we are heading toward a disaster of cosmic proportions, as the word itself indicates (*dis-astrum*). Our individual self-sufficiency is in crisis. We constantly run up one against the other, but we hardly have time to find our neighbor—because we do not find ourselves, being too busy with "businesses" of all sorts. "Qui enim se cognoscit, in se omnia cognoscet" (Who knows one-self, knows all things in one-self)—said the ancients, as formulated by Pico della Mirandola in his *Oratio.*

Our dealings with others are mostly either on the merely objective or on the purely subjective level, that is, either rational encounters or sentimental meetings. In the first case, we engage in "dialectical dialogues." We meet on supposedly neutral ground: the "arena" of doctrines and opinions. In the second case, we engage in "erotic dialogues." We meet on terrains of sympathy and antipathy at different levels: the agora of "personal" relationships.

Both encounters are part and parcel of our human condition, but if kept asunder, they are insufficient for a full human realization. Man is more than a thinking machine and a bundle of desires. The world is more than an objective fact, and the others more than separated individuals. "Semper occulta quaedam est concatenatio" (There is always a certain hidden connection between all things), to cite another phrase of Pico's in a wider context (*Opera omnia*, ed. Basileae, 1572, p. 235), which expresses what other traditions have termed as universal *harmonia*, *perichōrēsis*, *pratītiyasamutpāda*, *sarvam-sarvātmakam*, and the like. Our relationship with the other is not an external link but belongs to our innermost constitution, be it with the earth, the living beings—especially the humans—or the divine. The entire reality presents a "theoanthropocosmic" or, better sounding, a "cosmotheandric" nature.

When we limit our field to human relationships, we see that the other is not just a producer of ideas with which we agree more or less, or just a bearer of affinities that make possible a number of transactions; it is neither a mere (other) subject nor a mere (other) object. It is a person who is not my ego, and yet it belongs to my Self. This is what makes communication and communion possible. This awareness is the dawn of the "dialogical dialogue." The You emerges as different from the non-I.

When this encounter touches the depths of our intimate beliefs, when it reaches the ultimate questions of the meaning of life, in whatever sense, we have the "religious dialogical dialogue." Oftentimes this dialogue does not go beyond doctrinal levels or emotional projections. This is the "interreligious dialogue," which is generally carried on by experts or representatives of different belief systems or artistic sensitivities.

When the dialogue catches hold of our entire person and removes our many masks, because something stirs within us, we begin the "intrareligious dialogue." This is the internal dialogue triggered by the You who is not indifferent to the I. Something stirs in the inmost recesses of our being that we do not often dare to verbalize too loudly. That movement can lead to a purifying individual solitude or to a destructive individualistic isolation. The walls of "microdoxies" tumble down, and we can be buried under the rubble unless we succeed in clearing away the stones to build our house anew. The temptation may be twofold. For the powerful, it is to build a tower of Babel for the sake of unity—be it called one God, religion, or culture, or one world government, democracy, or the market. The human scale is lost. For the powerless the temptation is to construct for oneself an isolated shell instead of a home open to community. Again, the human scale is lost.

In brief, the intrareligious dialogue is itself a religious act—an act that neither unifies nor stifles but relinks us (in all directions). It takes place in the core of our being in our quest for salvific truth—in whatever sense we may understand these too-loaded words. We engage in such a dialogue not only looking above, toward a transcendent reality, or behind, toward an original tradition, but also horizontally, toward the world of other people who may believe they have found other paths leading to the realization of human destiny. The search becomes an authentic prayer, a prayer open in all directions.

The first steps of the intrareligious dialogue hardly make any sound. They take place in the depths of the person. This dialogue is *open*. It is no longer locked in the jail of egotism; it is open to the religiousness of our neighbors. How else could we love them as ourselves? Their beliefs become a personal religious question. It is also *profound*. It is no longer concerned with mere formulations (of our own tradition or of other people). It is a personal question concerning the meaning of reality—salvific truth, as we said before.

The intrareligious dialogue is an internal dialogue in which one struggles with the angel, the *daimon*, and oneself. How can we have access to the whole of a liberating truth if our neighbors seem to have other beliefs, which are sometimes totally incompatible with our own convictions?

This internal dialogue is neither a monologue nor a simple soliloquy with "God," nor a meditation on the partner's belief or on another religion. It is not research into a different worldview out of curiosity, or with a sympathetic mind. In this dialogue, we are in search of salvation, and we accept being taught by others, not only by our own clan. We thus transcend the more or less unconscious attitude of private property in the religious realm. Intrareligious dialogue is, of its very nature, an act of assimilation—which I would call eucharistic. It tries to assimilate the transcendent into our immanence.

But, one might say, the source of truth is found in God, or at least in transcendence, and not in Man. Truth manifests itself in enlightenment, the salvific experience, transcendence, or even evidence. In any event, this truth is not the result of my whim; it has a certain supraindividual character, be its name God, love, humanity, or ignorance. Why then seek religious truth among human opinions? Isn't there the beginning of a religious apostasy in intrareligious dialogue? Shouldn't I first try to understand better the riches of my tradition before venturing into unknown ways, trying to understand what others have said and thought? Can I be an orthodox Vedantin or a Roman Catholic, if I lend an attentive ear to foreign sirens? Do I no longer believe in the fullness of revelation crystallized in my tradition? Do I even have a right to serve myself a religious cocktail according to my own taste? In a word, doesn't intrareligious dialogue smack of a tendency toward eclecticism that betrays my lack of faithfulness and my shallowness?

It is precisely because these important queries have been ignored or interpreted as sectarian and fanatical attitudes that there is a growing proliferation of so-called new religious movements of all types. One is attracted by what is exotic; one misunderstands the meaning of newness and becomes uprooted. This explains both the attraction of the East for Western people and the exodus of young Orientals to the centers of science and technology. One should never mention the impact of the East on the West without, at the same time, underlining the greater impact of the West on the East—which Westerners sometimes seem to take for granted.

Undoubtedly, it is imperative to know first of all one's own tradition. However, to affirm contentedly that we should be able to find in our own tradition all that we are seeking is neither convincing nor sufficient. In the first place, very often we only discover the profound meaning of our own world after we have tasted something exotically different. One discovers "home, sweet home" when one returns from elsewhere. The prophet is almost always someone who has come from the outside, and often from exile. In the second place, to think of ourselves, even collectively, as self-sufficient implies a certain condemnation of others. We respect them and even accept that they may have their own subjective justification, but we consider them to be in error in whatever does not conform to our own criteria of truth, which are set up as absolute parameters. Even those who believe in an absolute revelation must admit that their interpretation of that revelation is limited and hence incomplete.

All this is very complex, but intrareligious dialogue transcends the purely sociological and historical levels. It belongs also to the realm of philosophical anthropology, if we wish to force it into categories. It is, in a word, a constitutive element of Man, who is a knot in a net of relationships, that is, a person—and not an isolated individual, conscious atom, or mere number within an undifferentiated democratic complex. It is our human nature that beckons to discover within ourselves the whole human world and also the entire reality. We are constitutively open—not only because the whole universe can penetrate us, but also because we can permeate all of reality. *Anima quodammodo omnia* (the human soul is, in a certain way, all things), said the scholastics, repeating Aristotle. When we speak of Man as a microcosm, this does not mean that we are another world in miniature, side by side with a multiplicity of small worlds; it means that Man is the "miniaturization" of the (only) world, that we are the world on our human scale. The other is certainly an *alius*, another nucleus in the network of relationships, an "other" individual, but not an *aliud*, another "thing," another (human) atom with no relatedness other than that defined by space or time narrowly considered as external elements to the human monads.

Intrareligious dialogue, by helping us discover the "other" in ourselves—is it not written, love your neighbor as yourself, as your "same" self?—contributes to the personal realization and mutual fecundation of the human traditions that can no longer afford to live in a state of isolation, separated from each other by walls of mutual mistrust, or in a state of war that may be more or less camouflaged by emulation and competition. Even peaceful coexistence is often but one form of political strategy for maintaining the status quo—preferable, undoubtedly, to war.

All in all, the intrareligious dialogue is not a minor affair; it is neither a strategy for peace nor even a method for better understanding. It is all this, and more, because it implies, first of all, a vision of reality that is neither monistic nor dualistic or atomistic. I am not the other, nor is the other I, but we are together because we are all sharers of the word, as the *ṚV* (I.164.37) says. We *are* in dialogue.

"When two will be made one, both the inside and the outside, the outside and the inside, the superior and the inferior . . . then you will enter [into 'the Kingdom']," says the *Gospel of Thomas* 22. When I shall have discovered the atheist, the Hindū, and the Christian in me, when I shall consider me and my sister as belonging to the same Self (Being, destiny, reality, mystery . . .), when the "other" will not feel alienated in me, nor I in the other . . . then we shall be closer to the Reign, *nirvāṇa*, realization, fullness, *śūnyāta*. . . .

Santa Barbara (California)
Pentecost 1983

Preface to the Original Edition

There is a long way—painful, but at the same time purifying—that is leading contemporary Christian consciousness from a self-understanding of being a historically privileged people, bearing an exclusive or inclusive message of salvation for the entire world, to an awareness of self-identity that, without weakening the strength of a conviction of uniqueness and fidelity to its own calling, does make room for different ultimate and salvific human experiences.

For thirty years the author has written extensively on such problems. The present essays (most of them written in the "ghats" of the Ganges) are here gathered as stepping-stones of that way. They were written in the middle of the internal struggle of the ecclesial self-reflection. They have been detached from another collection of studies—*Myth, Faith, and Hermeneutics*—because although they complement the chapters of the other book, their internal unity appears clearer as an independent volume.

The Sermon on the Mount of Intrareligious Dialogue

The aim of this book is to contribute toward peace and mutual understanding between religions and peoples by examining some examples lying at the root of human conflicts, whether still latent or manifest in our day and age. The spirit of this book may perhaps be expressed by drawing inspiration from an ancient text, the Sermon on the Mount.

When you enter into an intrareligious dialogue, do not think beforehand what you have to believe.

When you *witness* to your faith, do not defend yourself or your vested interests, sacred as they may appear to you. Do like the birds in the skies: they sing and fly and do not defend their music or their beauty.

When you dialogue with somebody, look at your partner as a revelatory experience, as you would—and should—look at the lilies in the fields.

When you engage in intrareligious dialogue, try first to remove the beam in your own eye before removing the speck in the eye of your neighbor.

Blessed are you when you do not feel self-sufficient while being in dialogue.

Blessed are you when you trust the other because you trust in Me.

Blessed are you when you face misunderstandings from your own community or others for the sake of your fidelity to Truth.

Blessed are you when you do not give up your convictions, and yet you do not set them up as absolute norms.

Woe unto you, you theologians and academicians, when you dismiss what others say because you find it embarrassing or not sufficiently learned.

Woe unto you, you practitioners of religions, when you do not listen to the cries of the little ones.

Woe unto you, you religious authorities, because you prevent change and (re)conversion.

Woe unto you, religious people, because you monopolize religion and stifle the Spirit, which blows where and how she wills.

1

The Rhetoric of the Dialogue

. . .e aquí preseren comiat los tres savis la un de l'altre molt amablement e molt agradable; e cascù qués perdò a l'altre si havia dita contra sa lig nulla vilana paraula; e la un perdonà l'altre. E quan foren en ço que's volgren departir, la un savi dix:

—De la ventura que'ns és avenguda en la forest on venim, seguir-se-n'ha a nosaltres alcun profit. ¿Parria-us bo que, per la manera dels cinc arbres e per les deu condicions significades per lurs flors, càscun jorn una vegada, nos deputàssem, e que seguissem la manera que la dona d'Intel. ligència nos ha donada: eque tant de temps duràs nostra desputaciò tro que tots tres haguéssem una fe e una lig tan solament, eque enfre nòs haguéssem manera d'honrar e servir la un L'altre, per ço que enans nos puscam concordar? Car guerra, treball e malvolença, e donar dan e honta, empatxa los hòmens a ésser concordants en una creença.*

—Ramon Llull
Libre del gentil e los tres savis (in finem)

. . . and here the three sages took leave of each other with great love and in a very agreeable way: each of them asked forgiveness of the others in case he might have proffered any unkind word against the religion of the other; and each of them did pardon the others. And when they were about to leave one of the sages said: Some profit should result from the venture that has happened to us in the forest. Would it not be good that, following the model of the five trees and the ten conditions represented by their flowers, we could discuss once every coming day the indications given to us by Dame Intelligence?

* *Sic, sed legendum* "desputàssem."

Our discussions should continue as long as necessary until we arrive at one faith and one religion so that we will have a form of honoring each other and serving each other. This would be the quickest way to come to our mutual concord. For war, strained works, and ill will produce harm and shame, hindering people in their efforts to reach an agreement on one belief.

—*Ramon Llull, Obres essencials, Barcelona (Editorial Selecta, 1957), 1:1138*

The chapters that follow do not elaborate a theory of the religious encounter. They are part of that very encounter. And it is out of this praxis that I would like to propose the following attitudes and models for the proper rhetoric in the meeting of religious traditions.

I do not elaborate now on the value of these attitudes or the merits of these models. This would require studying the function and nature of the metaphor as well as developing a theory of the religious encounter. I only describe some attitudes and models, although I will probably betray my sympathies in the form of critical considerations. The dialogue needs an adequate rhetoric—in the classical sense of the word.

Five Attitudes

Exclusivism

A believing member of a religion in one way or another considers his own religion to be true. Now, the claim to truth has a certain built-in claim to exclusivity. If a given statement is true, its contradictory cannot also be true. And if a certain human tradition claims to offer a universal context for truth, anything contrary to that "universal truth" will have to be declared false.

If, for instance, Islam embodies the true religion, a "non-Islamic truth" cannot exist in the field of religion. Any long-standing religious tradition, of course, will have developed the necessary distinctions so as not to appear too blunt. It will say, for instance, that there are degrees of truth and that any "religious truth," if it is really true, "is" already a Muslim one, although the people concerned may not be conscious of it. It will further distinguish an objective order of truth from a subjective one so that a person can be "in good faith" and yet be in objective error, which as such will not be imputed against that person, and so forth.

This attitude has a certain element of heroism in it. You consecrate your life and dedicate your entire existence to something that is really worthy of being called a human cause, to something that claims to be not just a partial and imperfect truth, but a universal and even absolute truth. To be sure, an absolute God or Value has to be the final guarantee for such an attitude so that you do not follow it because of personal whims or because you have uncritically raised your point of view to an absolute value. It is God's rights you defend when asserting your religion as "absolute religion." This does not imply an outright condemnation of the beliefs of all other human beings who have not received the "grace" of your calling. You may consider this call a burden and a duty (to carry vicariously the responsibility for the whole world) more than a privilege and a gift. Who are we to put conditions on the Almighty?

On the other hand, this attitude presents its difficulties. First, it carries with it the obvious danger of intolerance, *hybris*, and contempt for others. "We belong to the club of truth." It further bears the intrinsic weakness of assuming an almost purely logical conception of truth and the uncritical attitude of an epistemological naïveté. Truth is many-faceted, and even if you assume that God speaks an exclusive language, everything depends on your understanding of it so that you may never really know whether your interpretation is the *only* right one. To recur to a superhuman instance in the discussion between two religious beliefs does not solve any question, for it is often the case that God "speaks" also to others, and both partners relying on God's authority will always need the human mediation so that ultimately God's authority depends on Man's interpretation (of the divine revelation).

As a matter of fact, although there are many de facto remnants of an exclusivistic attitude today, it is hardly defended *de iure*. To use the Christian *skandalon*, for instance, to defend Christianity would amount to the very betrayal of that saying about the "stumbling block." It would be the height of hypocrisy to condemn others and justify oneself using the scandal of God's revelation as a rationale for defending one's own attitude: divine revelation ceases to be a scandal for you (for you seem to accept it without scandal)—and you hurl it at others.

Inclusivism

In the present world context one can hardly fail to discover positive and true values—even of the highest order—outside of one's own tradition. Traditional religions have to face this challenge. "Splendid isolation" is no longer possible. The most plausible condition for the claim to truth of one's own tradition is to affirm at the same time that it includes at different levels all that there is of truth wherever it exists. The inclusivistic attitude will tend to reinterpret things in such a way as to make them not only palatable but also assimilable. Whenever facing a plain contradiction, for instance, it will make the necessary distinctions between different planes so as to be able to overcome that contradiction. It will tend to become a universalism of an existential or formal nature rather than of essential content. A doctrinal truth can hardly claim universality if it insists too much on specific contents because the grasping of the contents always implies a particular "*forma mentis*." An attitude of tolerant admission of different planes, on the contrary, will have it easier. An umbrella pattern or a formal structure can easily embrace different thought-systems.

If *vedanta*, for example, is really the end and acme of all the Vedas, these latter understood as an expression of all types of ultimate revelation, it can seemingly affirm that all sincere human affirmations have a place in its scheme because they represent different stages in the development of human consciousness and have a value in the particular context in which they are said. Nothing is rejected, and all is fitted into its proper place.

This attitude has a certain quality of magnanimity and grandeur in it. You can follow your own path and do not need to condemn the other. You can even enter into communion with all other ways of life, and if you happen to have the real experience of inclusivity, you may be at peace not only with yourself but with all other human and divine ways as well. You can be concrete in your allegiances and universal in your outlook.

On the other hand, this attitude also entails some difficulties. First, it also presents the danger of *hybris* because it is only you who has the privilege of an all-embracing vision and tolerant attitude, you who allot to the others the place they must take in the universe. You are tolerant in your own eyes but not in the eyes of those who challenge your right to be on top. Furthermore, it has the intrinsic difficulties of an almost alogical conception of truth and a built-in inner contradiction when the attitude is spelled out in theory and praxis.

If this attitude allows for a variegated expression of "religious truth" so as to be able to include the most disparate systems of thought, it is bound to make truth purely relative. Truth here cannot have an independent intellectual content, for it is one thing for the parsi and another for the *vaiṣṇva*, one thing for the atheist and another for the theist. So, it is also another thing for you—unless you jump outside the model because it is you who have the clue, you who find a place for all the different worldviews. But then your belief, conception, ideology, intuition, or whatever name we may call it becomes a super-system the moment that you formulate it: you seem to understand the lower viewpoints and put them in their right places. You cannot avoid claiming for yourself a superior knowledge even if you deny that your conviction is another viewpoint. If you "say," furthermore, that your position is only the ineffable fruit of a mystical insight, the moment that you put it into practice, nothing prevents another from discovering and formulating the implicit assumptions of that attitude. Ultimately you claim to have a fuller truth in comparison with all the others, who have only partial and relative truths.

As a matter of fact, although there are still many tendencies in several religious traditions that consider themselves all-inclusive, there are today only very few theoretical and philosophical formulations of a purely inclusivistic attitude. The claim of pluralism today is too strong to be so easily bypassed.

Parallelism

If your religion appears far from being perfect, and yet it represents for you a symbol of the right path and a similar conviction seems to be the case for others, if you can neither dismiss the religious claim of the other nor assimilate it completely into your tradition, a plausible alternative is to assume that all are different creeds, which, in spite of meanderings and crossings, actually run parallel, to meet only in the ultimate, in the *eschaton*, at the very end of the human pilgrimage. Religions would then be parallel paths, and our most urgent duty would be not to interfere with others, not to convert them or even to borrow from them, but to deepen our own respective traditions so that we may meet at the end and in the depths of our own traditions. Be a better Christian, a better Marxist, a better Hindū, and you will find unexpected riches and also points of contact with other people's ways.

This attitude presents very positive advantages. It is tolerant; it respects the others and does not judge them. It avoids muddy syncretisms and eclecticisms that concoct a religion according to our private tastes; it keeps the boundaries clear and spurs constant reform of one's own ways.

On the other hand, it too is not free of difficulties. First of all, it seems to go against the historical experience that the different religious and human traditions of the world have usually emerged from mutual interferences, influences, and fertilizations. It too hastily assumes, furthermore, that every human tradition has in itself all the elements for further growth and development; in a word, it assumes the self-sufficiency of every tradition and seems to deny the need or convenience of mutual learning or the need to walk outside the walls of one particular human tradition—as if in every one of them the entire human experience were crystallized or condensed. It flatters every one of us to hear that we possess *in nuce* all we need for a full human and religious maturity, but it splits the human family into watertight compartments, making any kind of conversion a real betrayal of one's own being. It allows growth but not mutation. Even if we run parallel to each other, are there not *sangama*, *prayāga*, affluents, inundations, natural and artificial dams, and above all, does not one and the same water flow "heavenward" in the veins of the human being? Mere parallelism eschews the real issues.

Notwithstanding, this attitude presents on the other hand more prospects for an initial working hypothesis today. It carries a note of hope and patience at the same time: hope that we will meet at the end and patience that meanwhile we have to bear our differences. Yet when facing concrete problems of interferences, mutual influences, and even dialogue, one cannot just wait until this *kalpa* comes to an end or the *eschaton* appears. All crossings are dangerous, but there is no new life without *maithuna*.

Interpenetration

The more we come to know the religions of the world, the more we are sensitive to the religiousness of our neighbor, all the more do we begin to surmise that in every one of us the other is somehow implied and, vice versa, that the other is not so independent from us and is somehow touched by our own beliefs. We begin to realize that our neighbor's religion not only challenges and may even enrich our own, but that ultimately the very differences that separate us are somewhat potentially within the world of my own religious convictions. We begin to accept that the other religion may complement mine, and we may even entertain the idea that in some particular cases it may well supplement some of my beliefs, provided that my religiousness remains an undivided whole. More and more we have the case of Marxists accepting Christian ideas, Christians subscribing to Hindū tenets, Muslims absorbing Buddhist views, and so on, and all the while remaining Marxists, Christians, and Muslims. But there is still more than this: It looks as if we are today all intertwined, and that without these particular religious links my own religion would be incomprehensible for me and even impossible. Religions are un-understandable without a certain background of "religion." Our own religiousness is seen within the framework of our neighbor's. Religions do not exist in isolation but over against each other. There would be no Hindū consciousness were it not for the fact of having to distinguish it from Muslim and Christian consciousness, for example. In a word, the relation between religions is neither of the type of exclusivism (only mine), or inclusivism (the mine embraces all the others), or parallelism (we are running independently toward the same goal), but one of a sui generis *perichōrēsis* or *circumincessio*, that is, of mutual interpenetration without the loss of the proper peculiarities of each religiousness.

The obvious positive aspect of this attitude is the tolerance, broadmindedness, and mutual confidence that it inspires. No religion is totally foreign to my own; within our own religion we may encounter the religion of the other; we all need one another; in some way we are saying not just the same but mutually complementing and correcting things. And even when religions struggle for supplementation, they do it within a mutually acknowledged religious frame.

On the other hand, this attitude is also not free from dangers. First of all, one has to ask if this thinking is not a little wishful. Are we so sure of this interpenetration? So "*karma*" and "Providence" interpenetrate or exclude each other? On what grounds can we establish it? Is this attitude not already a modification of the self-understanding of the traditions themselves? This could be answered by justifying the role of creative hermeneutics. Each interpretation is a new creation. But can we say that such hermeneutics really exist in all the minutiae of the world religions? Or is it not a kind of new religiousness that makes selective use of the main tenets of the traditions while neglecting the others? There may be a religious universe, but is it sufficiently broad as to allow for insuperable incompatibilities?

But again this attitude may offer perspectives that the others lack. It may put us on a way that is open to all and that nobody should feel reluctant to enter. It can contribute to the spiritual growth of the partners: even interpreting other beliefs as exaggeration or distortions of our own, we touch a more fundamental frame of reference, and without losing our identity, we weaken our assertive ego. It can contribute to a mutual enrichment within a synthesis. The values of the other tradition are not merely juxtaposed to those of our tradition but truly assimilated and integrated to our beliefs and in our own being. It is an open process.

Pluralism

We should stress here that we use this polysemic word not as a super-system, which gives a more complete answer to the vexing problem of the relationship among religions, criticizing all the others as one-sided, but as denoting an attitude. It is the attitude of not breaking the dialogue with the other opinions, because having renounced any absolutization, it keeps the intrareligious dialogue permanently open.

The aim of the intrareligious dialogue is understanding. It is not to win over the other or to come to a total agreement or a universal religion. The ideal is communication in order to bridge the gulfs of mutual ignorance and misunderstandings between the different cultures of the world, letting them speak and speak out their own insights in their own languages. Some may wish even to reach communion, but this does not imply at all that the aim is a uniform unity or a reduction of all the pluralistic variety of Man into one single religion, system, ideology, or tradition. Pluralism stands between unrelated plurality and a monolithic unity. It implies that the human condition in its present reality should not be neglected, let alone despised in favor of an ideal (?) situation of human uniformity. On the contrary, it takes our factual situation as real and affirms that in the actual polarities of our human existence we find our real being.

Pluralism takes very seriously the fact that during the last six to eight thousand years of human history our fellow beings have not come to an agreement concerning religious beliefs. Our ancestors were not unintelligent, nor were they blind partisans of the respective establishments. A certain evolutionistic thinking, making us believe that we are at the top of the spiritual insights of the human race, and all the others were "undeveloped," smacks of modern *hybris* and ignorant naïveté.

For this very confidence it has in Man and not because of tired skepticism, the pluralistic attitude is not stuck at resolving the objective quandaries of religious divergencies and turns to the subjective, that is, human side of the problem. Could it not be that the dream of the mind to understand everything, because ultimately everything is intelligible, is a gratuitous and uncritical assumption? Pluralism is inclined to overcome the monopoly of the mental over everything. We are more, not less, than "rational." And perhaps the more realistic basis on which to ground human conviviality is not rational knowledge but loving awareness.

In other words, the pluralistic attitude dares not to accept the Parmenidean dogma of the bi-univocal correlation between thinking and being. We are aware of the unthinkable, for instance. Patience, tolerance, love, and the role of the heart are not accidental to human life and reveal to us aspects of ourselves and of reality that cannot be reduced *ad unum*—without, for that matter, having to accept duality.

Having dealt with this problem elsewhere, this brief description may suffice here.

*

I have described these five attitudes as examples of basic postures that when put to work become, of course, much more sophisticated. When the encounter actually takes place, be it in actual facts or in the more conscious dialogue, one needs some root-metaphors in order to articulate the different problems. It is here that some models may prove useful. I briefly describe five of them.

Five Models

I repeat that these root-metaphors are only ways to present the problematic of the religious encounter and instruments for expressing different views but not criteria to discriminate between good and bad distinctions, true and false theories, or even authentic and inauthentic religions. This is why they are paradigms. They serve many purposes and certainly too many for those who would like to maintain a particular opinion. This is not only a legitimate wish; it is ultimately a necessity lest we fall prey to sheer chaos, but this is not our concern here. Our models are such precisely because they are polyvalent. They open the dialogue; they do not close it.

The Geographical Model: The Ways to the Mountain Peak

It would be hard to argue that human beings are complete and perfect or that they have already fulfilled their destiny. No matter how we express it, we all agree that in some manner or another we have not yet reached the goal, be it God, salvation, annihilation, peace, progress, success, happiness, power, security, and so forth. A way of saying it makes use of a geographical paradigm: we are still pilgrims toward the summit (of life). Ultimately, we do not even know what shape this summit has, whether it is a peak or a plane, whether it is one or many. To be sure, prophets and holy founders, saints and philosophers, mystics and theologians as well as visionaries and charlatans have told us lofty things about those heights. Many speak about it, but their language is not unanimous. Many affirm that behind the snowclad peaks lies a sunny valley, while others shout that it has been revealed to them that the "summit" lies in the cave of the heart. Some state that the peak is the void, a total abyss of nothingness, or even that all there is is the absurd or the disenchantment that inevitably attends our alienating dreams of a Promised Land.

Still others claim that there is fullness at the summit, that it is permeated with peace and joy. In any case, however much the religious cartographers may dispute the nature of it, all will admit there is indeed some kind of summit to be reached.

In this context, then, we can consider a religion to be a way that claims to lead to the summit—whether this summit is transcendent or immanent, whether the goal is conquered by individual effort or is received in and enhanced by grace, and so on.

This summit has many names. Yet no matter how pertinent these names may be, they do not properly describe the actual peak, which is generally considered to be ineffable and inaccessible as long as we are in our present human condition. There are, in fact, many ways claiming to lead to the summit, and all of them are more or less arduous. In other words, the paths are climbs toward one mountain or steps toward one abyss: the mountain inverted.

Elaborating on the metaphor, we may also point out that at the foothills you may not even be aware of the efforts and accomplishments of the other traditions, for many ridges and valleys may separate you from them and prevent you from seeing the trail they have blazed. In the lower ranges the paths are wide apart, while higher up they come closer to each other.

Moreover, although your tradition has marked off a way for you, you still have to follow it on your own. You have to travel on it, and within the larger avenue that has been set out, you somehow have to find or create your own trail. Religion is a very personal concern and thus has an intimate and social dimension.

Furthermore, the geographical model clarifies the fact that if you go on jumping from one way to another you will certainly not reach the goal. You may stop to catch your breath, to enjoy the view, or to harvest a bouquet of wildflowers, but if you reject your calling simply because it is difficult for you and you refuse to climb, you will not reach the top. You have to continue steadfastly on your way.

The way, however, may not conform to your preconceptions, and these may have to be abandoned: you have to make your own way. There you may discover hidden paths and shortcuts, as ascetics and guides will tell you. This does not mean that at a certain moment of your pilgrimage you may not discover another trodden path that is more convincing and congenial to you. You may change your way, but nobody can erase your previous pilgrimage. In other words, conversion is a legitimate step when it is not a total rejection of what you have been going through all the way up until then. You can go back at a point where you think you departed from your right path, but even then you cannot begin again as if it were the first step of your journey. Rather, you carry the bundle of your experience with you as you enter into another tradition. You may have discovered that your *dharma* now leads you along a different avenue. Authentic conversion is not a move against your *svadharma*, but rather a movement that tries to regain harmony with your innermost nature.

The changing of ways is no simple affair; it is laden with unforeseen consequences. In spite of yourself, you not only bring all your former equipment over from the other tradition, but you also initiate a complicated process of metabolism. Depending on many factors, some things are discarded and others are assimilated and transformed into the new tradition.

More complex is the case in which wayfarers would like to follow a path different than their own without abandoning the original one. A new way must be cleared. If successful, this may become a path on which many others may also go. The ways may actually come nearer or extend further when such a passing over takes place on a sociologically relevant scale.

These considerations lead to a very broad understanding of the word *way*. Each traditional way is then a slope of the mountain on which people find their paths. Valleys may separate the traditional ways at points far away from the peak, but at a certain height two watersheds may meet, and the valleys are left behind.

As any mountaineer knows, you need a kind of faith to follow the path, for often the peak remains invisible and ultimately you do not know whether you will have to double back to a safer byway. The trail you have taken may suddenly fall off into sheer space or end abruptly at a granite wall. Nor is this all: landslides, floods, and even earthquakes may have blocked ancient trails. Indeed, religions change, degenerate, and even die. A jungle of routine and ritualism may have covered up the classical routes, or the weeds of misunderstanding and pride may have chocked off the way of the Golden Age.

This model of the religious quest seems to offer a suitable language to express almost anything about the religious dialogue: that not only your way leads to the top, that all the ways may reach the goal, that only some are traversable, that there are meandering trails and dead ends, that at a certain moment no way is of any avail. Another opinion will strike a compromise affirming that the paths exist only on the lower slopes of the climb and that afterward there is no way whatsoever, and so on. It also tells us that, whatever the summit may be, if we destroy all the paths, the summit will collapse. If you erode the slopes, the peak crumbles down. The way is somehow the goal.

The most *jñānic* or Gnostic attitudes may tell us that there is no way because "*saṃsāra* is *nirvāṇa*," or "you are that" or some similar intuition. The advocates of such ideas, however, cannot deny that the "no way" of the realization is also a way to be discovered by the wayfarer.

Moreover, the way must traverse not only the ruggedness of the geographical terrain, but also the psychic topography and inner landscape of the pilgrim, or more simply: the way is only a way if you go through it, if you walk on it and make it your own. We can speak authoritatively only concerning the ways through which we have gone. Yet we must be careful not to limit ourselves to an individualistic interpretation that would rob the metaphor of its flexibility. What may be the proper way for you may not be the true path for me. You may not be able to climb along cracks in the sheer granite walls, while I have an allergy to a path that goes through tropical bushes; you may have vertigo and not tolerate a precipice, while I may get sick from too many curves. I will have to trust you when you say that you will also reach the top safely, although for me your way would not be a "way" for me.

In our modern technological era there may be people who think that the old ways are well and good for times past but that nowadays we must have new "pontiffs," that is, new bridge builders and a priesthood of professionals who can assist us along the way better than the popes and bonzes of olden times. The "new" or "modern" ways would then be trying to construct the superhighways of a linear morality, a secure and well-measured success, and a well-engineered evolution of human nature. They claim to bridge over the cliffs of ignorance and superstition and to race forward toward the goal in vehicles better designed and equipped than the *mahāyāna* and *hīnayāna* of old. This sometimes shallow interpretation of the model, however, should not be cast aside too quickly, but rather it should be understood in terms of its depth of intuition: that we are not only wayfarers, but also pathfinders and waymakers; that we are the human engineers who construct the roads for a better, more human, and thus more divine life—or for worse. This modern spirit has, in fact, historically changed the course of traditional ways such that, while before they were parallel and mutually ignorant, today, willy-nilly they meet and cross. While apparently dealing with only secular pursuits, modern communication systems have actually made a significant contribution to the meeting of religious ways.

Finally, this model may also serve to explain the obvious differences among religions. If one religion *believes* that the summit is a purely transcendent peak that has little in common with our present status, it would consider the way to be one of renouncing anything earthly. If another religion *believes* that the peak is at the very end of the way, it would not ask for an initiation with a leap of faith or a rupture of planes, but rather it would consider the way to be a march through personal effort toward that end. If the peak is inaccessible, grace is needed; if the peak can be seen, intuition is required; if the summit is invisible, faith is indispensable; if the goal is in yourself, interiority is the way; and so on and so forth.

The Physical Model: The Rainbow

The different religious traditions of mankind are like the almost infinite number of colors that appear once the divine or simply white light of reality falls on the prism of human experience: it diffracts into innumerable traditions, doctrines, and religions. Green is not yellow, Hinduism is not Buddhism, and yet at the fringes one cannot know, except by postulating it artificially, where yellow ends and green begins. Even more, through any particular color, namely religion, one can reach the source of the white light. Any follower of a human tradition is given the possibility of reaching his or her destination, fullness, salvation, provided there is a beam of light and not sheer darkness.

If two colors mix, they may sire another. Similarly with religious traditions, the meeting of two may give birth to a new one. In point of fact, most of the known religions today are results of such mutual fecundations (Aryans-Dravidians, Jews-Greeks, Indians-Muslims, etc.). Besides, it is only from an agreed point of view that we can judge a religion over against another. Regarding social concern, for instance, one tradition may be more fruitful than another, but the latter may be more powerful than the former in securing personal happiness. We may begin the rainbow with the infrared or with the ultraviolet or choose, for instance, 5,000 angstroms as the central point, and so forth. Furthermore, within the green area all will appear under that particular light. A similar object within the red area will look reddish. This model reminds us that the context is paramount in comparing "religious truths."

Nor is this all. Just as the color of a body is the only color generally not absorbed by that body, this model would remind us also that a religion similarly absorbs all other colors and hides them in its bosom so that its external color is in truth only its appearance, its message to the outer world, but not the totality of its nature. We come to this realization when we attempt to understand a religion from within. The real body that has received the entire beam of white light keeps for itself all the other colors so that it would not accord with truth to judge a religion only from its outer color. This metaphor can still take more refinements. One particular religion may include only a few beams of light while another may cover a wider aspect of the spectrum. Time and space may (like the principle of Doppler-Fizeau) introduce modifications in the wavelength of a particular tradition so that it changes down the ages or along with the places. What is a Christian in the India of the twentieth century may be far different from what was considered such in tenth-century France.

This metaphor does not necessarily imply that all the religions are the same, that there may not be black or colorless spots, that for some particular problems only one particular color may be the appropriate one, and so on.

The metaphor, moreover, could still serve to contest the right of something that does not have light in it to be called a religious tradition. A humanistic critique of traditional religions, for instance, may well call obscurantistic all the religions of the past and deny to them the character of bearing light; only the Enlightenment traditions of rationalism, Marxism, and humanism, let us say, would come into consideration. I am citing this extreme case in order to clarify the immense variation possible in the use of this root-metaphor. It could even provide an image for the conception of one particular religion considering itself as the white beam and all the others as refractions of that primordial religiousness, or, on the contrary, it may offer an example of how to say that the variety of religions belongs to the beauty and richness of the human situation because it is only the entire rainbow that provides a complete picture of the true religious dimension of Man.

Yet the value of a model comes not only from its possible applicability, but also from its connaturality with the phenomenon under analysis. The physical fact of the rainbow in this case helps us to explain the intricacies of the anthropological phenomenon of religion.

The Geometrical Model: The Topological Invariant

If in the first model diffraction is what produces the different lights, or religions, transformation is the cause of the different forms and shapes of geometrical figures—of religions—in our third model.

In and through space and also due to the influence of time, a primordial and original form takes on an almost indefinite number of possible transformations through the twisting of Men, the stretching by history, the bending by natural forces, and so on. Religions appear to be different and even mutually irreconcilable until or unless a topological invariant is found. This invariant does not need to be the same for *all* religions. Some may prefer to hold the theory of families of religions, while others may try to work out the hypothesis that all the different human ways come from a fundamental experience transformed according to laws, which as in any geometrical universe have first to be discovered. Again, others may say that religions are actually different until the corresponding topological transformations have been constructed.

The model is polyvalent. Homeomorphism is not the same as analogy: it represents a functional equivalence discovered through a topological transformation. Brahman and God are not merely two analogous names; they are homeomorphic in the sense that each of them stands for something that performs an equivalent function within their respective systems. But this can only be formulated once the homeomorphism of a topological equivalence has been found. Religions that may appear at first sight to be very different from each other may find their connections once the topological transformation is discovered that permits connecting the two traditions under consideration.

This model offers a challenge to further study and prevents us from drawing hurried conclusions. A literal use of the topological model would assume not only that all religions are transformations of a primordial experience, intuition, or datum (as would be the case with the rainbow model), but also that each religious tradition is a dimension of the other, that there is a kind of *circumincessio* or *perichōrēsis* or *pratītyasamutpāda* among all the religious traditions of the world so that mere contiguity models are insufficient to express their relation. Religions do not stand side by side, but they are actually intertwined. Viṣṇu dwells in the heart of Śiva and vice versa. Each religion represents the whole for that particular human group, and in a certain way "is" the religion of the other group, only in a different topological form. Perhaps this may be too optimistic a view, but the model provides also for the necessary cautions or restrictions. One cannot, a priori, for instance, formulate this theory, but it may well be a working hypothesis spurring our minds toward some transcendental unity of the religious experience of the human race. It is clear that this model excludes neither a divine factor nor a critical evaluation of the human traditions. Sometimes we may not succeed in finding the corresponding topological equivalence, but sometimes it may also be the case that such a transformation does not exist.

According to this model, then, the comparison among religions would not be the business of finding analogies, which are bound to be always somewhat superficial and need a *primum analogatum* as point of reference (which should already belong to the traditions compared if the comparison is to be fair), but would rather be the business of understanding religions from within and discovering their concrete structures and of finding out their corresponding homeomorphisms. Religious variety would appear here not so much as a bountifully colorful universe as different appearances of an inner structure detectable only in a deeper intuition, be this called mystical or scientific.

Now, the topological laws do not need to be merely of a rational or logical nature, as is the case with geometrical topology. They could as well be historical or sui generis. In a word, the topological model is not only useful for possible doctrinal equivalents; it could also serve to explore other forms of correspondence and equivalence. We may succeed in explaining, for instance, how primitive Buddhism was reabsorbed in India through a certain *advaita* by means of finding the proper topological laws of transformation.

The Anthropological Model: Language

Whatever theory we may defend regarding the origin and nature of religion, whether it be a divine gift or a human invention or both, the fact remains that it is at least a human reality and as such coextensive with another also at least human reality called language. This model considers each religion as a language. This model has ancient antecedents. To the widespread old belief that there were seventy-two languages, some added the conviction that there were equally seventy-two religions. "Item dixit"—say the proceedings of an inquisitorial process of the thirteenth century in Bologna, condemning a Cathar—"quod sicut sunt LXXII lingue, ita sunt LXXII fides."

Any religion is complete just as is any language that is capable of expressing everything that it feels the need to express. Any religion is open to growth and evolution as any language is. Both are capable of expressing or adopting new shades of meaning, of shifting idioms or emphases, refining ways of expression, and changing them.

When a new need is felt in any religious or linguistic world, there are always means of dealing with that need. Furthermore, although any language is a world in itself, it is not without relations with neighboring languages, borrowing from them and open to mutual influences. Yet each language only takes as much as it can assimilate from a foreign language. Similarly with religions: they influence each other and borrow from one another without losing their identity. In an extreme case a religion, like a language, may disappear entirely. The reasons also seem very similar—conquest, decadence, emigration, and so forth.

From the internal point of view of each language and religion, it makes little sense to say that one language is more perfect than another, for you can in your language (as well as in your religion) say all that you feel you need to say. If you felt the need to say something else or something different, you would say it. If you use only one word for *camel* and hundreds for the different metals, and if another language does just the opposite, it is because you have different patterns of differentiation for camels and metals. It is the same with religions. Yours may have only one word for *wisdom*, *God*, *compassion*, or *virtue*, and another religion may have scores of them.

The great problem appears when we come to the encounter of languages—and religions. The question here is translation. Religions are equivalent to the same extent that languages are translatable, and they are unique as much as languages are untranslatable. There is the common world of objectifiable objects. They are the objects of empirical or logical verification. This is the realm of terms. Each term is an epistemic sign standing for an empirically or logically verifiable object. The terms *tree*, *wine*, *atom*, *four* can be translated into any given language if we have a method of empirically pointing out a visible thing (tree), a physically recognizable substance (wine), a physicomathematically definable entity (atom), and a logical cipher (four). Each of these cases demands some specific conditions, but we may assume that these conditions can all be empirically or logically verifiable once a certain axiom is accepted. In short, all terms are translatable insofar as a name could easily be invented or adopted even by a language that might lack a particular term (*atom*, for instance). Similarly, all religions have a translatable sphere: all refer to the human being, to his well-being, to overcoming the possible obstacles to it, and the like. Religious terms—qua terms—are translatable.

The most important part of a language as well as of a religion, however, is not terms but words, that is, not epistemic signs to orient us in the world of objects but living symbols to allow us to live in the world of Men and Gods. Now, words are not objectifiable. A word is not totally separable from the meaning we give to it, and each of us in fact gives different shades of meaning to the same word. A word reflects a total human experience and cannot be severed from it. A word is not empirically or logically detectable. When we say "justice," *dharma*, *karuṇā*, we cannot point to an object but have to refer to crystallizations of human experiences that vary with people, places, ages, and so on. We cannot, properly speaking, translate words. We can only transplant them along with a certain surrounding context that gives them meaning and offers the horizon over against which they can be understood, that is, assimilated within another horizon. Even then the transplanted word, if it survives, will soon extend its roots in the soil and acquire new aspects, connotations, and so forth.

Similarly with religions: they are not translatable like terms; only certain transplants are possible under appropriate conditions. There is not an object "God," "justice," or "Brahman," a thing in itself independent of those living words, over against which we may check the correction of the translation. In order to translate them we have to transplant the corresponding worldview that makes those words say what they intend to say. A nonsaying word is like a nonsung song: if the word is not heard as saying what it intends to say, we have not actually translated that word. The translation of religious insights cannot be done unless the insight that has originated that word is also transplanted. Now for this, a mere "sight" from the outside is not sufficient. We may then translate only the outer carcass of a word and not its real meaning. No word can be cut from its speaker if it has to remain an authentic word and not a mere term. The translator has to be also a speaker in that foreign language, in that alien tradition; he has to be a true spokesman for that religion; he has to be, to a certain extent (that I shall not describe further here), convinced of the truth he conveys, converted to the tradition from which he translates. Here I am already in the intrareligious dialogue.

The translator has to speak the "foreign" language as his own. As long as we speak a language translating from another, we shall never speak fluently or even correctly. Only when we speak that language, only when you "speak" that religion as your own, will you really be able to be a spokesman for it, a genuine translator. This obviously implies at the same time that you have not forgotten your native tongue, that you are equally capable of expressing yourself in the other linguistic world. It is then that one begins to wonder at the exactness of the translations or, as the expression still goes, at the "fidelity" of many a translation. Are you keeping fidelity to both Brahman and God, *dharma* and religion (or justice, or order?) when you translate in that way; or are you obliged to enlarge, to deepen, and to stretch your own language in order to make place for the insights of the other? This may be the case even with terms that are in part empirically verifiable. Are you so sure that when you translate *gau* with "cow" you are not misleading the modern English reader if you let him believe that you speak merely of a bovine female related perhaps to cowboys but not to the *kāmadhenu*? *Gau* is more than a zoological name, as *sūrya* (sun) is more than a mere name for an astronomical or physical body. *Dhvani* is a reality all poets know.

The linguistic model helps also in the complicated problem of comparative religion. Only when we have a common language can we begin to compare, that is, to weigh against a common background. Only then may a mutual understanding take place. This model, moreover, makes it clear that we cannot compare languages (religions) outside language (religion) and that there is no language (religion) except in concrete languages (religions). Comparative religion can only be comparative religions from the standpoint of the concrete religions themselves. This demands an entirely new method from that arising out of the assumption that there is a nonreligious neutral "reason" entitled to pass comparative judgments in the field of religions.

The Mystical Model: Silence

It should not be too quickly retorted that silence cannot be a model because it simply eliminates the problem by not wanting to detect the differences. There is certainly a silence of indifference as well as a silence of skepticism. But there is also a silence that does not deny the word but is aware that the silence is prior to the word and that the word simply words the silence that makes the word possible. The second person of the Trinity, the Logos, came out of the Silence of the first person, some church fathers used to say.

Mystics of all types and times have privileged this model. They tell us that every word is only a translation. There may be better and worse translations, and we may have lost the original and are bound to struggle with translators, but whenever we forget that the image is not the thing, this model will help us.

The true silence keeps quiet and is put to the test when we become convinced that a particular interpretation is not correct. The temptation is then strong to postulate a "transcendental unity of religions" or an "essential harmony." This may be the case, but the moment that we formulate it, we break the silence and with it the unity and the harmony.

Perhaps this model is not a full-fledged model, but only a canvas on which other models can be better situated.

*

Our aim was not to list a complete typology of opinions on our problem, but only to show what we called "the rhetoric of the dialogue," that is, the more subjective and human approach to the diversity of religions and ways to deal with the question that is neither a merely psychological perspective nor a purely objective classification.

Our double, fivefold description is neither exhaustive, of course, nor are the different points mutually exclusive. We find sometimes in the same person the use of more than one model and the adoption of more than one attitude.

2

The Dialogical Dialogue

Tat tvam asi
That are you.

—*CU VI.8.7*

Background

The overall background of these pages is constituted by the awareness of the pluralistic and cross-cultural nature of our present-day human situation: pluralistic because no single culture, model, ideology, religion, or whatnot can any longer raise a convincing claim to be *the* one, unique, or even best system in an absolute sense; cross-cultural because human communities no longer live in isolation, and consequently any human problem today that is not seen in pluri-cultural parameters is already methodologically wrongly put.

The philosophical background of this discussion can be seen in the urge to overcome the unconvincing monistic and dualistic answers to the fundamental problem of the "one and the many." Ultimately I am pleading for an advaitic or a-dualistic approach. Its theological horizon is the same philosophical dilemma that takes the form of a God who cannot be totally different from or totally identical with Man and/or World without disappearing. Ultimately, it is a challenge to monotheism and to polytheism alike. At this level, atheism belongs morphologically to monotheism. I am here making the plea that God is neither the Other nor the Same but the One: the one pole in a cosmotheandric insight. The cosmotheandric vision sees the entire reality as the interaction of a threefold polarity: cosmic, divine, and human.

The epistemological formulation of the same problematic voices the inadequacy of the subject-object paradigm of knowledge. My contention here is that no knower can be known as knower—it would then become the known—and yet is. Being is more than consciousness, although the latter is the manifestation of the former. Both are "coextensive" from the point of view of consciousness but not necessarily identical.

Its sociological aspect is evident in the apparent aporias that any serious study of comparative civilizations encounters. No religion, system, or tradition is totally self-sufficient. We need each other and yet find our ideas and attitudes mutually incompatible and ourselves often incapable of bridging the gulf between different worldviews and different basic human attitudes to reality.

The anthropological assumption is that Man is not an individual but a person—that is, a set of relationships of which the I-You-It, in all the genders and numbers, is the most fundamental.

With all the qualifications that the foregoing affirmations need, I submit that one of the causes of this present state of affairs lies in the fact that we need a fundamental reflection on method as well as on the nature of pluralism. This study concerns the first issue, although it is intimately bound up with the second.

The immensity of the problem would require a whole treatise. I shall limit myself to describing a possible method to deal with the particular problem of the cross-cultural encounter, on an ultimate level obviously, and to unveil some of its assumptions. Let us begin in medias res. I have taken as a motto the most important of the Upanishadic *mahāvākya* or Great Utterances: *tat tvam asi.* This mantra is not just a repetition of the other Great Utterances affirming that *brahman* is the *ātman*, consciousness, and the I. It means properly the discovery of the you: *brahman* is The You. "That (subject) are you (predicate)." *Brahman* cannot be the predicate of anything, so the text does not say you are that—that is, *brahman*—but *that* (that is, *brahman*) *are you.* The text does not speak in the third person. It is a dialogue, and thus it does not affirm *brahman* is you, but it reveals to Śvetaketu "*brahman* are you." Transposing it in the third person, it says that (*brahman*) is a you in you—because *that* (is what) *you are.* But I am not indulging here in Vedic hermeneutics. I am only underscoring the fact that besides the *it*, the objective world, and eventually the *I*, the subjective realm, there is also the *you*, which is neither the objective world of the *it* nor the subjective realm of the *ego*.

In other words, I am trying to overcome both the Cartesian dualism of the *res cogitans* and the *res extensa*, and the idealistic dichotomy of the *Ich* and the *Nicht-Ich*. In the last instance, I am criticizing any type of dualism without, for that matter, subscribing to any kind of monism. I am submitting that we have also the sphere of the *you*, which presents an ontonomy irreducible to the spheres of the *I* and the *it.* The *you* is neither autonomous vis-à-vis the I nor dependent heteronomically on it. It presents a proper ontonomical relation, that is, an internal relation constitutive of its own being. The you is therefore neither independent of nor dependent on the I, but interrelated. Consciousness is not only I-consciousness, but it entails also a you-consciousness, that is, not my consciousness of you but "your" consciousness, you as knower, irreducible to what you (and I) know. Because you-consciousness for you takes the form of I-consciousness, the "It-Philosophy" has tried to lump all consciousness together and forged the concept of a *Bewusstsein überhaupt*, a general consciousness. Then it has hypostasized it on an absolute subject. Whatever this supreme consciousness may be, it cannot be the sum total of all I-consciousness because many of those I-consciousnesses are contradictory and irreducible. If at all, it would have to be a supreme *coincidentia oppositorum* or a purely formal consciousness without any content. This conception, be it called God or Brahman or whatever, is what I have designated as monotheism.

Now, coming back to the sublunary world, as the ancients loved to say, in the realm of our human experiences, this implies that in order to have an undistorted vision of reality, we cannot rely exclusively on "our" consciousness but have somehow to incorporate the consciousness of other people about themselves and the world as well. In order to do this, a thematically new method is suggested: the dialogical dialogue. I say "thematically," meaning a conscious reflection on the topic, because the method has been spontaneously employed since many times the dialogue among people is more than "academic"—and even contemporary anthropology tends to it by stressing participatory approaches and the like.

The perceptive reader will of course discover that the background of the following reflections is also constituted by the contemporary insights of the sociology of knowledge (M. Scheler et al.), of hermeneutical criticism (Gadamer et al.), existential phenomenology (Strasser et al.), personalism of all sorts (Ebner et al.), and social theory (Habermas et al.), plus the age-old philosophical self-consciousness that goes from Parmenides to Heidegger and from the *Upaniṣads* to K. C. Bhattacharya, passing through Husserl, Śankara, et al.

The relevance of the dialogical dialogue for the encounter of religious traditions and the so-called comparative religion is obvious. I cannot really know—and thus compare—another ultimate system of beliefs unless somehow I share those beliefs, and I cannot do this until I know the holder of those beliefs, the you—not as other (that is, nonego), but as a you. Please note that I speak of beliefs and not just objectified opinions about things.

This much for an overcondensed introduction to the problematic.

Thesis

The foundation for the thesis of this chapter rests on the assumption that the ultimate nature of reality does not have to be dialectical. If we postulate it to be so, we do it by the already dialectical axiom that affirms reality to be solely or ultimately dialectical. Reality has no foundation other than itself, and if we assume it to be dialectical we are already postulating what reality has to be and imprisoning it in the dialectical frame, large and flexible as one may conceive this latter to be. The postulate of the dialectical nature of reality is an extrapolation of the conviction about the dialectical nature of the mind; it subordinates reality to mind.

My thesis is that the dialogical dialogue is not a modification of the dialectical method or a substitution for it. It is a method that both limits the field of dialectics and complements it. It *limits* dialectics, insofar as it prevents dialectics from becoming logical monism, by putting forward another method that does not assume the exclusively dialectical nature of reality. It *complements* dialectics by the same token. It is not a direct critique of dialectics, but only a guard against dialectical totalitarianism.

The thesis says, further, that the dialogical dialogue is the proper, although not exclusive, method for what I have called "*diatopical*" hermeneutics. By diatopical hermeneutics I understand a hermeneutic that is more than the purely morphological (drawing from the already known deposit of a particular tradition) and the merely diachronical one (when we have to bridge a temporal gap in order to arrive at a legitimate interpretation). It is a hermeneutic dealing with understanding the contents of diverse cultures that do not have cultural or direct historical links with one another. They belong to different loci, *topoi*, so that before anything else we have to forge the tools of understanding in the encounter itself, for we cannot—should not—assume a priori a common language. The privileged place of this hermeneutic is obviously the encounter of religious traditions. A Christian cannot assume at the outset that he knows what a Buddhist means when speaking about *nirvāṇa* and *anātman*, just as a Buddhist cannot immediately be expected to understand what a Christian means by God and Christ before they have encountered not just the concepts but their living contexts, which include different ways at looking at reality: they have to encounter each other before any meeting of doctrines. This is what the dialogical dialogue purports to be: the method for the encounter of persons and not just individuals, on the one hand, or mere doctrines on the other.

Dialogue and Dialectics

Let me emphatically assert that this essay is neither an attack on dialectics nor a critique of rationality. Dialectics, in spite of its many meanings, stands for the dignity of the human logos endowed with the extraordinary prerogative of discriminating between truth and error by means of thinking: *ars iudicandi*, said the Scholastics, condensing Cicero's definition of dialectics as *veri et falsi iudicandi scientia*. It is of course a matter of philosophical dispute where to locate this human power, its name and nature; at any rate we may accept the well-known Hegelian description of dialectics as *die wissenschaftliche Anwendung der in der Natur des Denkens liegenden Gesetzmässigkeit* (the scientific application of the inner structure [the internal law, the law-governedness] inherent in the nature of thinking).

We could, of course, try to harmonize most of the thinkers who have in the past used this word (in the present, the inflation makes any overview almost impossible) and define it as διαλεκτική τεχνή or as *ars scientiaque disputandi*, that is, the craft of human verbal intercourse. In this definition we would embrace Plato's "conversation" in questions and answers, as well as Aristotle's conception of reasoning on probable opinions, Kant's logic of appearances and, through

Hegel's dictum that *das Selbstbewusstsein wesentliches Moment des Wahren ist* (self-consciousness is an essential moment of truth), the Marxist's interpretation of dialectics as the method of true thinking because it constitutes the expression of the dynamic coherence of otherwise contradictory historical reality. In this wider sense the dialogical dialogue is still dialogue and thus dialectical or conversational. But we may legitimately assume that nowadays when people use the word *dialectic* they imply that tight relationship between thinking and being about which I shall later express my critical doubts. They mean also a technique that empowers one to pass judgments on other people's opinions and not a mere art of conversation. In this sense the dialogical dialogue lies outside the sphere of dialectics. *Dia-logical* here would stand for piercing, going through the logical and overcoming—not denying—it. The dialogical dialogue is in its proper place when dealing with personal, cross-cultural, and pluralistic problems. In all three cases we deal with situations not totally reducible to the *logos*.

Personal problems are those in which the complexity of the whole human person is at stake and not merely mental quandaries or, for that matter, any other partial queries. A personal problem is not a sheer technical puzzle of how to reestablish the proper functioning of the human organism. The human being is certainly a rational animal and rationality may be its most precious gift, but the realm of reason does not exhaust the human field. It is not by dialectically convincing the patients that the psychotherapist will cure them. It is not by proving one side to be right that a war can be avoided. There is no dialectical proof for love. Not less but something more is required.

A *cross-cultural* problem arises from the encounter of two cultures, for example, when somebody insists that the earth is a living being and should be treated as such against a technological view of the planet. It cannot be solved dialectically. We should avoid using the word *cross-cultural* when we mean only the study of another culture different from our own but still with the categories of the latter. A cross-cultural approach to Asia, for instance, does not mean "Orientalism" in the Victorian sense of the word. Cross-cultural studies deal with the very perspective in which the "problem" is approached. They reformulate the very problem by using categories derived from the two cultures concerned. Scholastically speaking, we may say that cross-cultural studies are not characterized by their "material object" (say, India or Hinduism from a Western stance), but by their "formal object" (say, the scale of values, perspectives, views, and categories we apply to apprehend the very "problem"). I am saying here that dialectics are not cross-cultural enough. Dialectics are a knowledge with an "interest" arising from a particular worldview, and the very interest in universalizing the dialectical method—especially the historical dialectics—reinforces our affirmation. We need another method for cross-cultural studies before any discussion in the dialectical arena.

Dialectical Dialogue

The dialectical dialogue supposes that we are rational beings and that our knowledge is governed above all by the principle of noncontradiction. You and I admit it as a given, and if you lead me into contradiction I will either have to give up my opinion or attempt to overcome the impasse. We present our respective points of view to the Tribunal of Reason, in spite of the variety of interpretations that we may hold even of the nature of reason. The dialectical dialogue trusts Reason and in a way the reasonableness of the other—or of the whole historical process. It admits, further, that none of us exhausts the knowledge of the data. On this basis we engage in dialogue. If we refuse the dialogue it is because, even without saying it, we assume that someone is motivated by ill will and not ready to abide by the fair play of dialectics or else is mentally weak, fears defeat, or the like. It is obvious that there are fields proper to the dialectical dialogue, and even that it can never be bypassed. If we deny reason or reasonableness, we make impossible any type of dialogue.

As we shall expound later again, the dialectical dialogue is a necessary intermediary in the communication between human beings. Dialectics have an irreplaceable mediating function at the human level. The dialectical dialogue cannot be brushed away in any truly human exchange. We have the need to judge and to discriminate for ourselves—not necessarily for others—between right and wrong. It would amount to falling into sheer irrationalism to ignore this essential role of dialectics.

Dialogical Dialogue

The dialectical dialogue is a dialogue about objects that, interestingly enough, the English language calls "subject matters." The dialogical dialogue, on the other hand, is a dialogue among subjects aiming at being a dialogue about subjects. They want to dialogue not about something, but about themselves: they "dialogue themselves." In short, if all thinking is dialogue, not all dialogue is dialogical. The dialogical dialogue is not so much about opinions (the famous *endoxa*, ἔνδοξα of Aristotle with which dialectics deal) as about those who have such opinions, and eventually not about you, but about me to you. To dialogue about opinions, doctrines, views, the dialectical dialogue is indispensable. In the dialogical dialogue the partner is not an object or a subject merely putting forth some objective thoughts to be discussed, but a you—a real you and not an it. I must deal with you and not merely with your thought—and of course, vice versa, you yourself are a source of understanding.

Now, two persons cannot talk each other; they have to talk *to* each other. This means that the talk has to be mediated by something else. The medium is a language, and if there is language there is thought. They cannot dialogue themselves; they need the mediation of language. In any dialogue there is something outside of and in a way superior to the partners that link them together. They have to be speaking about something, and this something has an inner structure that the participants have to respect and acknowledge. But this something is only a mediator conveying to each of them not just "thoughts," that is, objectifiable ideas, but thematically a part of themselves. In other words, this something is not made independent, "objective," but is seen in its peculiar *dialogical intentionality*.

In order to describe the characteristics of this dialogical dialogue, we have been contrasting it with the dialectical one. It should be made clear that the relation between the two is not dialectical; they are two intertwined moments of the dialogical character of the human being. There is no pure dialectical dialogue. When two persons enter into dialogue, in spite of all the efforts to keep the "personal" to a bare minimum, it emerges all along. We never have an encounter of pure ideas. We always have an encounter of two (or more) persons. This aspect of the human being often emerges conspicuously in the actual praxis of the dialectical dialogue, in which the partners, forgetting that they are supposed to be thinking beings, indulge in getting involved in quite different but also real aspects of human life. To discard those aspects as "sentimental" or as "passions" obscuring the work of Reason misses the point. Sentiments also belong to the human being. There are, further, cases in which what is at issue are not emotional ingredients but fundamental options stemming from different self-understandings. But there is much more than this. There is no pure *theory*. It is always "tinged" with interests and connected with the milieu that accepts it as theory.

Similarly, there is no dialogical dialogue alone. Two subjects can only enter into dialogue if they "talk" about something, even if they are interested in knowing each other and in wanting to know themselves better by means of the mirror-effect on the other. The dialogical dialogue is not a mute act of love. It is a total human encounter, and thus it has an important intellectual component. It is precisely the importance of the very subject matter of the dialogue that unveils the depths of the respective personalities and leads to the dialogical dialogue proper.

This emphasizes a fact that is often only latent in the merely dialectical dialogue: the will to dialogue. This will is paramount here. It is not that if I do not will to enter into dialogue I keep my mouth shut. It is that if I do not have that will even if I speak with my partner I will not enter into any dialogical dialogue. Here no pretense would do. The dialectical dialogue can be an instrument to power and can be a means to the will to power. This is not the case with the dialogical dialogue. It is for this reason that any further intention—the intention, for example, to convert, to dominate, or even to know the other for ulterior motives—destroys the dialogical dialogue.

The trusting in the other, considering the other a true source of understanding and knowledge, the listening attitude toward my partner, the common search for truth (without assuming that we already know what words mean to each of us), the acceptance of the risk of being defeated, converted, or simply upset and left without a north—these are not pragmatic devices to enable us to live in peaceful coexistence because the other is already too powerful or vociferous and cannot be silenced. It is not because reason has failed us or that humankind has suddenly experienced a disenchantment with the idea of a possible *pax mundialis* as it is traditionally expressed in the models of One God, One Church, One Empire, One Religion, One Civilization, and now One Technology. The justification of the dialogical dialogue lies much deeper; it is to be found in the very nature of the real, namely in the fact that reality is not wholly objectifiable, ultimately because I myself, a subject, am also a part of it, am *in* it, and cannot extricate myself from it. The dialogical dialogue assumes a radical dynamism of reality, namely that reality is not given once and for all, but is real precisely in the fact that it is continually creating itself—and not just unfolding from already existing premises or starting points.

This is certainly what the modern understanding of dialectics also espouses: Reality is in a state of constant flux, everything depends on everything else, and immutability is not a feature of reality. Still more: modern dialectics accepts the changing nature of reality in such a way that change is made imperative. Change is not contingent but necessary, and it brings about qualitative leaps in the order of things. The overcoming of internal contradictions belongs to the very nature of reality. All this is dialectics. But there is one thing that dialectics cannot give up: the pliability of reality to the dialectical laws of thinking. It is here that the ultimate character of the dialogical dialogue appears clearly, as we shall see in a moment.

From what has been said so far, we may gather the impression that the dialogical dialogue is inbuilt in any authentic and deep dialogue. This is certainly so, but the evolution of human culture, especially in the West, has given predominance to the dialectical aspect of the dialogue, and the dialogical one has been relegated to playing second fiddle. We would like now to unearth some of the assumptions underlying this dialogue. We will then better see its revolutionary character. It challenges, in point of fact, many of the commonly accepted foundations of modern culture. To restore or install the dialogical dialogue in human relations among individuals, families, groups, societies, nations, and cultures may be one of the most urgent things to do in our times, which are threatened by a fragmentation of interests that threatens all life on the planet. In point of fact, one feature of contemporary Western culture—mainly subcultures—is the praxis of a certain approach to the dialogical dialogue in the form of social work and psychotherapies. Yet in many cases, the lack of the "dialogical intentionality" makes such methods ineffective.

Thinking and Being

The dialogical dialogue assumes, we said, that nobody can predict or fathom the dynamism of being because this latter is not mere evolution but also creativity. We could say, paraphrasing an *Upaniṣad*, that even the mind has to recoil and stand back. Science is that astonishing feat made possible because our thinking can foretell how beings are going to behave. This is an incontrovertible fact. But nothing stands in the way of reality expressing itself freely in ways not predictable by thinking of any kind. The spontaneity and creativity of Nature may be hidden in its very recesses, perhaps at the origins of time and at the infra-atomic levels, as modern science begins to surmise, but certainly (the human) being possesses a factor of creativity and spontaneity that cannot be encapsulated in any a priori scheme. This creativity constitutes the locus of the dialogical dialogue. To sum up: Dialectics, in one way or another, deals with the power of our mind but assumes a peculiar relation between thinking and being.

Here comes the great divide. It is one thing to assert that thinking tells us what being is and another thing to make being utterly dependent on thinking. In other words, the justification of dialectics does not depend on the often uncritically accepted hypothesis that the nature of reality is dialectical. Reality certainly has a dialectical aspect, but this aspect does not have to be all of the real. It is in this hiatus between thinking and being that the dialogical dialogue finds its *ultimate* justification. There are human situations that do not necessarily fall under the jurisdiction of the dialectical dialogue because reality does not have to be exhaustively dialectical. The laws of thought are laws of being, and this makes science possible, but not necessarily vice versa. Rather, being does not have to have—or always follow—laws, however useful such a hypothesis may be. Being is not exclusively restricted to be what thinking postulates. This makes ontic freedom possible and constitutes the ultimate onto-logical problem: The *logos* of the *on* is only the *on* of the *logos*, but this latter is not identical with the former. The *on* is "bigger" than the *logos*. The *logos* may be coextensive with the *on*, but still there "is" the *pneuma* "between," and "where Spirit, freedom." And where there is freedom, thought cannot dictate, foresee, or even necessarily follow the "expansion," "explosion," life of Being. We recall that Plato believed ideas have a life of their own.

"Being is said in many ways": τό ὀν πολλαχῶς λέγεται is the famous sentence of Aristotle. But being "is" also unsaid, at least inasmuch as it has not yet been said. Further, we cannot think how being will speak, that is, will say itself. Yet this unsaid accompanies being. This silent companion may not be in principle unspeakable, but it is actually unspoken. Real silence is not repression of the word and incapacity to think, but absence of the word and transcending of thought.

The dialogical dialogue makes room for this sovereign freedom of being to speak new languages—or languages unknown to the other.

Be this as it may, even without this ultimate foundation, there is place for the dialogical dialogue.

Subject and Object

The most immediate assumption of the dialogical dialogue is that the other is not just an other (*alius*) and much less an object of my knowledge (*aliud*), but another self (*alter*) who is a source of self-understanding, and also of understanding, not necessarily reducible to my own.

Another way of putting it: Reality is not totally objectifiable. The dialectical dialogue takes place in the sphere of the objectifiable reality. We discuss, agree, or disagree on objective grounds, following objective rules. Something is objectifiable when it is in principle conceptualizable. It can then be an object of some thought. What is objectifiable is the conceptual aspect of reality apprehended as such by the subject. But this apparently leaves the subject out of it.

Anything we say about an objective state of affairs is an abstraction. It abstracts from the subject and ignores its influence on the object. It is like freezing the flow of the real. This freezing may well be necessary for a moment in order more easily to apprehend something, but it can become a trap we fall into the moment we forget that it is only a device, and a provisional one, a scaffold we use to reach outside ourselves and grasp something. In other words, the trap is to mistake the objective idea for the real, the concept for the thing—eventually identifying the two. In this setting the others are able only somewhat to qualify or correct my assertions, but certainly not to convert me radically, that is, to throw me out of the fortress of my "own" private world. From here to an ideology of power there is only a short way to go.

The dialogical dialogue, on the other hand, considers the other as another subject, that is, as another source of (self-)understanding. The others as subjects do not have to be necessarily reduced to an ultimately unique source. This is the question of pluralism (that we said we were leaving aside) and its connection with monotheism: the different subjects participating, each in their own way, from the one single Source of intelligence and intelligibility.

The dialogical dialogue is not concerned so much about opinions as about the different viewpoints from which the respective opinions are arrived at. Now, to deal with a perspective means to deal with very fundamental springs in the knowing subject. A new epistemology is required here. Just as any knowledge of an object requires a certain connaturality and identification with the object to be known, any knowledge of the subject necessitates also a similar identification. This is what has led me to formulate the principle of "Understanding as Convincement." We cannot understand a person's ultimate convictions unless we somehow share them.

I and You

This is not the place to describe the rich evolution of the idea of dialectics. Suffice it to say that it was probably F. H. Jacobi, who first saw, in the post-Cartesian age, the implicit solipsism of any idealism (including Kant's) and began to develop the idea of a dialogical thinking transcending the constriction of objective dialectics. But it was Feuerbach criticizing Hegel who tried to develop a dialogical dialectic that is a forerunner of the dialogical thinkers of the beginning of this century: Buber, Rosenzweig, and Ebner. Feuerbach says, "Die wahre Dialektik ist kein Monolog des einsamen Denkers mit sich selbst, sie ist ein Dialog zwischen Ich und Du" (The true dialectic is not a monologue of the individual thinker with himself, but a dialogue between the I and the You).

Yet, without now entering into a detailed analysis of those predecessors, I may add that the dialogical dialogue I am espousing claims to transcend the realm of dialectics by realizing that the relation I/Thou is irreducible to any relation I/It or I/Non-I, and thus equally ultimate.

A certain type of philosophy, which could be designated broadly as Idealism, has potentiated the knowledge of all potential subjects and called it the ultimate or true I as the bearer of all knowledge, as absolute consciousness. Over against this I, there remains only the Non-I, be it called world, matter, extension, evil, illusion, appearance, or whatever.

Another type of philosophy, which could broadly be called sociology of knowledge, has stressed the fact of the dependency of the thinking individual on both collectivity and environment. Any individual's thinking expresses only what is thinkable within the community in which that individual thinks, and one's personal contribution makes sense only within the larger context of the community. Furthermore, one's thinking is also a part of human thinking and not only a disconnected heap of human thoughts.

In the first case we have the ultimate dialectical opposition between the I and the Non-I. The individual is part of that I, and when in dialogue with other egos it has only to deepen its participation in the absolute consciousness. The other as subject is invited to do the same; as object it belongs to the sphere of the Non-I.

In the latter case, the individual's thinking is situated vis-à-vis the collectivity, of which it is also a part. The others are members of the same or a different community sharing in the same or another *Zeitgeist*, as it were.

In both cases the dialogue with the other is directed toward the source of our understanding of reality by means of a sharing in either an absolute consciousness or a collective consciousness of a group in space and time, or even the entire humanity.

This may be true, but there is still more to it. When the individual thinks, he does not think individualistically; he does not think out of himself alone, nor only in contemplation of God or intercourse with the world, that is, with the object of his thinking (his thought), but he thinks already in conformity, harmony with, and/or reaction to, stimulated by, and in dialogue with other people. Thinking is not an individualistic process, but an act of language.

But language is primarily neither a private activity nor a mystical act in connection with Consciousness or Humanity. It is an exchange with someone in front of us and at our level. It is fundamentally a dialogical activity. What the two just-mentioned considerations have overlooked is precisely that our first verbal relationship is not dialectical but dialogical. We begin by listening, learning, assimilating, comparing, and the like. We are not confronting a non-ego but a "you" with whom we have a common language or with whom we strive to have one.

In order to think, we cannot succeed alone. We need dialogue with the *you.* In point of fact, the *I* can only express "itself" in intercourse with the *you* or with the *it.* We need the living dialogue because the "I love," "I will," and even "I think" acquires its full meaning only in confrontation with what a "you" loves, wills, and thinks. This amounts to saying that thinking is only possible within one—our—world, and thus one language, our language.

I am not excluding the dialogue with the it, that is, with things. This is one of the fascinations of Science, and I am even prepared to reinstate animism in the traditional sense of the *anima mundi* and the belief that in one way or another everything is alive, conscious of the fact that this position introduces a revolution in Science: not only does physics become biology, but Science itself becomes dialogical. But in the human dialogue with things, in spite of the fact that things react, offer resistance, are not pliable to the wishes of the human intellect, and in a certain way respond to the human dialogue, they do not have the same interiority and consciousness as human beings. In brief, for the full development of human thinking, even when thinking about things, human dialogue is imperative.

The dialogical dialogue takes you my partner as seriously as myself and by this very fact wakes me up from the slumber of solipsistic speculations, or the dreaming fantasies of a docile partner. We encounter the hard reality of an opposition, another will, another source of opinions, perspectives. The dialogue maintains the constitutive polarity of reality that cannot be split into subject and object without the previous awareness of different subjects speaking. There is not only a subject and an object, but also a subject and another subject, although mediated by an object. This is even inbuilt in language itself. The I-and-You statements can never set the speaking subject aside; they cannot be substantives in the sense of being reified, cut off from the I and the You and made into eternal, immutable "truths." In the dialogue we are reminded constantly of our temporality, our contingency, our own constitutive limitations. Humility is not primarily a moral virtue but an ontological one; it is the awareness of the place of my ego, the truthfulness of accepting my real situation, namely, that I am a situated being, a vision's angle on the real, an existence.

As already indicated, the rationale for the dialogical dialogue is that the *you* has a proper and inalienable ontonomy. The you is a source of self-understanding that I cannot assimilate from my own perspective alone. It is not as if we all would see "the same thing" but from a different vantage point. This may be true, but the dialogical dialogue is not just the locus for perspectivism. It does not assume a "thing in itself," the elephant in the dark room of the Indian story (one witness describing "reality" as a shaft, the other as a pillar, the third as a winnowing fan, and so on). Nor does it assume a mere atomistic view, as if each human being were an independent monad without windows. It assumes, on the contrary, that we all share in a reality that does not exist independently and outside our own sharing in it, and yet without exhausting it. Our participation is always partial, and reality is more than just the sum total of its parts.

Myth and *Logos*

To be sure, many things happen in the dialectical dialogue: there are winners and losers, some conclusions are arrived at, some new light is shed on the subject matter, new distinctions are made, and so on. Besides and above those things the dialogical dialogue changes the partners themselves in unexpected ways and may open new vistas not logically implied in the premises. The very "rules" of this dialogue are not fixed a priori; they emerge out of the dialogue itself. The dialogue is not a "duologue," but a going through the *logos*: *dia ton logon*, διά τόν λόγον, beyond the logos-structure of reality. It pierces the *logos* and uncovers the respective myths of the partners. In the dialogical dialogue, we are vulnerable because we allow ourselves to be "seen" by our partner, and vice versa. It is the other who discovers my myth, what I take for granted, my horizon of intelligibility, the convictions of which lie at the source of my expressed beliefs. It is the other who will detect the hidden reasons for my choice of words, metaphors, and ways of thinking. It is the other who will interpret my silences and omissions in (for me) unsuspected ways.

Now, in order to allow this to happen we need to unearth our presuppositions. But this we cannot do alone. We need the other. We are more or less conscious of our assumptions, that is, of the axioms or convictions that we put at the starting point and use as the foundation of our views. But those very assumptions themselves rest on underlying "pre-sub-positions" that for us "go without saying" and are "taken for granted." But this does not need to be the case for our partner, and he will point them out to us and bring them to the forum of analysis and discussion. We may then either discard them or convert them into conscious assumptions as bases for further thinking.

The dialogical dialogue challenges us on a much deeper level than the dialectical one. With the dialectical dialogue we are unable to explore realms of human experience, spheres of reality, or aspects of being that belong to the first and second persons, that is, to the "*am*" and [you] "*are*" aspects of reality. In other words, with the dialectical dialogue we can only reach the "*it is*" aspect of the real and cannot be in full communication with other subjects and their most intimate convictions. With the dialectical dialogue, we may discuss religious doctrines once we have clarified the context, but we need the dialogical dialogue to discuss beliefs as those conscious attitudes we have in face of the ultimate issues of our existence and life.

In the dialogical dialogue, I trust the other not out of an ethical principle (because it is good) or an epistemological one (because I recognize that it is intelligent to do so), but because I have discovered (experienced) the "*you*" as the counterpart of the I, as belonging *to* the I (and not as not I). I trust the partner's understanding and self-understanding because I do not start out by putting my ego as the foundation of everything. It is not that I do not examine my partner's credentials (he could be wicked or a fool), not that I fall into irrationalism (or any type of sentimentalism), giving up my stance, but that I find in his actual presence something irreducible to my ego and yet not belonging to a non-ego: I discover the you as part of a Self that is as much mine as his—or to be more precise, that is as little my property as his.

Now, this discovery of the *ātman*, the human nature, a common essence or divine undercurrent, is not, properly speaking, *my* discovery of *it*, but my discovery of *me*, the discovery of myself as me—and not as I: "*me-consciousness*."

Further, this dawning of me-consciousness cannot occur without the "you" spurring it on, and ultimately the real or ultimate I (*aham*) performing it. Leaving aside now the awareness of the transcendent-immanent I, the fact still remains that without a "you" calling and challenging me, my "me-consciousness" would not emerge. In the dialogical dialogue my partner is not the *other* (it is not he/she, and much less it), but the You. The You is neither the other nor the non-ego. The You is the very "you" of the I in the sense of the subjective genitive.

It is the cross-cultural challenge of our times that unless the barbarian, the *mleccha*, *goy*, infidel, "nigger," *kafir*, foreigner, and stranger are invited to be my *you*, beyond those of my own clan, tribe, race, church, or ideology, there is not much hope left for the planet. This on a world-scale is a *novum*, but an indispensable element for a present-day civilization worthy of humanity. We have mentioned already the importance of the dialogical dialogue for the Encounter of Religions. It is, I submit, the neglect of this method and the application of a predominantly dialectical dialogue among religious traditions that is at the root of so many misunderstandings and enmities among the followers of so many religions. The lack of proper understanding among religions is not so much matter of doctrinal differences—these exist also among schools of the same religion—but of existential attitudes—down often to economic, administrative, and political reasons.

And so, we close the circle. We began by saying that true dialogue is a dialogue among human beings and have underscored that a person is more than a thinking subject; persons are fields of interaction where the real has been woven or striped by means of all the complexity of reality; they are knots in the continuous weaving of the net of reality.

*

Millennia ago, Chuang Tsu said,

> Assume you and I argue. If you win and I lose, are you right and I wrong? If I win and you lose, am I right and you wrong? Are we both partially right and wrong? Are we both right or both wrong? If you and I cannot see the truth, other people will find it harder.
>
> Whom shall we ask to be the judge? Someone who agrees with you? If he agrees with you how can he be a fair judge? Shall I ask someone who agrees with me? If he does, how can he be a fair judge? Shall I ask someone who agrees with both of us? If he already agrees with both of us, how can he be a fair judge? If you and I and other cannot decide, shall we wait for still another?
>
> Since the standard of judging right or wrong depends on the changing relative phenomena, then there is fundamentally no standard at all.
>
> Seeing everything in relation to the natural cosmic perspective, argument stops, right and wrong cease to be. We are then free and at ease.
>
> What do I mean by "seeing everything in relation to the natural cosmic perspective, then argument stops"? This is to say that "right" *can be said* to be "wrong," "being," "non-being." If something is really right, it naturally has its distinction from wrong. There is no need for argument.
>
> Being is naturally distinguished from non-being. There is no need for argument either. Forget all about differentiation between life and death, right and wrong. Be free. Live and play with the infinite.*

---

* On the basis of the published version of G.-F. Fend and J. English, retranslated by Agnes Lee, whom I thank.

3

Faith and Belief

A Multireligious Experience

te 'pi mām eva, . . . yajanti
Me they also worship.

—*BG IX.23*

Whoever wishes to care for me,
let him look after the sick ones.

—*VP I.302*

εμοί εποιήσατε
mihi fecistis
You did it unto me.

—*Mt 25:40*

Introduction

The distinction between faith and belief, along with the thesis that faith is a constitutive human dimension, represents more than just an intellectual venture. It is equally an existential adventure: a human pilgrimage within religious traditions divided by multisecular walls of history, philosophies, theologies, and prejudices. It has been my *karma* to undergo such experiences without artificially or even reflectively preparing them. A decade ago, after fifteen years' absence from the European literary scene, the plainest and yet the most searching question to ask me was: How have I fared? Although my human pilgrimage was not yet finished, I used to give a straightforward—obviously incomplete—answer: I "left" as a Christian, I "found" myself a Hindū, and I "return" a Buddhist, without having ceased to be a Christian. Some people nevertheless wonder whether such an attitude is objectively tenable or even intelligible. Here is a reply in outline that I hope will also throw some light on the spiritual condition of humankind today—even if it belongs to my historical past.

Ecumenism Today

In ancient Greece, *oikumene* referred to household management. When the domestic sense broadened, the word came to mean the world, but still within a rather narrow compass—just as when someone says "everybody" has left Madrid for August vacation, although the only water most of the people ever see is the trickle in their own channeled river Manzanares. Our age prides itself on its ecumenical spirit and has indeed risen above the clan mentality far enough to acknowledge the right of other clans to exist, whether they call themselves philosophical systems, religious beliefs, races, or nations. But for all their importance, these ecumenisms generally remain very restricted, still far removed from an *ecumenical ecumenism* that means more than the mere notion that people everywhere are human or that my own views and judgments can be exported quite safely to other countries.

The great temptation for ecumenism is to extrapolate—to use a native growth beyond the bounds of its native soil. We have seen what comes of exporting European and American democracy; we know that the baffling population explosion over much of the world's surface comes of exporting antibiotics, know-how, and the like. No one-way movement—certainly not exporting a Gospel—can solve our present problems. I do not for a moment suggest that there be no crossing of borders. I am only saying that most solutions to our problems remain terribly provincial; we do not yet have categories adequate to the exigencies of our *kairos.*

The Province and the Parish

The confrontation of religions provides an instructive instance of what I am trying to say. Western culture constructs a philosophy or theology of religion and considers it universal. To be more precise, it dashes off Judeo-Greco-modern categories and with these attempts to lay hold of religious, cultural, and philosophical phenomena lying many a mile beyond the remotest colony (as it is called), the farthest outpost of its *oikumene.* Thus Asia, for example, compelled to speak in some European language, will have to say "way" instead of *dao*, "God" instead of Brahman, and "soul" instead of *ātman*; it must translate *dharma* as "justice," *ch'an* as "meditation," and so forth. But the problem lies even deeper than the difficulty of suitably translating ideas belonging to other cultural contexts. The problem cannot be "computerized," so to speak, because it involves the very laws that govern the working of our minds—and of computers to boot.

This "neocolonialistic" situation prompts me to observe that while the *province* may betoken narrowness of mind bordering on myopia and may lead to fanaticism and intolerance, the *parish* might connote safeguarding a particular reality, a human scale of things, organic and personal life. The parish is by its very nature a miniature universe quantitatively speaking but is also the entire universe speaking qualitatively (although symbolically). Nevertheless, from the steeple of the parish church many other steeples can be seen. A theological hermeneutic of this symbol tells us that the parish will be whole only when the Pantocrator, the Lord of all the universe, is at its center and there holds communion (this is the right word) with the whole world. Wisdom reaches its pinnacle in a happy commingling of universal and concrete, intellectual and vital, masculine and feminine, divine and human—in short, in cosmotheandric experience.

"Ecumenical ecumenism," a phrase I diffidently put forward some years ago and that now seems to be sweeping the board, might well express this blend of household hearth and universal humanness. The parish lived in all its depth and scope stands for the same thing: homey, down-to-earth, regional things; it means dialect, personal roots, personalizing forms, and at the same time an awareness that we all draw nourishment from a common sap, that one sky arches over us all, that a single Mother Earth sustains us all.[1]

Ecumenical ecumenism does not mean cloudy universalism or indiscriminate syncretism; or a narrow, crude particularism or barren, fanatical individualism. Instead it attempts a happy blending—which I would boldly call androgynous before calling it theandric—of these two poles, the universal and the concrete, which set up the tension in every creature. In other words, the identity our age so frantically seeks is not individuality (which ends in solipsism) nor generality (which ends in alienation), but the awareness of that constitutive relativity that makes of us but connections in the mysterious warp and woof of being. But I should not go on cheering *pro domo mea* when I am saying my house is the cottage of mankind.

An Objectified Autobiographical Fragment

Before embarking on a clearer, more scholarly treatment of the subject, I should like to present it in a personal way, psychological if you will—although not strictly autobiographical.

Here I am, a person brought up in the strictest orthodoxy, who has lived as well in a milieu that is "microdox" from every point of view. It will not do to say now that if I managed to survive, it was thanks to seeds of true life sown even before I had reached the age of reason. This person goes forth, forsaking the land of Ur, to dwell in the land of "Men" (indeed he knew it before, but not through experience, not in his flesh like Job). Instantly he finds himself confronted by a dilemma: either he must condemn everything around him as error and sin, or he must throw overboard the exclusivistic and monopolistic notions he has been told embody truth—truth that must be simple and unique, revealed once and for all, that speaks through infallible organs, and so on. None of the answers people

---

[1] No need to remind the reader that *parish*, Latin *paroecia*, comes from the Greek πάροικος, made of πάρά and οἰκος, "to sojourn, dwell beside, be beside the house, a neighbor," but also a stranger. See πάροκος, a public purveyor.

give to this dilemma satisfy him. The eclectic answer flouts logic and sometimes common sense as well. He cannot make do with the "orthodox" answer that merely concocts casuistic shifts so that some nook is left for those who profess error through no fault of their own; it does not convince him either as a whole or in its details. So he overcomes the temptation of *relativism* by acknowledging *relativity*. Instead of everything falling into an agnostic or indifferent relativism, everything is wrapped in an utter relativity of radical interdependence because every being is a function in the hierarchical order of beings and has its own place in the dynamism of history, a place not incidental to the thing but actually making the thing what it is.

But the personal problem went deeper still. It involved more than rising above provincialism or acknowledging that today philosophy must recognize cultural differences and account for Man's pluralism. One had to safeguard the parish, uphold one's identity, live by one's faith and yet not cut oneself off from others, not look on oneself as a special, privileged being. Can this man keep his feet firmly planted on the ground—on his native soil—while his arms embrace the most distant heavens? Indeed, the problem was trying to live one's faith without an exclusivity that appears outrageously unjust and false even when decked out in notions of grace, election, or what have you. In other words, the whole idea of belonging to a chosen people, of practicing the true religion, of being a privileged creature, struck me not as a grace but a disgrace. Not that I felt myself unworthy, but I thought it would ill become me to discriminate in such a fashion, and I thought it would ill become God to do so.

I am well aware of the innumerable theoretical ways to get around the objection. I do not claim that this idea runs counter to God's goodness or justice, which presumably is not affected by our revulsion; I contend only that this idea contravenes the freedom and joy I would look for in a belief that enables the human being to grow to full stature. It is not as though the conception of God could not outride such objections; it is rather that such a conception of God reflects little credit on the person who thinks it up. I share, if you like, the well-known outlook of the *bodhisattva*, who forestalls his own beatitude until the last sentient being has attained it; or of Moses and Paul who would rather be stricken from the Book of Life than saved alone. In short, can one live a religious faith to the full without being cut off from others either quantitatively or qualitatively—either from the whole of mankind down the ages or from whatever is human in them and in oneself?

Universality and Concreteness

The problem comes down to this: can one lead a universal life in the concrete? Is it feasible to live by faith that is at once embodied—incarnational—and transcendent? Is the concrete incompatible with the universal, the categorical with the transcendental?

But here we have only the first part of the problem. The second part emerges when we must contend with people holding different views who claim the right to argue just as we do and to draw conclusions in favor of their own views. After all, the rules must be the same for both sides; I may embrace my neighbor only if I let her embrace me at the same time; I may universalize my belief and reform my religion only if, at the same time, I let my neighbor do the same with hers. Taking this attitude, am I not endangering an entire conception of truth based on the principle of property?

But once our seven-league boots have swept us to the pinnacle of the problem, it is best to start down again along one particular path, to try to shed light on a single facet of the problem and afterward cite an example to corroborate our words.[2] The aspect I would like to rough out may be focused in the distinction already made between faith and belief.[3]

The Encounter of Beliefs

Let us return to our point of departure and say that I (who for the present purposes can be anybody) live by certain underlying persuasions that express themselves in my personal act of faith: I believe in a God who made the universe, in a Christ who redeemed mankind, in a Spirit who is our pledge of everlasting life, and so forth. For me all these phrases are just translations into a given language understandable in a given tradition of something that transcends all utterance. I refer to those dogmas (as they are called) that make sense of my life and convey what truth is for me. I cannot dispense with these phrases because they make up my belief, but neither must I forget that they are phrases, neither more nor less.

On this level I encounter a person who belongs to another religious tradition. She tells me she does not believe in God, she has no idea who Christ is, and she thinks there is no life but the present one we all experience. She may tell me further that she believes in Buddha as an Enlightened One who has pointed out the road to salvation and that salvation consists in blotting out all existence.

The first requisite for dialogue is that we understand each other. The first prerequisite for this understanding on the intellectual level is that we speak the same language, lest we use different words to convey the same idea and therefore take them to mean different things. Now in order to know we speak the same language, we need a lodestar somewhere outside the framework of language: We must be able to point with the finger of the mind, or some other sign, to the "thing" when we use the same or different words.

Let us assume (which is assuming a great deal, but so we must if we are to make any headway) that we have reached agreement about our language and

---

[2] See R. Panikkar, *Myth, Faith, and Hermeneutics: Cross-Cultural Studies* (New York: Paulist Press, 1978), chapter 14 on *karma*, which expands this example.

[3] See ibid., chapter 6.

we are using words to signify ideas defined sharply enough to make discussion possible.

The exchange might then take some such form: "I believe in God as embodying the truth that makes sense of my life and the things around me." "I, on the other hand, believe in the nonexistence of such a being, and this nonexistence is precisely what enables me to believe in the truth of things and to make sense of my life and the things around me." Here one person makes "God" the keystone of her existence, salvation, and so on, while the other makes her conviction of "no God" the keystone of the same thing. More simply put: The first declares "God is the truth"; the second says, "no-God is the truth."

Both believe in truth, but the phrase "God exists" sums up the truth for one, while for the other the phrase "God does not exist" sums it up. At this point the more exact statement enters: both have *faith* in the truth, but for the one this faith expresses itself in the *belief* that "God exists," while for the other it expresses itself in the contrary proposition that "God does not exist."

If one said "God exists" and the other, "God does not exist," then *faith* would be the ground of each one's conviction of what her own proposition means, and *belief* would be the conviction set forth in each one's proposition. Even to bluntly refuse any dialogue implies the faith that one possesses the truth and the belief that the formula cannot be sundered from the thing formulated. Affirming absurdity or postulating nothingness can be *beliefs* of the *same faith* that moves others to believe in God or in Humanity.

Kṛṣṇa and Christ

Here, by acknowledging that a single faith may express itself in contrasting and even contradictory beliefs, dialogue would start. The next step is to understand the other's position, and at once a tremendous difficulty arises. I can never understand her position as she does—and this is the only real understanding between people—unless I share her view; in a word, unless I judge it to be somewhat true.

It is contradictory to imagine I understand another's view when at the same time I call it false. I may indeed say I understand my partner in dialogue better than she understands herself. I may say she is mistaken because she contradicts herself, even say I understand her position because I understand her premises; but clearly I cannot uphold her view as she does, unless I share it. When I say I understand a proposition and consider it untrue, in the first place I do not understand it because, by definition, truth alone is intelligible (if I understand a thing I always understand it *sub ratione veritatis*); in the second place I certainly do not understand it in the way of someone who holds it to be true. Accordingly, to understand is to be converted to the truth one understands.[4]

[4] See R. Panikkar, "Verstehen als Überzeugtsein," in *Neue Anthropologie*, vol. 7, ed. H. G. Gadamer and P. Vogler (Stuttgart: Thieme, 1975), 132–67.

Now the problem becomes even more involved. Let us consider an example: my partner declares that one arrives at salvation through Kṛṣṇa, the supreme epiphany of the Godhead. If I understand *what* he is saying I must simply yield my assent, as he does his, to the truth of that declaration; that is, I share his point of view—even though I may still believe that mine may be subtler and may in fact incorporate his. Otherwise I must say I do not understand *it*, or withdraw intelligibility to an earlier level: I understand *him*, I know what he *means* because I understand that his declaration follows from a series of assumptions that lead him to believe what he says; but I do not share his belief in the truth of those assumptions. Then the problem comes down to understanding these assumptions and their intelligibility. Hence dialogue serves the useful purpose of laying bare our own assumptions and those of others, thereby giving us a more critically grounded conviction of what we hold to be true.

To my mind the most far-reaching conclusions follow from what has been said up to this point, but I have yet a good deal more to say. The real religious or theological task, if you will, begins when the two views meet head-on inside oneself; when dialogue prompts genuine religious pondering, and even a religious crisis, at the bottom of one's heart; when interpersonal dialogue turns into intrapersonal soliloquy.

Let us suppose I have grasped the basic belief of a *vaiṣṇava* and therefore share it; in other words I can honestly affirm what an orthodox *vaiṣṇava* believes. Does this mean I have deserted my original religious position? Are the two beliefs not essentially irreconcilable? Either I believe in Kṛṣṇa or I believe in Christ. Either I am a Christian and declare Jesus as the Savior of mankind, or I follow Kṛṣṇa and acknowledge him as the true Savior of humanity. Is it not a double betrayal to try to reconcile these two beliefs, which conflict at every point? Can we find any way out of this dilemma?

At this juncture, the dialogue of which I speak emerges not as a mere academic device or an intellectual amusement, but as a spiritual matter of the first rank, a religious act that itself engages faith, hope, and love. Dialogue is not bare methodology but an essential part of the religious act par excellence: loving God above all things and one's neighbor as oneself. If we believe that our neighbor lies entangled in falsehood and superstition we can hardly love him as ourselves, without a hypocritical, pitying love that moves us to try plucking the mote out of his eye. Love for our neighbor also makes intellectual demands, for as the Christian tradition has said over and over again, you cannot love your neighbor as yourself without loving God. Perhaps I can love the other person as *other*, which means as an object to me (as useful, pleasant, kind, beautiful, complementary to me, something of this sort), but I cannot love him as *myself* unless I take my place on the one bit of higher ground that will hold us both—unless I love God. God is the unique *locus* where my selfhood and my neighbor's coincide, consequently the one place that enables me to love him as he loves his own self without any attempt at molding him.[5]

---

[5] See Pannikar, *Myth, Faith, and Hermeneutics*, chapter 9.

For this very reason I cannot love God unless I love my neighbor because God is that transcending of my "I" that puts me in touch with my neighbor. Saint Augustine (could we expect otherwise?) says so word for word: "In fact, a Man loves his neighbor as himself only if he loves God" (*Diligit enim unusquisque proximum suum tamquam seipsum, si diligit Deum*). Understanding my neighbor means understanding him as he understands himself, which can be done only if I rise above the subject-object dichotomy, cease to know him as an object, and come to know him as myself. Only if there exists a Self in which we communicate does it become possible to know and love another as Oneself. Anyone with half an eye can see what follows and how it upsets the false privacy in which we are inclined to shut ourselves away. True intimacy does not stiffen or mortify us because within that Self (God is not the Other, he is the One) dwell life, dialogue, and love. This is in fact the Trinitarian mystery, but we must not wander from our present topic.

Let no one object that the Gospel commission is not to dialogue with all nations but to go and teach them—in the first place, because here we are not conducting apologetics of any sort and so feel under no obligation to prove the orthodoxy of any view; and in the second place because that commission is cited in a mutilated form and altogether out of context. The complete text makes it quite clear that the "discipleship" it refers to consists precisely in serving one's fellows and loving them, and they are not served if I am the one who lays down how the master is to be served. Moreover, the commission is purely charismatic—it calls for the power to work miracles. Who would like to throw the first stone?

Be that as it may, no one can fail to see the religious challenge of the situation I have set forth. A really devout mind will ask how we can embrace the faith of our neighbor without going astray in our own. Indeed, how can we embrace it at all? Can my faith absorb another's belief? Here I think we have the touchstone for any genuine life of faith in our day: We must believe those who do not believe, just as we must love those who do not love.

The Multireligious Experience

Now I should like to sketch the religious attitude of one embarked on such a venture. She starts by making a real, heartfelt, unselfish effort—a bold and hazardous one—to understand the belief, the world, the archetypes, the culture, the mythical and conceptual background, the emotional and historical associations of her friends from the inside. In short, she seriously attempts an existential incarnation of herself into another world—which obviously involves prayer, initiation, study, and worship. She does this not by way of trial but rather with a spirit of faith in a truth that transcends us and a goodness that upholds us when we truly love our neighbor—which does not mean, as I have said, eliminating the intellect from this enterprise. It is not experimentation but a genuine experience undergone within one's own faith.

Consequently that experience is forbidden, or rather does not become possible, unless she has established in herself the distinction between her faith (ever transcendent, unutterable, and open) and her belief (an intellectual, emotional, and cultural embodiment of that faith within the framework of a particular tradition that, yes, demands her loyalty but not that she betray the rest of humankind). I need hardly add that not everyone is called to such an undertaking, nor is everyone capable of it. Besides a particular cast of mind, it presupposes perhaps a special constellation in one's character and background that enables one to undergo the experience without any taint of exoticism, exhibitionism, or simply unremitting intellectualism. In a word, we need a kind of connaturality to go through that venture in a genuine way. I repeat: it does not mean experimenting either with one's own faith or with that of others. Faith can only be lived, but living it may at times demand risking it in order to remain faithful.

Moreover, this risk of faith must be understood as emerging from one's own faith itself—not from doubting what one believes, but deepening and enriching it. This risk should not be understood as an intellectual or religious curiosity but as a dynamic of faith itself, which discloses another religious world in one's neighbor that we can neither ignore nor brush aside, but must try to take up, integrate into our own. What is more, when faith claims universality, the faith of the neighbor automatically becomes a problem that cannot be evaded.

Abstract principles do not enable one to foresee what will happen in such an encounter; she must be prepared to stake everything she is and believes, not because she harbors doubts about it, nor yet because she says at the back of her mind that she is conducting some sort of methodological *epochē* (which at this juncture in history would be unnatural and unthinkable),[6] but because the venture hazards—or, to be more precise, let us say makes possible—a conversion so thoroughgoing that the convictions and beliefs she had hitherto held may vanish or undergo a far-reaching change. Unquestionably the venture is perilous; you gamble your life. Hardly anyone would be equal to it but for the very drive of faith that invites us to hazard our life without fear, even to lose it.

Interpreting Experience

Only afterward can we describe what happens. I shall attempt to do this in the space of a few paragraphs.

We can live only by truth; falsehood offers the mind no nourishment.[7] If my

---

[6] See chapter 5 of this volume, "*Epochē* in the Religious Encounter."

[7] See the two following quotations, the first of Thomas Aquinas citing St. Ambrose (*Glossa Lombardi*, PL 191.1651): "Omne verum, a quocumque dicatur, a Spiritu Sancto est" *Summa Theologiae* I-II, q. 109, a. I, ad 1). And the second from Meister Eckhart: "Falsum vero, a quocumque dicatur, nulli dicitur" (*In Iohan*. I.51 [N. 277 of the *Opera omnia*]). See also *Sermo* XX (N. 198).

partner believes in Kṛṣṇa, it is because he believes Kṛṣṇa embodies truth, and this belief enters into the very truth of what he believes. I can understand this only if I also believe in the truth he believes, perhaps under rather a different guise. Whatever can be said of objective truth, religious belief is a highly personal and so subjective thing; the faith that saves is always personal and subjective. The Kṛṣṇa of our dialogue is not a historical or mythological figure but the Kṛṣṇa of faith, of my interlocutor's personal faith. His belief is the one I must assume, sharing his truth, the truth of the Kṛṣṇa of faith.

My own faith must be strong enough for me to do this—open and deep enough to work its way into the *vaiṣṇava* world and share that world's ups and downs. First of all, my faith must be naked enough to be clothed in all those forms with no misgivings about slipping into heresy or apostasy. (Anyone who *thinks* he will be betraying his faith should not and cannot embark on this venture.) Then, in a second moment, my intrareligious soliloquy will have to blend my earlier beliefs with those acquired later, according to my lights and conscience (this entire procedure, of course, is also valid for my partner).

My partner in dialogue will then judge whether what I have learned of Kṛṣṇa is sound or not. I will have to give him an account of my belief, and he will tell me whether what I say about Kṛṣṇa—one of the epiphanies of God and his love for humanity, eminently one of God's names, a real symbol of the freedom of God, and so forth—represents fundamental belief in Kṛṣṇa or not.

Once this first step has been taken, I must next explain to myself and also to my interlocutor how I blend this new religious experience of mine with belief in Christ.

Here an alternative lies before me: either I have ceased to be a Christian—belief in Kṛṣṇa has supplanted my belief in Christ; I have found a loftier, fuller divine reality in Kṛṣṇa than in Christ—or else I am able to establish a special kind of bond between the two that both religions, or at least one of them, *can* acknowledge and accept (I do not say they already *have* accepted it).

If the specific problem is talked over not only with the uninvolvement befitting investigators into religion but also on a spiritual level high enough to rule out what may be called fundamentalist microdoxy, then we could in most cases reach a solution where each tradition finds the other's reading of it valid, therefore at least partially orthodox. I say "partially" because each belief is integrated into a wider whole, which does not need to be accepted by the other party.

This example brings in a set of propositions that may answer the requirements of orthodoxy on both sides. With regard to traditional Christianity, I would say: the unutterable, transcendent, everlasting God has never left us without witness to the divine reality, and God has always wisely looked after God's creatures. That one mystery at work since the dawn of time, whose delight is to be with the children of "Men," has disclosed to them God's kindness, the godliness of love, the gladness of living, the nature of worship, and a set of rites with which to give their earthly existence meaning. That same mystery, hidden away for eons, unveils itself in Christ in the last days with a special historical consciousness so that the incorporation of the peoples into the *historical* dynamism of the world entails a certain relationship with Christ.

What may trouble the Christian mind about this sketch is the nature of the relationship between Christ and Kṛṣṇa. I shall make no attempt to deal with this problem at present. It is enough to say, first, that the difficulty strikes me as Greco-Western, or rather philosophical, more than strictly Christian; second, that the identity need not be one of personal substance—a functional identity will do. I am not evading the problem; I merely point out its parameters. Perhaps mythic terms best serve to intimate the connection between Christ and Kṛṣṇa, but obviously the connection is something other than flat identity. I mean there is no need to say Christ is Kṛṣṇa, or the one a foreshadowing or fulfillment of the other in order to indicate their special relationship. At this point we feel the lack of a theology dealing with the encounter between religions. The problem of the one and the many also crops up here, albeit in a new form. But the place of *Vaiṣṇavism* in the Christian economy of salvation might very well be found here, within the framework of a universal economy of salvation and in a certain mysterious presence of the Lord in a multitude of epiphanies. Something parallel could be said from the *vaiṣṇava* side. We do not propose to argue whether the theology of Kṛṣṇa is the most perfect there is, blending the human element in its fullness with the godly one within the strictest demands of the Absolute. What may trouble the *vaiṣṇava* mind is the peculiar emphasis laid upon historicity, perhaps to the detriment of an ever-original and genuine religious experience that does not need to rely on the faith of others but discovers by itself the living symbol of belief. What may further bother a devotee of Kṛṣṇa is what he feels to be the Christian reductionism of religion to morals and of Christ to a single man. Perhaps Christians could answer and the dialogue could go on, but we merely wish to show that belief in Kṛṣṇa need not rule out acknowledging Jesus as an epiphany of God at one particular moment in history.

The basic issue for discussion would be the ultimate nature of the two divine epiphanies. While the Christian will say that Christ is the fullness and apex of God's every *epiphany*, the *vaiṣṇava* will be moved to say that nothing can outdo the *theophany* of Kṛṣṇa. Nevertheless the difficulty can be overcome by mutual understanding. In terms of belonging to one or the other religious body (according to traditional standard, although nothing can halt the growth of tradition), the difficulty is for the time being insuperable, but we are now talking about something else, about dialogue that *is* true dialogue and therefore brings each side to understand and share the basic attitude of the other.

Here the difficulty is not insuperable because, in the first place, when the matter is raised in this down-to-earth, existential way, one may perfectly well say that the heart of the matter is not deciding who holds the "objective" primacy, because by living in accordance with their particular persuasions and beliefs both will attain to what they sincerely believe; in the second place, because the question of Christ and Kṛṣṇa is not a speculation outside time and so defies answer by a timeless and abstract reason alone. Only historical eschatology can adequately tell us whether Christ fulfills Kṛṣṇa, or Kṛṣṇa, Christ, or neither supersedes the other.

The question *as such* is childish, as though I were to argue that my daddy writes better poetry than your daddy (forgetting that each poem is unique for each child and there can be no comparing of poems qua poems). *In you* and *in me* the question is premature (neither of us need be argued out of his belief); *in us*—that is, insofar as it helps us toward mutual understanding and the ultimate goal of all mankind—history (personal and collective) will have the last word. Meanwhile a wholesome emulation will harm neither side. Things might go further; the *vaiṣṇava* may perhaps admit the also-historical nature of Kṛṣṇa, thereby opening the door for the Christian to acknowledge the growth—hence the metamorphosis—Christ "undergoes" down the ages. The Christian may perhaps admit the also-transhistorical nature of Christ, thereby opening the door for the *vaiṣṇava* to acknowledge the mystery—hence the pluriformity—Kṛṣṇa "undergoes" down the ages. But this is only a beginning because the continuation of the dialogue has to produce its own rules and categories.

Faith and Beliefs

I need hardly say that neither every *vaiṣṇava* nor every Christian is automatically prepared, in intellect and spirit, to come thus face-to-face—at bottom because very few have had the experience and so it has not been worked out theologically. Here history might teach a mighty lesson by reminding us how Jewish, Greek, Zoroastrian, and other "dogmas" seeped into the Christian mind, making themselves part of what we nowadays call the common Christian heritage. The same would apply for a theology of Kṛṣṇa—in both cases.

For the moment let us content ourselves with some philosophical and theological considerations centering on the distinction we have drawn between faith and belief. For the sake of simplicity I shall start from Christian assumptions that commend themselves as a succinct and intelligible frame of reference to the Western mind, but that can be readily transposed into those of other religious traditions. Let me add at once that in so doing I jump to no conclusions as to whether the Christian approach can be universalized in a way others cannot. At the present time I do not wish to grapple with that problem.

The main function of faith is to connect me with transcendence, with what stands above me, with what I am not (yet). Faith is the connection with the beyond, however you choose to envision it. So one thing faith effects is salvation: the business of faith is preeminently to save us. Now for this, faith cannot be couched in universal forms that express it fully. If this were possible, faith would become so earthbound that it would no longer provide a bridge "binding" us (Latin: *religare*) to something loftier than ourselves. Faith may lend itself more or less to ideation, but no set of words, no expression, can ever exhaust it. Yet it needs to be embodied in ideas and formulas—so much so that faith incapable of expressing itself at all would not be human faith. Such expressions we have called beliefs, in accordance with what tradition has always felt.

Were things otherwise, my faith would cut me off from others rather than unite me with them, faith would estrange us from each other instead of binding us together, and religion would express horizontal divergences instead of vertical convergence. That history, for countless reasons, both bears witness to trends in the actual evolution of religions and does not invalidate what I am saying; it only shows that faith has been confused with belief. The moment dialogue ceases and we live isolated from one another, faith inevitably becomes identified with belief and fosters exclusivism with all the results that history in general and the history of religions in particular have made so painfully familiar.

Yet our distinction presents special features. Faith cannot be equated with belief, but faith always needs a belief to be faith. Belief is not faith, but it must convey faith. A disembodied faith is not faith. A belief that does not always point to a beyond that outsoars and in a sense annihilates it is not belief but fanaticism. Faith finds expression in belief, and through it people normally arrive at faith. Where people live in a homogeneous cultural world, most never notice the tension between faith and belief. They look on dogmas, which are simply authoritative formulations of belief, almost as if they were faith itself, half forgetting that they are dogmas of faith. When cultural change or an encounter between religions robs the notions hitherto bound up with faith of their solidity and unmistakable correspondence to faith, naturally a crisis erupts. But this is a crisis of belief, not faith. Undoubtedly the bond between the two is intimate; it is in fact constitutive because thought itself requires language, and belief is the language of faith. Hence what begins as a crisis of belief turns into a crisis of faith, as a rule due to the intransigence of those who will tolerate no change because they do not distinguish between faith and belief.

When a Christian says she believes in God the Father, in Christ, and in the Holy Spirit, she does not believe in a *deus ex machina ad usum christianorum*, but a reality of truth subsisting everywhere, even outside the bounds of her own experience. But she conveys this truth in language inherited from her own tradition, and she can grasp its meaning only in those terms. When she comes into contact with a different form of religious expression, her first impulse will be to suppose her interlocutor is talking about some reality apart from and essentially different from her own: she will think of false "Gods," false religion, and so on. After a deeper look, she will perceive that at bottom they mean a similar thing, although the other refers to it with concepts she may judge inadequate or erroneous.

Thus one of the primary tasks facing theology is the tremendous one of finding parallels and features in other religions that complement each other, as well as points of conflict. But no one can deny that the ultimate purpose of the two religions is the same. Unless the spadework, entailing all we have indicated, is done at the outset, and a good deal more besides, misunderstandings will almost inevitably accumulate, even today, to bedevil nine-tenths of the relations among religions and therefore among people.

At times the obvious will have to be explained, but patience seems to be an intellectual as well as a moral virtue. Doesn't faith itself call on us to break out of our limitations and constantly die to ourselves to rise again in newness of life? I mean that the Christian's connatural attitude toward the faith of others seems to embrace, absorb, and embody rather than repulse, expel, and shut out. Possibly these are two anthropological bents marking different cultural situations, but in any event the disposition to attract rather than repel strikes me as more consonant with the Christian dynamism.

I will not attempt now to develop an entire doctrine of the Mystery—whom Christians recognize in Christ and other religions in other symbols—present and at work in every religion, usually in a dark and enigmatic way. I will only try to set forth the spiritual attitude that impels me to seek to integrate, as far as possible, the religiousness of others into my own before asserting mine in order to compare and judge. Let us only dip into the experience of trying to understand a form of religion from inside, and we will perceive the authenticity and truth with which it is charged, whatever the weakness and even immorality its outward features exhibit (as in certain forms of devotion to Kṛṣṇa or certain interpretations of Christianity). What I should like to stress is the way faith prompts one to link up different kinds of religion. We may not see eye to eye about how to do this, but theology today must work out the means if it is to survive and stop being archaeology.

The solution is not so easy, not only due to historical and cultural estrangements but also because the relation between faith and belief is not so simple that we might consider belief the mere costume of faith and so infer that it is all a matter of taste for one vestment or another. Belief, the garb or expression of faith, is part and parcel of faith itself inasmuch as our self-understanding belongs to the very nature of that being whose nature is precisely understanding—even if it is not exclusively understanding. I cannot strip off my belief—insofar as it is a real belief, that is, insofar as I believe in "it" (or more simply said, I believe)—without touching and even transforming my faith.

In a word, I am not simplistically saying that all beliefs are merely expressions of one and the same faith, because faith without belief does not exist—not for those who believe. We are not *logos* alone, but the *logos* is something more than the mere instrument of us. This is why to speak of the transcendent unity of religions is true as long as it does not remain the immanent "truth" of the different religious traditions under discussion.[8] The *relativity* of beliefs does not mean their *relativism.* Our human task is to establish a religious dialogue that, although it transcends the *logos*—and belief—does not neglect or ignore them.

I am only trying to say that faith must not be confused with belief. Many a misunderstanding has risen from confusing them, or rather from not adequately distinguishing between them.

The experience of faith is a primal anthropological act that every person performs in one way or another, rather like the way we begin to use reason upon its awakening, although no one can foresee along what lines our minds will work or what our first thoughts will be. The act of faith itself has saving power. Theologians will hasten to say (and we need not contradict them) that the act of faith can be made by a human being only when God's grace prompts it. In any event the act of faith is not only transcendent, uniting us with what surpasses us, but also transcendental. It exceeds all possible formulations, and it makes them possible because it also precedes them. Faith is a constitutive human dimension.[9]

At any rate the experience of faith is a human experience that will not be contained in any formula but in fact couches itself in what I have called formulas of belief. Each of us perforce gives utterance to the deepest of our impressions, but to this end we must use language that binds it up with a given human tradition; we lay hold of images and symbols that belong to a cultural group. We will make our faith known in a set of beliefs that we will perhaps call dogmas, expressing in intellectual terms what we wish to convey. Obviously these terms may be multifarious; in fact, they are necessarily multivalent.

I am not suggesting that all beliefs are equal and interchangeable; I am saying that in a certain respect they exhibit the same nature, which makes dialogue, and even dialectics, possible. Moreover, I assert they are generally equivalent in that every belief has a similar function: to express our faith, that faith that is the anthropological dimension through which we reach our goal—in Christian language, our salvation.

Clearly there remains the major difficulty of ascertaining how deep each belief delves into faith or how satisfactorily it expresses faith. Certain belief formulas deriving from a naive, underdeveloped cast of mind may not answer the needs of more highly developed people. This truth emerges at every turn in the history of

---

8 See F. Schuon, *De l'unité transcendante des religions* (Paris: Gallimard, 1948), of which there is an English translation (London: Faber and Faber, 1953) and which has recently been resurrected in North America (see *Journal of the American Academy of Religion* 44, no. 4 [December 1976]: 715–24).

9 See *Myth, Faith and Hermeneutics*, chapter 6.

religions, in the encounter and cross-fertilization between differing religious traditions, in the dialogue and sometimes the skirmishes between different schools of thought within the same tradition. We have an example of it in much of what goes on in the cultural and religious world of the Catholicism people call "Roman": The noble monolithic solidity of that world breaks down into various parts, into all the colors of the rainbow, through a thoroughgoing change of beliefs within a single experience of faith.

The problem we are considering reaches far beyond these limits and lights on the furthest human horizon where the issue of religious encounter presents itself. For obvious reasons we can only rough out the problem here. One way or another we are all embarked on the venture. Dead calm is as fraught with danger as a roaring gale. While we are on the high seas, we must have oars and sails.

4

The Rules of the Game in the Religious Encounter

Śastra-yonitvāt
Learned traditions being the
source (of knowledge)

—*BS 1.1.3*[1]

The meeting of religions is an inescapable fact today. I would like to formulate one principle that should govern the meeting of religions and draw from it a few corollary consequences.

The principle is this: *The religious encounter must be a truly religious one.* Anything short of this simply will not do.

Some consequences are as follows.

It Must Be Free from Particular Apologetics

If the Christian or Buddhist or believer in whatever religion approaches another religious person with the a priori idea of defending his own religion by all (obviously honest) means, we shall have perhaps a valuable defense of that religion and undoubtedly exciting discussions, but no religious dialogue, no encounter, much less a mutual enrichment and fecundation. One need not give up one's beliefs and convictions—surely not, but we must eliminate any apologetics if we really want to meet a person from another religious tradition. By apologetics I understand that part of the science of a particular religion that tends to prove the truth and value of that religion. Apologetics has its function and its proper place, but not here in the meeting of religions.

It Must Be Free from General Apologetics

I understand very well the anguish of the modern religious person seeing the wave of "unreligion" and even "irreligion" in our times, and yet I would consider it misguided to fall prey to such a fear by founding a kind of religious league—not

[1] Brahman is the *yoni* of the *śāstrat*, says *Śaṅkara* in his commentary. The Great Scriptures, the human traditions, are the womb of knowledge and *brahman* also is the source, not in a vicious, but in a vital circle.

to say crusade—of the "pious," of religious people of all confessions, defenders of the "sacred rights" of religion.

If forgetting the first corollary would indicate a lack of confidence in our partner and imply that he is wrong and that I must "convert" him, neglecting this second point would betray a lack of confidence in the truth of religion itself and represent an indiscriminate accusation against "modern" Man. The attitude proposing a common front for religion or against unbelief may be understandable, but it is not a religious attitude—not according to the present degree of religious consciousness.

One Must Face the Challenge of Conversion

If the encounter is to be an authentically religious one, it must be totally loyal to truth and open to reality. The genuinely religious spirit is not loyal only to the past; it also keeps faith with the present. A religious person is neither a fanatic nor someone who already has all the answers. She is also a seeker, a pilgrim making her own uncharted way; the track ahead is yet virgin, inviolate. She finds each moment new and is but the more pleased to see in this both the beauty of a personal discovery and the depth of a perennial treasure that the ancestors in the faith have handed down.

Yet to enter the new field of the religious encounter is a challenge and a risk. The religious person enters this arena without prejudices and preconceived solutions, knowing full well that she may in fact have to lose a particular belief or particular religion altogether. She trusts in truth. She enters unarmed and ready to be converted herself. She may lose her life—she may also be born again.

The Historical Dimension Is Necessary but Not Sufficient

Religion is not just *Privatsache*, nor just a vertical "link" with the Absolute, but it is also a connection with humanity; it has a tradition, a historical dimension. The religious encounter is not merely the meeting of two or more people in their capacity as strictly private individuals, severed from their respective religious traditions. A truly religious person bears at once the burden of tradition and the riches of her ancestors. But she is not an official representative, as it were, speaking only on behalf of others or from sheer hearsay: She is a living member of a community, a believer in a living religious tradition.

The religious encounter must deal with the historical dimension, not stop with it. It is not an encounter of historians, still less of archaeologists, but it is a living dialogue, a place for creative thinking and imaginative new ways that do not break with the past but continue and extend it.

This is hardly to disparage historical considerations; quite the contrary, I would insist on an understanding of the traditions in question that is at once deep and broad. The first implies not only that we be familiar with the age-old tradition but also with the present state of that particular religion. Taking as our example that bundle of religions that goes under the name of "Hinduism," I would contend that a profound understanding of this tradition cannot ignore its evolution up to the present day, unless we are ready to accept an arbitrary and skewed interpretation. A scholar may indeed limit herself to Vedic studies, for example, but someone engaged in a truly religious encounter can scarcely justify basing her understanding of Hinduism solely on Sāyana's interpretation of the Vedas while completely ignoring that of, say, Dayānanda or Aurobindo (the relative merits of various interpretations is not our concern here). Similarly no modern Christian can be satisfied with Jerome's interpretation of the Bible or with the medieval understanding of it.

Our point is that no study of an idea, cultural pattern, or religious tradition is adequate unless we consider all its possibilities, just as no botanist can claim to know a seed until he knows the plant that grows up from that seed. Moreover, in this case, the movement of understanding is dynamic and reciprocal. Thus I would contend not only that any study of the nature of *dharma*, for instance, is incomplete if it does not consider the present-day understanding of that concept, but also that the ancient notion is likely to be only partially understood if its development up to modern times is left aside. This approach also implies that someone who tries to understand the notion of *dharma*, whether in ancient or modern India, cannot do so *in vacuo*: The very words he uses are already culturally charged with meanings and values.

Further, the traditions must also be understood in a broader perspective, one that oversteps the provincial boundaries of geography and culture. To understand the Hindū tradition—staying with our example—we cannot limit ourselves to the Indian subcontinent: The impact of Buddhism on eastern and central Asia is so well known that I need only mention it; the *Rāmāyaṇa* and the *Mahābhārata* have been shaping forces in many countries south of Burma; Śiva is worshiped in Indonesia. Pursuing these avenues of research is not a mere academic tangent but serves to complete the picture we begin to see through indigenous sources.

Even more, we cannot limit our attention to past cross-cultural contacts and ignore the multitude of contemporary instances. Many an Indic value asserts itself today on the shores of California and in universities throughout Europe. Whether the change in climate distorts or enhances the original values is a separate question; the influence is unmistakable. In return, Western values have, for better or for worse, deeply penetrated not only the great cities but also the most remote villages of India. Given such developments, can our understanding of Indic religions remain imprisoned in a scholarly ivory tower whose drawbridge was raised when the Muslims arrived? The phenomenon of feedback does not refer only to the diffusion of gadgets and other technological paraphernalia throughout the world; popularized ideas from every continent now travel literally at the speed of light to the farthest corners of the planet and the deepest recesses of the human psyche.

The importance of the historical dimension notwithstanding, what is at stake in the religious encounter is not "History of Religions" or even "Comparative Religion," but a living and demanding faith. Faith is life, and life cannot be reduced to imitating the past or merely reinterpreting it. The religious encounter is a religious event.

It Is Not Just a Congress of Philosophy

Needless to say, without a certain degree of philosophy, no encounter is possible, and yet the religious dialogue is not just a meeting of philosophers to discuss intellectual problems. Religions are much more than doctrines. Within one religion there may even be a pluralism of doctrines. To pin down a religion to a certain definite doctrinal set is to kill that religion. No particular doctrine *as such* can be considered the unique and irreplaceable expression of a religion. Indeed, *denying* a particular doctrine without overcoming it or substituting another for it may be heresy, but no religion is satisfied to be *only* orthodoxy, ignoring orthopraxis. To be sure, creation, God, *nirvāṇa*, and the like are important concepts, but the real religious issue lies elsewhere: in the real "thing" meant by these and other notions. I may share with my Muslim colleague the same idea of the transcendence of God, and he may be of the same opinion as his Buddhist partner regarding the law of *karma*, and yet none of us may feel compelled to change our religion.

Clearly, I need to understand what the other is saying—that is, what the other means to say—and this involves a new understanding of interpretation itself. Now the golden rule of any hermeneutic is that the interpreted thing can recognize itself in the interpretation. In other words, any interpretation from outside a tradition has to coincide, at least phenomenologically, with an interpretation from within—that is, with the believer's viewpoint. To label a *mūrtipūjaka*, an idol-worshiper, for instance—meaning by "idol" what is commonly understood in the Judeo-Christian-Muslim context rather than beginning with what the worshiper affirms of himself—is to transgress this rule. An entire philosophical and religious context underpins the notion of *mūrti*; we cannot simply impose alien categories on it. Although the problem remains formidable, one of the most positive achievements of our times is that we have come to realize that no immutable categories can serve as absolute criteria for judging everything under the sun.

Briefly then, I would like to consider two principles that govern any sound hermeneutical method and the way in which they may be critically coordinated.

The principle of homogeneity. An ancient conviction, held in both East and West, has it that only like can know like. In other words, a concept can be properly understood and evaluated only from within a homogeneous context. Every cultural value has a definite sphere where it is valid and meaningful; any unwarranted extrapolation can only lead to confusion and misunderstanding. Nothing is more harmful than hurried syntheses or superficial parallelisms. Here is the place and the great value of traditional theology, which provides the internal understanding of a religion, the self-understanding of that religion as it is lived. Without this previous work, fruitful interreligious encounters would not be possible.

The dialogical principle. Applying the principle of homogeneity with strict rigor or exclusivity would paralyze a critical approach and halt any progress toward mutual understanding. I may understand the worldview that underlies the religious practice of another—human sacrifice, for instance—yet I may still consider it immature, wrong, even barbaric. Why is this? It may be that I have developed another form of awareness or discovered another principle of understanding that leads me to see the inadequacy of a certain notion (here that which upholds human sacrifice). I may have acquired a perspective under which I am able to criticize another point of view; perhaps I can now detect incongruencies or assumptions that are no longer tenable. In this sort of activity, the dialogical principle is at work. Only through an internal or external dialogue can we become aware of uncritical or unwarranted assumptions. This dialogue does not merely look for new sources of information but leads to a deeper understanding of the other and of oneself. We are all learning to welcome light and criticism, even when it comes from foreign shores.

Coordination. By themselves, each of these principles is barren and unsatisfying; together they provide a means of cross-cultural understanding that is both valid and critical. Those concerned with Indic traditions, whatever their background, are convinced that they cannot disregard the methodological principles of modern critical scholarship. At the same time, they are quite aware that neither science nor Western categories constitute an absolute standard, nor do they have universal applicability. These two insights give rise to the coordination of the two principles. Here we cannot elaborate the guidelines for such a coordination. It is enough to say that the effort must be truly interdisciplinary and interpersonal, involving not only the traditional fields of "academia," but also the people whose religions we are considering. No statement is valid and meaningful if it cannot be heard, understood, and, in a way, verified by all those concerned and not merely bandied about by the literati.

Indeed, philosophical clarification is today extremely important because by and large religions have lived in restricted areas and closed circles and have tended to identify a particular set of philosophical doctrines—because they were useful to convey the religious message—with the core of the religion. The mutual enrichment of real encounter and the consequent liberation may be enormous.

It Is Not Only a Theological Symposium

As an authentic venture, the true religious encounter is filled with a sort of prophetic charisma; it is not just an effort to make the outsider understand my point. Indeed, at least according to more than one school, true theology also claims to be a charismatic deepening in meaning of a particular revelation or religion. Generally, however, theologians are more concerned with explaining given data than with exploring tasks ahead. Obviously hermeneutics is indispensable, but still more important is to *grasp* what is to be interpreted prior to any (more or less plausible) explanation. Theology may furnish the tools for mutual understanding but must remember that the religious encounter imperative today is a new problem and that the tools furnished by the theologies are not fit to master the new task unless purified, chiseled, and perhaps forged anew in the very encounter.

As an example of what is needed, we may use the notion of homeomorphism, which does not connote a mere comparison of concepts from one tradition with those of another. I want to suggest this notion as the correlation between points of two different systems so that a point in one system corresponds to a point in the other. The method does not imply that one system is better (logically, morally, or whatever) than the other, nor that the two points are interchangeable: You cannot, as it were, transplant a point from one system to the other. The method only discovers homeomorphous correlations.

Now homeomorphism, as we have already said, is not identical with analogy, although they are related. Homeomorphism does not mean that two notions are analogous—that is, partially the same and partially different—because this implies that both share in a "tertium quid" that provides the basis for the analogy. Homeomorphism means rather that the notions play equivalent roles, that they occupy homologous places within their respective systems. Homeomorphism is perhaps a kind of existential-functional analogy.

An example may clarify what I mean.

It is quite clearly false, for instance, to equate the Upanishadic concept of *Brahman* with the biblical notion of YHWH. Nevertheless it is equally unsatisfactory to say that these concepts have nothing whatever in common. True, their context and contents are utterly different; they are not mutually translatable, nor do they have a direct relationship. But they are homologous; each plays a similar role, albeit in different cultural settings. They both refer to a highest value and an absolute term. On the other hand, we cannot say that *Brahman* is provident and even transcendent or that YHWH is all-pervading, without attributes, and so forth. Nevertheless we can assert that both function homologously within their own cultures.

To give another example, an examination of the traditional Indic notion of *karma* and the modern Western understanding of historicity under the aegis of this principle could reveal a common homologous role: each one stands for that temporal ingredient of the human being that transcends individuality.[2] Even more intriguing, perhaps, would be a consideration that homologizes the Indic notion of Īśvara (Lord) and the Western idea of Christ.[3]

Whatever shape it will take, whatever contents it will carry, I am convinced that a new theology (though this very name means nothing to a Buddhist) will emerge precisely out of these encounters between sincere and enlightened believers of the various religious traditions.

Yet the religious encounter is not a mere theological reflection. Theologies—in the widest sense of the word—have a given basis: they are efforts at intelligibility of a given religious tradition and generally within that tradition itself (*fides quaerens intellectum*). But here we do not have such a belief or such a basis. There is neither a common given nor an accepted basis, revelation, event, or even tradition. Both the very subject matter and the method are to be determined in the encounter itself. There is no common language at the outset. Short of this radical understanding, the encounter of religions becomes a mere cultural entertainment.

It Is Not Merely an Ecclesiastical Endeavor

To be sure, the dialogue among religions may take place at different levels, and on each level it has its peculiarities. Official encounter among representatives of the world's organized religious groups is today an inescapable duty. Yet the issues in such meetings are not the same as those in a dialogue that tries to reach the deepest possible level. Ecclesiastical dignitaries are bound to preserve tradition; they must consider the multitude of believers who follow that religion, for and to whom they are responsible. They are faced with practical and immediate problems; they must discover ways to tolerate, to collaborate, to understand. But in general they cannot risk new solutions. They have to approve and put into practice already proven fruitful ways. But where are those proofs to come from? The religious encounter we have in mind will certainly pave the way for ecclesiastical meetings and vice versa but must be differentiated and separated from them.

It Is a Religious Encounter in Faith, Hope, and Love

The word "religious" here does not stand for mere piety or commitment. It stands for the integrality of the total person engaged in the dialogue. In other words, it does not stand for "religious" ideas or ideals exclusively, as if the encounter

---

[2] See R. Panikkar, *Myth, Faith, and Hermeneutics: Cross-Cultural Studies* (New York: Paulist Press, 1979), chapter 14.

[3] See R. Panikkar, *The Unknown Christ of Hinduism*, revised and enlarged ed. (Maryknoll, NY: Orbis Books, 1981), 148–62.

may only deal with doctrinal issues of common interest. We are also discussing *ourselves* and putting the whole of us at the negotiation table, as already suggested in the third rule.

This means that a truly religious encounter is never totally objectifiable. We do not put objectified "beliefs" on discussion, but believers, we, ourselves. This is why the mere logical principle of noncontradiction is not enough (necessary as it is) to govern the entire meeting. I may believe that the doctrine *x* is the highest possible way to express one particular truth, or just the Mystery, so to speak. You may believe that the doctrine *y* fulfills the requirement, both being different. There is no possible compromise. There would be contradiction if some of us were to believe that within an agreed context *x* and *y* could be the case, but there is no contradiction in the fact that you believe *y and* I *x*. A believing *x* and B believing *y* are only contrary situations that can still communicate and struggle further.

I may put it with Christian vocabulary, apologizing for this, and yet I think it has a more universal meaning.

By *faith* I mean an attitude that transcends the simple data and the dogmatic formulations of the different confessions as well; that attitude that reaches an understanding even when words and concepts differ because it pierces them, as it were, goes deep down to that realm that is the religious realm par excellence. We do not discuss systems but realities and the way in which these realities manifest themselves so that they also make sense for our partner.

By *hope* I understand that attitude that, hoping against all hope, is able to leap over not only the initial human obstacles, our weakness and unconscious adherences, but also over all kinds of purely profane views and into the heart of the dialogue, as if urged from above to perform a sacred duty.

By *love*, finally, I mean that impulse, that force impelling us to our fellow beings and leading us to discover in them what is lacking in us. To be sure, real love does not aim for victory in the encounter. It longs for common recognition of the truth, without blotting out the differences or muting the various melodies in the single polyphonic symphony.

Some Practical Lessons

What do these rules mean in practice? The chief lessons gleaned from my experience could be summarized as follows:

There must be *equal preparation* for the encounter on both sides, and this means cultural as well as theological preparation. Any dialogue—including the religious one—depends on the cultural settings of the partners. To overlook the cultural differences that give rise to different religious beliefs is to court unavoidable misunderstandings. The first function of the dialogue is to discover the ground where the dialogue may properly take place.

There must be real *mutual trust* between those involved in the encounter, something that is possible only when all the cards are on the table, that is, when neither partner "brackets" his personal beliefs.[4]

The *different issues* (theological, practical, institutional, etc.) have to be carefully distinguished; otherwise there is going to be confusion.

A Christian Example

Christ is the Lord, but the Lord is neither only Jesus nor does my understanding exhaust the meaning of the word.

Church, as the sociological dimension of religion, is the organism of salvation (by definition), but "the church" is not coextensive with the "visible Christian Church."

Christendom is the socioreligious structure of Christianity and as such is a religion like any other. It must be judged on its own merits without any special privileges.

God wants all Men to reach salvation. Here salvation is that which is considered to be the end, goal, destination, or destiny of Man, however this may be conceived.

There is no salvation without faith, but this is not the privilege of Christians nor of any special group.

The means of salvation are to be found in any authentic religion (old or new) because a man follows a particular religion because in it he believes he finds the ultimate fulfillment of his life.

Christ is the only mediator, but he is not the monopoly of Christians, and in fact, he is present and effective in any authentic religion, whatever the form or the name. Christ is the symbol, which Christians call by this name, of the ever-transcending but equally ever-humanly immanent Mystery.

Now these principles should be confronted with parallel humanist, Buddhist, and other principles, and then one should be able to detect points of convergence and of discrepancy with all the required qualifications. Further, the Christian principles have no a priori paradigmatic value, so it is not a question of just searching for possible equivalents elsewhere. The fair procedure is to start from all possible starting points and witness to the actual encounters taking place along the way.

Summing Up

The religious encounter is a religious and hence sacred act through which we are taken up by the truth and by loyalty to the "three worlds" with no further aim or intention. In this creative religious act the very vitality of religion manifests itself.

---

[4] See chapter 5, this volume.

5

Epochē in the Religious Encounter

Nothing is more outwardly visible than
the secrets of the heart,
nothing more obvious than what one
attempts to conceal.

—*Chung Yung I.1.3*[1]

Prologue

Interreligious dialogue is today unavoidable; it is a religious imperative and a historical duty for which we must suitably prepare. But we often hear more talk about interreligious dialogue than actual dialogue. In order to sidestep this pitfall, I would like to begin again by stressing the often-neglected notion of an *intrareligious* dialogue, that is, an inner dialogue within myself, an encounter in the depth of my personal religiousness, having met another religious experience on that very intimate level. In other words, if *interreligious* dialogue is to be real dialogue, an *intrareligious* dialogue must accompany it; that is, it must begin with my questioning myself and the *relativity* of my beliefs (which does not mean their *relativism*), accepting the challenge of a change, a conversion, and the risk of upsetting my traditional patterns. *Quaestio mihi factus sum* (I have become a question to myself), said that great African, Augustine. One simply cannot enter the arena of genuine religious dialogue without such a self-critical attitude.

My point is this: I shall never be able to meet the other as the other meets and understands himself or herself if I do not meet and understand her in and as myself. To understand the other as "other" is, at the least, not to understand her as she understands her-self (which is certainly not as "other," but as self). Obviously this self that understands the other is not my previous ego that reduces the other to my own unchanged self. Each process of real understanding changes me as much as it changes the other. Real understanding transforms my ego as well as the *alius*. The meeting point—and this is my thesis—is not a neutral dialectical arena that leaves both of us untouched, but a self that besides being myself is also shared by the other. This is to say, among other things, that I am not advocating any reductionism. I have developed this point elsewhere; here I am only

[1] Ezra Pound's translation.

concerned about paving the way for such an approach by dismissing as insufficient a minimalistic attitude without, obviously, falling into the trap of exclusivism.

In a laudable effort to avoid an exclusivist and paternalist posture, some modern writers are tempted by the *phenomenological epochē*, improperly so-called in this context, which is interpreted to be the bracketing of one's "faith" as the necessary condition for fruitful "interfaith dialogue."

This attitude is more common than we usually suppose, although not always under the aegis of so scientific an expression. When a Christian, for example, thinks he can understand another religion or be a partner in dialogue without engaging his own religious convictions, he is trying to practice this kind of *epochē*. When a Hindū thinks he can genuinely experience another religion just by experimenting, by accepting—for the time being and the sake of the experiment—the rites, practices, and beliefs of the other, he also is intending to bracket his "faith" by the *epochē* we are discussing. Has the Hindū really bracketed his convictions when he claims to follow the Christian path for a time? Has the Christian shut off his Christian faith when he tries to forget his beliefs or preferences and accommodate himself to the forms and habits of another tradition? No one today, I guess, would say that Ramakrishna Paramahamsa or Roberto de Nobili practiced *epochē* when they sincerely tried to enter the heart of another religion. Rather, they were impelled by a belief that their personal religion was wide enough and deep enough to allow such an embrace.

Critique of the So-Called Phenomenological *Epochē* in the Religious Encounter

I shall offer here only some critical considerations of this attitude without, I hasten to add, tackling just now the many other problems involved in the phenomenology and philosophy of religious dialogue.

Although this chapter seems to have a negative character because it attempts to dispel a misunderstanding, it actually offers a positive standpoint, namely that inner dialogue involving the whole person is the necessary condition for a real and fruitful encounter of religions.

The opinion I am going to criticize understands *epochē* as putting aside one's personal religious convictions, suspending judgment on the validity of one's own religious tenets—in a word, bracketing the concrete beliefs of individual allegiance to a particular confession.

The good intention underlying this attitude is obvious: the *epochē* is put forward in order to prevent undue dominance from any one side or to be able to understand better without bias or prejudice. The *epochē* would thus provide a common ground, a necessary condition for genuine dialogue in which neither side predominates. It is feared that if I approach my partner with strong personal convictions, either

I shall not be able to listen to, much less understand, him, her, or it, filled as I am with my own tenets, or that we shall be unable to find a common language.

If I believe in God or Christ or *karma*, for instance, and my partner does not, unless for the sake of dialogue I "put off" my belief in God, Christ, or *karma*, we shall not be able to establish a real dialogue without privileges on either side. So it is said. The *epochē* procedure has been compared to a kind of methodological doubt. I temporarily suspend my judgment about some fundamental tenets I hold true, bracket my personal "faith," because I do not want to impose it on my partner nor influence her in the least regarding the contents of our dialogue. Thus I am ready to meet her on her own ground, having renounced my personal standing.

The positive aspect of such an attempt lies in the fact that it distinguishes between the conceptualized beliefs of a person and the underlying existential faith. If the subject matter of the *epochē* consists of the concepts we form about a particular idea, then we should be able to perform and even welcome such an operation. The problem arises when we pretend to bracket not a formulation, a notion, but a fundamental conviction of the person at the existential level. If we accept the distinction between faith and belief, we may be able to agree to a certain necessary *epochē* of our beliefs, but I would prefer to call for transcending them altogether as long as we are engaged in a serious interreligious dialogue. The *epochē* looks rather like a closet for temporarily storing one's personal convictions for the sake of the dialogue, whereas transcending our concepts is not simply a methodological device. A nonconceptual awareness allows different translations of the same transconceptual reality for different notional systems without methodological strategies.

The need and the place for a truly phenomenological *epochē* come in the introductory stage, getting to know a particular religiousness by means of an unbiased description of its manifestations.

Negative

My contention is that transferring the *epochē* to a field that is not its own, like that of ultimate convictions in the interreligious dialogue, would be

- Psychologically impracticable
- Phenomenologically inappropriate
- Philosophically defective
- Theologically weak
- Religiously barren

Before taking up the burden of proof, I wish to state emphatically, although very concisely, that I am not

- Speaking against phenomenology in general or against the phenomenology of religion, which has its own merits and justification, because there is room for a clear and valid description of religious phenomena.
- Attacking authentic phenomenological *epochē* or finding this procedure incorrect in phenomenological analysis.
- Belittling all the steps prior and necessary to an interreligious dialogue: human sympathy, for instance; capacity and willingness to listen and learn; sincere desire to understand; conscious effort to overcome preconceptions; and so on.
- Advocating sticking to one's own judgment about the other's religiousness or not performing a phenomenological reduction of my preconceptions regarding the other. I am not saying, for example, that a Protestant should from the outset judge a Roman Catholic as "idolatrous" because of his Marian cult.

Positive

On the contrary, I am saying that

- Precisely what I should not and cannot put into brackets are my religious convictions, my ultimate religious evaluations, for I must approach religious dialogue without putting my most intimate self on some safe ground outside the confrontation and challenge of the dialogue.
- Dialogue is neither teaching nor simply listening; in other words, interreligious dialogue presupposes a rather advanced stage in the confrontation between people of different religious allegiances. Obviously, before meaningful dialogue can take place, one must already know the religion of the partner. But one must be both intellectually and spiritually prepared. Dialogue is not mere study or understanding (although, indeed, by dialogue I may well deepen my understanding of my partner), but a total human contrast and participation in deeper communication and fuller communion.
- Interreligious dialogue demands a mutual confrontation of everything we are, believe, and believe we are in order to establish that deeper human fellowship without prejudicing the results, without precluding any possible transformation of our personal religiousness.

Thesis: The Phenomenological *Epochē* Is out of Place in the Religious Encounter

a. Such an *epochē* is *psychologically impracticable* if religious dialogue is to be more than merely doctrinal discussion, in other words, if it is a personal encounter with the whole human being. It would be a pretense to affirm that I do not know or am not convinced of my certainties. I cannot simply abstract my deepest convictions or concoct the fiction that I have forgotten or laid aside what I hold to be true. Just this would be required if I really had to bracket my "faith."

If, for instance, I am convinced that God created the world or that the law of *karma* is true, I cannot act (and dialogue is action) *as if* I did not believe in these tenets. Even if I sincerely tried to bracket these convictions, they would go on conditioning and generating a score of side issues. My partner simply would not understand why I maintain the fundamental goodness of this world against empirical evidence or why I see congruences where he does not, and so on. In other words, every reason I might adduce in our discussion regarding the ultimate nature of the world or human behavior would spring from my repressed convictions (the existence of a creator, the validity of the karmic line, and so forth).

Imagine I am reading a detective story. Just when I am at the climax, someone who has read the novel tells me "who did it." I cannot continue reading *as if* I did not know. Not only are the charm, interest, and tension gone, but the reading becomes insipid or at least qualitatively different. If I still read on, my interest will shift to checking plot consistency or, for example, the writer's skill and style.

On the contrary, the genuine phenomenological *epochē* is psychologically possible because it does not engage the entire *psychē*, the whole person; it is an intellectual attitude adopted to get at the phenomenon with the requisite accuracy. I can remain immobile if I like while speaking, but I must open and close my arms to embrace somebody.

b. This method is also *phenomenologically inappropriate*, and this for several reasons.

To ask for the psychological inhibition required to lock up all my religious convictions for the time being—when it is no longer a question of description and understanding but of confrontation and dialogue—is almost an offense against phenomenology, as if the latter feared our psychological constitution. If there is a foe to the now classical phenomenology, it is the so-called psychologism. It could even be said—as the first volume of Husserl's *Logische Untersuchungen* shows—that phenomenology emerges out of the effort to overcome and discard the psychological constituent aspects of human consciousness. Both the subjective attitude and the objective projection are overcome in phenomenology because they do not belong to the realm of "transcendental consciousness," the only place where the "appearance of the essences," of the phenomena, occurs. But dialogue comes only after the transcendental-phenomenological reduction has been used as a methodological device to discover the "transcendental ego" or "pure consciousness."

Submitting religious dialogue to phenomenological analysis—something quite apart from existentially performing the religious dialogue itself—one discovers that if the rule of *epochē* were valid, it should also be applied to the partner's personal convictions so that having thoroughly bracketed both sides, religious dialogue would be impossible. Such an analysis would still detect vestiges of a superiority complex on the part of whoever defends or practices this *epochē*: they think they can accommodate themselves to the mind of the other and put away their own preconceptions, while the partner is not asked to do so. I repeat: the phenomenological *epochē* has its place in the study and initial clarification of religious phenomena, but not in the actual performance of dialogue.

The authentic phenomenological *epochē*, further, does not bracket my convictions or my claim to truth. When dealing with the *noēmata*, the essences given in the "eidetic intuition"—that is, with the manifestation of pure objects in the "transcendental consciousness"—phenomenological investigation brackets the external "existence" (outside the mind) of the idea described. This makes sense within the Husserlian framework, but extending the *epochē* outside the limits for which it is intended amounts to an unwarranted extrapolation.

Phenomenology, and this is not its least merit, teaches precision in philosophical and prephilosophical investigation. It aims to lay bare the phenomenon so as to have, first, an "objective" description (as far as possible) and, second, to allow well-founded and justified interpretation. Phenomenology teaches us to listen to the phenomenon and to approach it with a minimum of presuppositions.

Now it is phenomenologically wrong, which amounts to saying it is a methodological error, to leave outside the dialogue an essential part of its subject matter.

In a Hindū-Christian dialogue on the nature and role of grace, for instance, neither participant can meaningfully lock away—for reasons of security or whatever—his personal commitment to and belief in grace. Otherwise the "dialogue" becomes one partner inspecting the other's opinions, and not a real existential exchange on the religious level.

As an analysis of the conditions for a meaningful *epochē* shows, the very possibility of the *epochē* rests on assumptions that do not exist in many cultures and religious traditions. There are, for example, systems of thought and ways of life that do not make room for such a distinction between my belief and the truth it embodies, much less for a separation between them. To understand what the *epochē* is about, and even more to perform it, a certain sort of mind is required and also to some extent a particular culture, which cannot presume to universality. There are in fact many cultures and religions in which the distinction between the truth and one's conviction of it is not possible, nor between ideas and what they "intend," the formulation and the formulated thing, and so on.

c. This phenomenological *epochē* is *philosophically defective* when applied to religious dialogue.

First of all, the Cartesian methodological doubt—whatever its other merits—is not applicable here. It would be a philosophical mistake. Nobody, not even a philosopher, can jump over his own shadow. You do not experiment with ultimate convictions. You experience them.

Ultimate convictions—and if they are religious they are ultimate—cannot be bracketed; there is no *doer* left to perform such a maneuver. I have nothing with which to manipulate what is by definition ultimate. Were such manipulation possible, it would mean either total suicide with no resurrection possible, or that my ultimate convictions are not ultimate, for beyond them the manipulator would remain pulling the strings.

If I believe in God, for example, I cannot pretend that I do not believe in God or speak and act *as if* there were no God when—by definition if I believe in him—it is God who lets me speak and act. Even methodologically I cannot put him aside when I am convinced that it is he who enables me to deny or bracket him. The "God" I can dismiss—even for a moment—as an unnecessary hypothesis is undoubtedly not a necessary Absolute.

We can obviously bracket formulations and stop pressing certain points if we "sense," whatever our motives, that they are not opportune. But the *epochē* in question does not intend to bracket only formulae. In other words, Descartes could very methodically doubt everything but his own method.

Were such an *epochē* maintained, the dialogue would not even reach the level of a philosophical encounter, for philosophy implies and requires a sincere and unconditional search for truth, and there can be no such search if my truth is removed from the sight of my partner, for fear of frightening him with my convictions or out of reverence for him, not wanting to dazzle him with the abundant light I keep for myself.

d. Such a procedure is *theologically weak.* Can I lay down my "faith"—even methodologically or "strategically"—like a hat?

This would imply that there is no fundamental understanding possible, no basic human accord unless I distance myself from any type of faith, thus reducing faith to a kind of luxury. Faith would then not be necessary for a full human life because we claim to encounter our fellow-being on the deepest religious level without it.

And, that my particular faith is so one-sided, so limited, that it represents an obstacle to human understanding, something that must be locked away or banished to some distant chamber of my being if I am to seek universal fellowship with other humans. If I keep my faith in brackets it is doubtlessly because I think it does not foster religious understanding, probably because my partner is not enough advanced to bear the "sublime heights" of my particular brand of faith, which I carefully try to withhold from his scrutiny.

It is not simply a question of human respect—in every sense—but of anthropological integrity. If faith is something a person can discard with impunity so that he can still meet his fellow beings religiously, meaningfully, and humanly, this amounts to affirming that what I happen to believe is simply supererogatory to my being and has no fundamental relevance for my humanity.

e. Finally, such an *epochē* would be *religiously barren*: at a stroke, it would delete the very subject matter of the dialogue. If in the religious dialogue I meet a person belonging to another religious tradition, we do not meet just to talk about the weather or merely to discuss some noncommittal doctrinal points, but to speak of her and my own ultimate concerns, about our ultimate convictions, about how we see and understand life, death, God, Man, and so on.

If I come to the encounter devoid of any religious commitment, so open and fresh that I have nothing, nothing of my own to contribute—besides the unbearable pretension of such a claim—I shall have frustrated any possible religious dialogue. We should be discussing precisely what I have bracketed. In order not to "hurt" the other fellow with my convictions (suspicious notion!), I offend her by pretending I can meet her without laying all my cards on the table. How am I going to start? Shall I examine her religious feelings and opinions before the higher tribunal of my uncommitted, unattached, and open attitude? Isn't the very opposite the case? Does this not betray an almost pathological attachment to my "faith," such a fear of losing it that I dare not risk it, but prefer instead to preserve it under lock and key? To exclude my religious convictions from religious dialogue is like renouncing the use of reason in order to enter a reasonable encounter.

Toward a Genuine Religious Encounter

It is not the purpose of these reflections to elaborate an alternative. To mention the following suggestions will suffice.

A religious dialogue must first of all be an authentic *dialogue*, without superiority, preconceptions, hidden motives, or convictions on either side. What is more, if it is to be an authentic dialogue it must also preclude preconceiving its aims and results. We cannot enter a dialogue having already postulated what will come of it or having resolved to withdraw should it enter areas we have a priori excluded. Dialogue does not primarily mean study, consultation, examination, preaching, proclamation, learning, and so on; if we insist on dialogue we should respect and follow its rules. Dialogue listens and observes, but it also speaks, corrects, and is corrected; it aims at mutual understanding.

Second, a religious dialogue must be genuinely *religious*, not merely an exchange of doctrines or intellectual opinions, and so it runs the risk of modifying my ideas, my most personal horizons, the very framework of my life. Religious dialogue is not a salon entertainment.

This amounts to saying that dialogue must proceed from the depths of my religious attitude to these same depths in my partner. In other words, I understand her, or try to, both from and within my faith, not by putting it aside. How could I possibly comprehend with mere reason something that very often, without necessarily being irrational, claims somehow to be more than sheer rationality?

Imagine we are discussing the meaning and function of sacrifice. Only if I believe, one way or another, in that act or event that makes sacrifice reasonable shall I be able to understand in depth what my partner really believes, and vice versa of course. Otherwise I may pretend I understand him (because I follow his description and know the effects of sacrifice, and so forth), but I shall miss the point of his belief and, in fact, whether I say so or not, most likely regard his belief as pure magic. In brief, the kernel of the purely religious act is phenomenologically undetectable, at least with the theory of phenomenology accepted up to now. I am saying that the *phenomenon* of religion does not exhaust the whole of religious *reality*, so that besides, not opposed to, phenomenology of religion there is yet room for philosophy and theology—and indeed for religion itself.

The peculiar difficulty in the phenomenology of religion is that the religious *pisteuma* is different from and not reducible to the Husserlian *noēma*. The *pisteuma* is that core of religion that is open or intelligible only to a *religious* phenomenology. In other words, the belief of the believer belongs essentially to the religious phenomenon. There is no "naked" or "pure" belief separate from the person who believes. This being the case, the *noēma* of a religiously skeptical phenomenologist does not correspond to the *pisteuma* of the believer. The religious phenomenon appears only as *pisteuma* and not as mere *noēma*. How to reach the *pisteuma* is an urgent and tantalizing task for religious phenomenology.

We lack a philosophy of religion. We have philosophies of religions, that is, philosophies of particular religious traditions, or we have—and this causes difficulty in the religious encounter—the extrapolation of one religion's philosophy to other religious traditions for which it was neither intended nor suitable.

It almost goes without saying that the philosophy of religion I anticipate would not reduce all religions to one homogeneous pudding. On the contrary, it would allow the most variegated beliefs and religious traditions to flourish in its field, uprooting only isolationism and misunderstanding (not to say resentment and envy) to make room for a healthy and natural pluralism. We will have a true philosophy of religion not by lumping everything together but by discovering our religious root, which grows, flowers, and gives fruit in the most multiform way. Only then may the walls fall and private gardens open their gates. . . .

Such a philosophy results only from the mystical adventure of seeing truth from within more than one religious tradition. Interreligious dialogue is undoubtedly a preparation for this, a stepping-stone to that intrareligious dialogue where living faith constantly demands from us a total renewal, or—in Christian terms—a real, personal, and ever-recurring *metanoia*.

6

The Category of Growth in Comparative Religion

A Critical Self-Examination

Ὀς γάρ ουκ ἐστιν καθ' ἡμῶν υπέρ ἡμῶν ἐστιν
Whoever is not against us,
is for us.

*—Mk 9:40 (Lk 9:50)**

The echo produced by some of my writings dealing with problems in comparative religion invites me to restate thematically one of the main issues in the encounter of religions.

This chapter tries to overcome the temptation of self-defense. I shall try to rethink my approach to the problem of the encounter of Christian faith with the religions of the world and present it for correction or even total eclipse. How can I put forward more than a hypothesis in this field of open dialogue just now emerging among religions?

Ultimately my aim is not to defend or attack either Christianity or any other religion, but to understand the problem. It is precisely because I take seriously Christ's affirmation that he is the way, the truth, and the life[1] that I cannot reduce his significance only to historical Christianity. It is because I also take seriously the saying of the *Gita* that all action done with a good intention reaches Kṛṣṇa,[2] and the message of the Buddha that he points the way to liberation,[3] that I look for an approach to the encounter of religions that will contain not only a deep respect for but an enlightened confidence in these very traditions—and eventually belief in their messages.

Because I am equally concerned with contemporary Man, only too often wearied by a certain "religious" inflation when it is a better world for his fellow-beings he wants to build, I cannot consider the meeting of religions exclusively

* Significantly enough, the *Vulgata* translated both Mark's and Luke's verses as, "Qui enim non est adversus *vos*, pro *vobis* est," probably in order not to contradict Mt 12:30 ("Qui non est *mecum* contra *me* est") and Lk 11:23.

1 See Jn 14:6.

2 See *BG* IX.26–34.

3 *SN* V.421–23.

as a problem concerned with the past or relevant only to traditional religions. It speaks to the modern secular individual as well.

The Insufficient Methodological Approaches

One main objection to some of my writings is that I have undertaken a totally "false method": instead of defending Christianity, showing the demonic character of paganism and "utilizing" the tools of Hinduism to proclaim the Christian gospel, I involved myself with "heathen" absurdities, daring to "interpret" positively pagan texts in a certain way and thus defending "paganism" instead of undermining it. The reason for this is alleged to be my assumption that Christ is already present in Hinduism. In short, I "interpret" paganism with "Christian concepts," that is, I misinterpret it instead of "utilizing" it for Christian apologetics; or, in the words of a benevolent Hindū critic, I do just the opposite: my interpretation of Christ is in fact a Hindū interpretation.

But my purpose is not Christian or Hindū apologetics. I am not concerned with defending one or the other religion, one or the other thesis. This does not mean I am betwixt and between and stand nowhere at all; rather I start from the existential situation where I happen to be. I am not assuming the position of the aseptic-scientific mind beyond good and evil or outside the dilemma that claims to be ultimate. I affirm only that I am starting from my personal situation, without caring at this moment to describe it further. I am not writing on behalf of one or another religious tradition. I am speaking for myself and inviting my contemporaries to sincere dialogue.

Now, and this has been sometimes a cause of misunderstanding, I cannot speak many languages at the same time or defend many fronts simultaneously. External circumstances have led me to write more often for Christians—trying to open them up to other religious intuitions—than for Hindūs or Buddhists. Some, contrary to the criticism voiced above, consider this a "proof" that I am still on the Christian side. Others have interpreted this in the opposite way, namely that I believe Christians are in more urgent need of that opening to others than Hindūs and Buddhists. Again, I am not defending myself but simply trying to understand.

It seems to me that my deepest divergence from some of my critics is not so much in method as in understanding the fundamental Christian fact. Ultimately I would not accept absolutizing Christianity in order to consider that its truth has an exclusive claim that monopolizes salvation. In other words, I would not equate historical Christianity with transhistorical truth, nor, for that matter, a-historical Hinduism with a historical message. Insofar as it is a historical religion, Christianity belongs to history and should not transgress the boundaries of history; insofar as it conveys ahistorical values, Hinduism should not be totally identified with a historical religion.

I am well aware, of course, that Christianity contains more than just a historical message, that the history of salvation implies the salvation of history, and that this latter has an eschatological value transcending history. I am convinced, similarly, that Hinduism is also a historical phenomenon and a cultural asset in the history of mankind.

Most of the misunderstandings in this field arise from the fact that only too often comparisons are made between heterogeneous elements: we judge one religious tradition from inside and the other from outside. Any vision from within, with belief and personal commitment, includes at once the concreteness (and so the limitations) of that particular religion and the universal truth it embodies. A view from outside cannot see this link and judges only by objectified values. But religion, by definition—that is, as what it claims to be—is not completely objectifiable, nor is it reducible to mere subjectivity.

For this reason I do not accept the *utilization-interpretation* dilemma, nor do I find that these approaches do justice to the dialogue among religions toward which we are today impelled.

The difference between an exposition of Christian mysteries by *utilizing* Indic or other concepts and images on the one hand and an *interpretation* of the religions of the world by means of Christian concepts on the other would be important were I engaged in the defense of a particular doctrine. But for one who sincerely strives to find and express the truth, for one who does not discard either Hindū or Christian tradition as demonic, the difference is not relevant. Indeed, someone who humbly desires to make a radical investigation cannot take as his starting point a position that fundamentally and inexorably begs the question. I do not think either Christian or Hindū has to start with a kind of entrenched a priori that makes any meeting and dialogue impossible from the outset.

I am not considering whether what Christ conveyed is the same message Hinduism conveys or not. I am, however, making a fundamental assumption: the *ultimate* religious *fact* does not lie in the realm of doctrine or even individual self-consciousness. Therefore it can—and may well—be present everywhere and in every religion, although its "explicitation" may require varied degrees of discovery, realization, evangelization, revelation, hermeneutics, and so on. This makes it plausible that this fundamental—religious—fact may have different names, interpretations, levels of consciousness, and the like that are not irrelevant but that may be existentially equivalent for the person undergoing the concrete process of realization.

In a word, I am pleading for the *de-kerygmatization* of faith. The *kerygma*—like myth—has its place within any religion, but the "proclamation of the message" should not be identified without qualifications with the reality religions aim to disclose. I would apply this in a very special way to Christianity, and I may also say my reason for this is a conviction that the living and ultimately the real Christ is not the kerygma of the Lord, but the Lord himself. The naked Christ means also the "dekerygmatized" Christ.

I would say there is a primordial theandric fact that appears with a certain fullness in Jesus[4] but that is equally manifested and at work elsewhere. This is the Mystery that exists since the beginning of time and will appear only at the end of time in its "capital" fullness.[5] It is in my opinion a disheartening "microdoxy" to monopolize that mystery and make it the private property of Christians.

The main difference between "interpretation" and "utilization" then seems to lie in this. The *utilization* of, say, Greek or Hindū concepts to expound a Christian doctrine implies that I know well what Christian belief is, and that I *use* some thought-patterns from an external source to expound that Christian doctrine.

The *interpretation* of, say, Hinduism or Greek religion along Christian lines implies that I know well what Hinduism or the Greek religion is, and that I interpose some thought patterns coming from an external source (Christianity) in order to explain those very religions.

Let us now analyze these two methodological approaches to the encounter of religions, *utilization* and *interpretation.* My contention is that these two methods are not valid methods for a fruitful encounter of religions. Moreover, they seem to be incompatible with at least a significant part of the Christian attitude. Further, I will contend that only the category of growth does justice to the real religious situation of our time.

Utilization

Time and again it is said that the proper Christian attitude in the encounter of religions is that demonstrated by the church fathers themselves: *utilizing* the elements of pre-Christian thought to expound Christian doctrine. Undoubtedly this opinion has been held by many Christians, and by people of other religions as well.

To begin with, historical evidence for the first generation of Christians utilizing already existing elements of thought merely to express their own Christian ideas as their main or only procedure is very questionable, and, although this may sometimes have been the method, it was never the creative nor the prevailing attitude in Christianity. History shows that precisely where the Christian message succeeded in transforming a society it was never by such a "utilization," but, on the contrary, by its being assimilated—the Christian word is *incarnated*—by that particular religion and culture, the Christian fact working as the leaven.

Very often, indeed, we cannot say whether the church fathers were the "utilizing" ones, or just the opposite. In fact, many controversies and tensions in

4 Col 1:19.

5 See 1 Cor 2:7; Eph 1:9–10.

the patristic period were due precisely to the coexistence of both processes: that of "utilizing" and that of being "utilized." Were Plato's ideas Christianized, or was Christianity "Platonized"? Were Aristotle's concepts of *ousia* and the like utilized for the Christian doctrine of the Trinity, or did the Christian idea of the Trinity evolve as it did because of the internal dialectic of the concepts thus introduced? To put it differently, is not a great part of what is today called Christian doctrine, or even Christianity, precisely the result of such a symbiosis?

"Christian doctrine" did not come out of nothing, but it was the expression of certain beliefs within a specific thought pattern, which, in the beginning, was either "Jewish" or "Gentile" (this word embracing more than one cultural form), but certainly not "Christian." No Christian doctrine of Trinity nor any Christology existed before its expression in Gentile or Jewish categories. The Christian experience—belief or whatever one wishes to call it, but assuredly not doctrine—was molded, found expression—in a word, became doctrine—by means of already existing thought-patterns. It could not be otherwise.

Early Christians did not "utilize" Greek or other thought categories of the time in order to convey what had not yet found a proper expression. On the contrary, only by means of those—Jewish and Gentile—categories could the Christian experience be expressed and understood at all. A cogent proof for this is the significant fact that both orthodox and heretical views, in the Trinitarian and Christological controversies of the age, used the terminology of their respective milieus. Thus, to say "three *ousiai*" or "three *hypostaseis*" (substances) meant one thing to Origen and another to Arius, or to say "three *prosopa*" (persons) meant one thing to Hippolytus and another to Sabellius. They were not utilizing Greek concepts to express one single Christian intuition, but they had a different understanding of the Christian fact, perhaps because they were carried away by the very concepts they used. One could almost say they were utilized, used, by those very concepts.

In fact, Greek concepts handled (and often mishandled) the Christian event. St. John, for instance, did not utilize (and transform) the Philonic concept of *logos* to convey his "message"; it was almost the other way around: the *logos* took flesh, I would say—begging not to be misunderstood—not only in the womb of Mary but also in the midst of the intellectual speculation on the *logos* at that time. To use utterly new words and expressions to say what Christ was all about would have been unintelligible—and impossible.

In order to give expression to the Christian faith not by dint of willful and calculated utilization, but through a natural, cultural, and spiritual process, the only possibility was—and always is—to let it take form, name, and flesh in the terms of the contemporary culture. In scholastic terms, the logical analogy of the concepts, necessary for their intelligibility outside their univocal realm, implies also an ontological analogy. If the Johannine concept of *logos* were not somehow analogous to the pre-Christian concept, if it did not start from an interpretation of a concept already existing, it could neither be intelligible nor in any way "inspired." A parallel example would be that of the Buddha interpreting the already existing concept of *nirvāṇa* in a new and original way.

But one may retort that the situation is different today: there *are* dogmas; there *is* a church; there is now a definite Christian doctrine, and even so-called Christian thought. But, it is further said, such "thought" can very well profit by concepts and ideas borrowed from other cultures and religions. This we may grant for the sake of the argument, but we should emphasize that such borrowing method will never go very deep, or lead us very far; it will touch only the surface and lead to an artificial and definitely shallow adaptation. There will emerge from it neither synthesis nor symbiosis, nor even a serious confrontation. It will all remain foreign and external, a mere superstructure.

The fact that there is now an elaborate Christian thought-system makes it all the more urgent to overcome the dangers of isolation and self-satisfaction by reaching out to meet other religious traditions, learning from them, and interpreting them in the light of one's own beliefs. Two main reasons seem relevant here. The first is the almost self-evident fact that the Western Christian tradition seems to be exhausted, I might almost say effete, when it tries to express the Christian message in a meaningful way for our times. Only by cross-fertilization and mutual fecundation may the present state of affairs be overcome; only by stepping over the current cultural and philosophical boundaries can Christian life become creative and dynamic again. Obviously, this applies to the other religions as well: it is two-way traffic. The encounter of religions today is vital for the religious life of our contemporary time; otherwise, traditional religions will remain altogether obsolete, irrelevant relics of the past, and what is worse, we will be uprooted and impoverished.

The time for one-way traffic in the meeting of cultures and religions is, at least theoretically, over. If there still are powerful vestiges of a past colonialist attitude, they are dying out by the very fact that they become conscious. Neither monologue nor conquest is tenable. The *spolia-aegyptiorum* mentality is today no longer possible, or in any way justifiable. To think that one people, one culture, one religion has the right—or the duty, for that matter—to dominate all the rest belongs to a past era in world history. Our contemporary degree of consciousness and our present-day conscience, East and West, finds, by and large, such a pretension utterly untenable. The meeting point is neither my house nor the mansion of my neighbor, but the crossroads outside the walls, where we may eventually decide to put up a tent—for the time being.[6]

Finally, there is a theoretical point to consider: if the use of a concept foreign to a given cultural setup is to be made viable, if it is to be grafted successfully onto

[6] See Mk 9:5.

another system of thought (the Christian one, for example), it will succeed only if it has somehow attained a certain homogeneity with the host cultural and religious world, so that it may live there. If this is the case, it amounts to recognizing that its possible use depends on a certain previous homogeneity, on a certain presence of the one meaning within the other framework; otherwise, it would be completely impossible to utilize the concept at issue. In spite of the heterogeneity between the Greek and the Christian conception of the Logos, for instance, the former had to offer a certain affinity with the new meaning, which would be enhanced once it was assumed. In other words, "utilization," even if it is admitted as a proper procedure, can be fruitful only if based on a previous relatedness that is the condition for its use. Only homogeneous materials can be used if any integration is to survive. The real problem, thus, lies deeper—and elsewhere.

Interpretation

Some critics maintain that it is quite wrong in the encounter of religions (at least from the Christian point of view) to interpret the texts and statements of other religious traditions in light of the Christian insight.

If the Christian faith were totally foreign to such traditions, if the Christian fact had nothing to do with the fundamental religious fact or human reality in its ultimate concern, then obviously to introduce a hermeneutical principle (the Christian one) completely alien to those traditions would be unwarranted. But this is not necessarily a Christian position.

Be this as it may, I would like to offer the following condensed remarks.

First, one could question the historical accuracy of the statement that true Christians never interpreted pre-Christian religions but only utilized them for their own kerygma. I wonder, then, what it was St. Paul did with the Jewish Bible if not interpret it, and rather drastically at that. Moreover, most church fathers and Scholastics undoubtedly did this very thing vis-à-vis "non-Christian" thinkers and Greek concepts; that is, they interpreted them according to what they thought to be the Christian line of development. In this way, the traditional doctrine of the *sensus plenior* was developed: the fuller meaning of pre-Christian ideas seen in the light of Christ. This idea underlies nothing less than the incorporation of the Old Testament into Christianity.

Second, the question becomes even clearer if we consider that ultimately we cannot use a concept without, at the same time, interpreting it in a certain way. If St. Paul, for instance, had "utilized" a Stoic or Gnostic concept of *sōma* (body) without interpreting it in his own way, this would have amounted to accepting fully its Stoic or Gnostic connotations. The work of polishing or emphasizing or even sometimes twisting, which theologians of every age have always done—what is this, if not simply interpreting, or, I would say, reinterpreting already existing concepts?

Third, the main objection to a Christian interpretation of the world religions seems to rest on a double assumption: on the idea that all that does not belong "officially" and "visibly" to historical Christianity, or to the church, is sinful and Satanic (an extrapolation of the saying that "everything not born of God is sin"[7]), and on the fear that such interpretation would mean recognizing that the Spirit of God has also been at work in other religious traditions[8] and that even Christ, who is before Abraham,[9] is somehow present and effective in those other religions. ("Lord, we have seen some performing miracles in your name, who do not belong to our group";[10] "The rock indeed was Christ!"[11]).

I personally cannot subscribe to any opinion that monopolizes God, *logos*, Christ, and even Jesus, and sets the rules for how the kingdom of God must work. I disagree from a purely human standpoint, as well as from scientific, theological, and Christian points of view. There were zealots even among the apostles, but Christ was not a zealot.

Finally, there remains the objection from the other side, that is, from the followers of other religious traditions. Are they going to be satisfied with a Christian interpretation?

One may answer, first of all, that these religions are going to be satisfied even less by the other method, which simply uses their own tools to preach something apparently contrary to their traditions and beliefs. Yet the force of the argument clearly does not come from this quarter.

The one reason supporting the resistance to a Christian interpretation seems to be that, with few exceptions, Christ has been considered the monopoly of Christians, as if Christ were *ad usum Delphini*, solely for the benefit of orthodox believers. So, when one simply mentions the name of Christ, other religions understand it in a polemical way, or at least as foreign stuff.

Now, it is clear that any genuine "Christian" interpretation must be valid and true, and for this very reason it must also be acceptable to those who are being interpreted: a basic methodological rule for any interpretation. This means that no interpretation of any religion is valid if the followers of that religion do not recognize it as such. But this means also, by the same token, that nobody can propose as Christian something that Christians do not recognize as such. On the other hand, the history of religious traditions is not closed, and it shows that certain ideas or conceptions, denounced as heretical at a given moment, were accepted later. In point of fact, the evolution—and, as I am going to say, the growth—of any religion has been brought about mainly by "foreign" ideas incorporated into the body of beliefs.

---

7 See Rom 14:23.

8 Rom 10:10.

9 Jn 8:58.

10 Lk 9:49; Mk 9:38.

11 1 Cor 10:4.

Furthermore, there is another, though ambivalent, reason for the "Christian interpretation" or any interpretation of one religion by another, for that matter. I will point out pros and cons.

Pro. If the Christian interpretation of, say, *karma* has to be a valid one, as it has already been said, it has to be valid for both traditions. This is to say that such an interpretation will have to reach a depth where the one tradition does not find itself deformed, and the other one finds it acceptable. Obviously, the new interpretation, because of its incorporation into Christianity, may imply some shades of meaning that Hindūs and Buddhists may not accept; but, provided that they recognize the starting interpretation as a legitimate one, nothing stands in the way of the new step.

Contra. Religions are organic wholes, and each particular tenet makes sense within the entire body of doctrine. Now, to transplant one particular notion into another body is not only a delicate operation but it also requires a homogeneous body to receive it. Otherwise, what we have done is to get stimulated by the "foreign" tenet, but in fact we have not crossed the boundaries of our own tradition. This is particularly visible with the very words we use. Words are meaningful within a context, and mere translation may not do. In other terms, not everything is amenable to an exogenous interpretation.

Here we must confess that a great deal of fundamental work still has to be done. I would like now to state tentatively the direction in which I would be inclined to look for further research.

Philosophies and Philosophy of Religion

One fact should be clearly and sincerely acknowledged: by considering the geographical and historical coordinates of our times, we do not find a philosophy of religion worthy of the name. What is termed *philosophy of religion* is usually a particular philosophy of a particular religion expressed in more or less vague or universal terms, and then applied almost a priori to all other "religions" of the world. Undoubtedly, mankind can be considered a unity, and from the reflection of a particular group one may sometimes draw conclusions that are valid for the entire human race, but this approximate method is distinctly insufficient as a working and effective philosophy of religion for our times. Even if in the past such efforts were made, the worldview that prompted such attempts has been superseded today, when the whole earth—for good or ill—begins to form a geographical and historical unit for the first time in human existence.

The fact that traditional religions are mainly oriented to the past, for instance, and that the religious vitality of mankind has produced new forms of religiousness marginal to, if not in conflict with, traditional religions, is part of the same problem: namely, we do not have a philosophy of religion. Ideologies and other secular forms that claim a total hold on the human person, and thereby the right to direct our lives, are numberless in our times. Morphologically, in fact, they are religions, but few would call themselves like that, because the very name of religion has fallen into widespread disrepute.

Our main point follows. We may easily agree that one cannot even envision the possibility of a philosophy of religion without the inner experience peculiar to religion. In the classic terms of Christian Scholasticism, theology is a *charisma*, and faith is required for a real and creative theologian—and here the philosophical and the theological activity should not be artificially severed.

Now, in spite of the claim of every religion to touch the very core of the human being, *the* "experience of religion" does not exist. What is given is a religious experience within one particular context—that is, there is a peculiar inner experience of, or within, *a* particular religion. A religion "in general" does not exist.

This could justify *a* philosophy of *a* religion, but not the philosophy of religion. Either, then, we agree that it is possible to experience, inwardly and authentically, more than one religion, or we renounce forever a philosophy of religion valid for the different world religions. Or else, as it is generally the case today, the philosophy of religion is merely replaced by a phenomenology of religions—and even then the problem is not solved, as we show in the following chapter.

In no way do we belittle the phenomenology of religion, which has earned many merits in recent times; but to consider it a substitute for philosophy of religion would be a serious mistake. *Unicuique suum.*

I am not maintaining that no philosophy of religion is possible without the specific "theological" *charisma* in the Scholastic sense. Whatever conception of philosophy (or theology, if we prefer) we may have, only a philosophy or theology of religion that takes into account the facts, categories, and insights of a particular religion is able and entitled to handle the phenomena of that religion. But for this we must know such data not merely by hearsay but through a genuine effort to understand. Even the strictest philosophical positivism makes no exception. If, as this latter will tell us, philosophy of religion is only the scientific analysis of religious language, one must nevertheless know the particular language, which originated from assumptions rather different, perhaps, from the language of the positivist philosopher himself. In brief, it is not only a question of proper translation; we need a common symbolism not only to check the translation and establish a two-way communication but also to make the translation itself. In order to say, "*Tisch* means table," I need another common term of reference (my finger, my eyes, and so on) that is able to transfer (translate) the meaning.

The philosophy of religion is only made possible by a prior philosophy of religions. Only after this, which is more than just a digest of philosophies of religions, will we be on the way to a philosophy of religion capable of fulfilling the task that falls to such a discipline today. To elaborate a philosophy of religion we need to take religions seriously and, further, to experience them from within—to believe, in one way or another, in what these religions say. Otherwise, we remain floating on the surface. To know what a religion says, we must understand what it says, but for this we must somehow believe in what it says. Religions are not purely objectifiable data; they are also and essentially a personal, subjective issue. As we have said, the specific belief of the believer belongs essentially to religion. Without that belief, no philosophy of religions is possible. Merely to describe the tenets or practices that the followers of a particular religion claim to acknowledge is not yet a philosophy of religions, much less the philosophy of religion. Needless to say, this is only a necessary precondition or requirement, insufficient by itself for a critical philosophy of religion.

This seems to be a major challenge in our times; lacking an authentic philosophy of religion, we will not be able to understand the different world religions nor the people and cultures of this Earth, for religion is the soul of a culture, and one of the most important factors in the shaping of human character, both individually and collectively.

Undoubtedly, the extrapolation of a particular philosophy into fields beyond the scope of its original application is no longer justifiable, yet this still happens in many philosophical, theological, and religious quarters. Christianity is perhaps the religion that has been most concerned with this problem, and yet, not only does it not possess any philosophy of religion, but it continues to extrapolate unawares. When, for instance, St. Paul talks about the Gentiles or the idolaters, he has the people of Corinth or Asia Minor in his mind, or those whom he thinks deserve that name for whatever reason. To apply the Jew-Gentile dichotomy outside its sphere and call "heathens" the Hindūs and Buddhists (or even Muslims!) is an unwarranted extrapolation, to say the least.

Biblical scholarship today does not insist on the doctrine that the entire planet was underwater in Noah's time, or in utter darkness at the crucifixion of Christ. It has set geographical boundaries to those statements, but it still has not sufficiently examined the anthropological, metaphysical, and religious boundaries of the Old and New Testaments.

Is such an enterprise—a philosophy of religion—possible? I believe it cannot be affirmed a priori that it is impossible, although it may remain only an ideal. Philosophy can encompass more than one religion, because one can have a true, inner religious experience in more than one religious tradition without betraying any of them, and of course without confusing genuine experience with artificial experiment. One cannot experiment with religions as if they were mice or plants, but one can believe in them as authentic paths, and try to understand, and eventually to integrate more than one religious tradition. After all, most of mankind's great religious geniuses did not create or found new forms of religiousness out of nothing; they rather united more than one religious stream, melting them by their own prophetic gifts. But one need not be a prophet or a religious founder to be creative in this new field of research; the philosopher of religion needs, however, to be a believer, and to be sufficiently humble, ready to undergo—with his faith—not an experiment but an experience.

I have said that a philosophy of religion is not impossible, but I should have immediately added one condition. This condition links us, once more, with the traditional philosophical or theological activity, in contradistinction to the individualistic character of Western modernity. This condition is, in old parlance, the scholastic (in the basic sense of "school"), corporate, or ecclesial character of the philosophical enterprise. In present-day terms, we may like better to speak of the dialogical character of the philosophy of religion.

A genuine philosophy of religion in our times, if it is to keep the claim to speak about the religious dimension of Man, has to be critically aware that neither a single individual nor any single religious tradition has access to the universal range of the human experience. It must then pull together the findings, experiences, and data coming from the four directions of the Earth; it has to be dialogical and, like a net, encompass the different religious experiences of humanity.

The main thing favoring such an enterprise is not the individual's psychological capacity to experience sincerely more than one religious tradition but the fact that there exists something like a fundamental religiousness, a constitutive religious dimension in us, an inbuilt religious or basically human factor, however we may call it. Surely no religious tradition today takes such hold of the entire human being that it leaves no room for communication and dialogue. Man indeed transcends his own historical and cultural boundaries.

Human nature is a meta-ontological one. This allows the possibility of an experience that certainly implies an overcoming of the actual boundaries of a particular religion, though without betraying it.

The Vital Issue: Growth

We said that neither the *use* of a foreign tradition to enrich another one, nor the *interpretation* of one religion in the light of another, is adequate or appropriate to the philosophical task and to the religious needs of our times. I submit that the one category able to carry the main burden in the religious encounter and in the further development of religion (and religions) is *growth*. Theology or philosophy, and much more religion, are not simply matters of archaeological interest, nor is religion mainly directed to the past. On the contrary, the future, hope, eschatology, the end of human life and the world are fundamental religious categories. Religion is inclined toward the future; it is full of that *epektasis* we find in the Greek Christian patristic writings, that is, an attitude of more than expectation, of constantly leaning toward our transhuman or superhuman end. In the life of religion, as in the life of a person, where there is no growth there is decay; to stop means stagnation and death.

It would be wrong and methodologically false to restrict the theological task to just imitating the elders. Obviously it is a risky adventure to start toward the terra incognita of a really new land in religious consciousness and proceed in the discovering of new paths. "Men of Galilee, what are you doing here just gazing at the skies?"[12]

After much effort and many painful misunderstandings, Christian theology has accepted as a fact what in certain theological circles is called the development of dogma. This seems to be a good starting point, but it would hardly suffice, if interpreted merely as a kind of explication of something that was already there. Were religious consciousness static, our task would be only to unfold what was already there, nicely "folded." There is, however, undoubtedly a development in religious consciousness. Two points should be immediately stressed in this connection.

First, religious consciousness is something more than an external development of a knowing organ, which at a certain moment discovers something of which it was not previously aware. Besides, since religious consciousness is an essential part of religion, the development of this consciousness means the development of religion itself.

Second, it amounts to more than just a development in personal consciousness; at the very least, human consciousness is set in evolution. What develops, in fact, is the entire cosmos, all creation, reality. The whole universe expands. In a word, there is real growth in Man, in the World, and I would also add, in God, at least inasmuch as neither immutability nor change is a category of the Divine. Divinity is constant newness, pure act, as the Scholastics said.

So there is not only a development of dogma; there is also a real development of consciousness. We may—or may not—have a system of thought sufficiently elaborated to express this fact adequately, but it is one thing to underscore the limitations of the human mind struggling to find a proper expression, and another thing to dismiss an intuition because it is still in the throes of birth, still a *concipiendum* and not yet a *conceptum.* After all, what, here on Earth, is born into life already complete? Only something that is already dead, stillborn. As it is often remarked, only dead languages do not tolerate mistakes (nobody being left to accept them), but a living language makes a lot of room for today's mistakes, which may become tomorrow's rule. The physical theory of an expanding universe may furnish a fair image of what happens in the ontological realm as well.

Without allowing for such growth, no religious maturity is possible. But here growth means not only linear development. In spite of all Christian theological contrivances, the Jewish point of view is quite right when it judges not only Paul but also Christ as real innovators. Given this perspective, the members of the Sanhedrin were not so wrong in condemning Jesus. They really understood what it was all about: not merely evolution, reform, or improvement, but a real mutation,

---

[12] Acts 1:11.

a new step, another sphere, more akin to revolution than to evolution. It is almost a platitude to say that if Jesus were to come to Earth now, the church would put him to death. I interpret this not in the sense that the church has betrayed the message of Jesus (this is not my point now), but that Christ would introduce another revolution, another step, a new wine that he would not allow to be poured into old skins.[13] This constant growth should be a fundamental element of sacramental theology, especially of the liturgical Eucharist.

Growth is perhaps the most pertinent category to express this situation, which is more than simple development or explication. In growth there is continuity as well as novelty, development as well as a real assimilation of something that was outside and is now incorporated, made one body. In growth there is freedom. Perhaps nowhere else is human freedom more visible and more magnificent than in the consciousness of the religious person who discovers that he or she is the cocreator, the shaper and builder not only of his or her own life but also of the life of the cosmos: Man is the artist of the Mystical Body, the free agent who can make himself and the world go one way or another, who can lead history in one or another direction. Nothing is more fascinating than the religious existence being seen and lived as such a dynamism.

I repeat: Growth means continuity and development, but it also implies transformation and revolution. Growth does not exclude mutation; on the contrary, there are moments even in the biological realm when only a real mutation can account for further life. We know roughly the law of growth for a plant or a child's body; we do not know, and—in a way—we cannot know, the ways growth may possibly grow further. The future is not just a repetition of the past. (I hope one result of the landing on the moon will be to free us from provincial horizons and foreshortened views.) How Hinduism needs to grow, or how Christianity or modern humanism has to grow, we cannot know yet. The prophet's function is not precisely to know in advance, but to point out the direction and to go ahead, to ascend the ladder of time, space, and the spirit. There are false prophets, too, of course, but this happens for the same reason for which there exists false silver and not, so far, false earth or water: we only falsify things worth falsifying.

Growth does not exclude rupture and internal or external revolution. We know what the growth of an adolescent means only once the evolution is completed. We do not know where we are going. Yet, in this common ignorance, genuinely religious people experience real fellowship and fraternal communion.

Growth does not deny a process of death and resurrection; quite the contrary. If growth is to be genuine and not merely a cancer, it implies a negative as well as a positive metabolism, death as well as a new life. That we must constantly kill the idols that creep in from all sides, this we are prepared to accept; we also

---

[13] Lk 5:37–38.

know that the prophets' lot is to be crushed between the temple and the palace. It seems, at least to me, an empirical truth that *metanoia* is the first condition for sound growth and real life.

But what about Islam, Hinduism, Christianity? I am tempted to give the answer Jesus gave to a similar question, asked by Peter: "If I will that he remain till I come, what is that to you? You follow me!"[14]

In the contemporary scene, where everything is in the fires of revision and reform, in which every value is contested, a total *metanoia* is needed; the authentically religious person cannot shut himself off, close his ears and eyes, and simply gaze toward heaven or brood over the past; he cannot ignore his fellow human beings and act as if religion has assured him that he has no more to learn, nothing to change. He must throw himself into the sea and begin to walk, even if his feet falter and his heart fails.[15] Who are we to stifle the growing seed, to choke humble and personal buds, to quench the smoking wick?[16]

Bibliographical Note

Besides the more than one hundred book reviews scattered among specialized journals and the discussion that took place (over a period of several years) in the Bombay weekly *The Examiner* (from 1965 onward), see:

D. Reetz, "Raymond Panikkar's Theology of Religion," *Religion and Society* (Bangalore, September 1968), 32–54; D. E. Mulder, "Raymond Panikkar's Dialog Met Het Hindoe'isme," *Gereformeers Theologisch Tiydschrift* (August 1969), 186–98; and F. Molinario, "L'evangelizzazione della cultura e della religione nell'esperienza e negli scritti di R. Panikkar," *Testimonianza* (No. 144, 1972).

Regarding specific points, see the author's answers to:

J. A. Cuttat, "Vergeistigungs 'Technik' und Umgestaltung in Christus," *Kairos* (Salzburg, 1/1959): 18–30; P. Hacker, "Magie, Gott, Person und Gnade in Hinduismus," *Kairos* (Salzburg, 4/1960): 225–33; and K. Rudolph, "Die Problematik der Religionswissenschaft als akademisches Lehrfach," *Kairos* (Salzburg, 1/1967): 22–42 (all of which may be found in *Kairos* [Salzburg, 1/1960]: 45 *et seq.*; [2/1961]: 112–14; and [1/1968]: 56–67, respectively).

As for the negative criticism, which these pages have tried to meet without polemics, see:

The article-review by P. Hacker of the author's *Kultmysterium in Hinduismus und Christentum* in *Theologische Revue*, no. 6 (1967): 370–78; and also Hacker's short essay "Interpretation und 'Benutzung,' 'Kleine Beitrage,'" in *Zeitschrift für Missionswissenschaft und Religionswissenschaft* 51, no. 3 (July 1967): 259–63.

---

[14] Jn 21:22.

[15] Mt 14:28ff.

[16] Mt 12:20; see Isa 42:3.

7

Intrareligious Dialogue according to Ramon Llull

The dialogue in *Llibre del gentil e los tres savis*[1] takes place in a land that Jews, Christians, and Muslims all considered as their own. Ramon Llull speaks to us of the concord needed between the three most important Western powers. If we had listened to him, history would have been different. But perhaps we can still take heed today. . . .

*

Putting to one side the powerful imagery of the "beautiful maiden" riding her "handsome palfrey," and the symbolism of the five trees and the 217 flowers, I shall restrict myself to commenting on Llull's prophetic and ecumenical vision, so rich in teachings for our own time.

I would like *first of all* to stress his boldness in heaping praise not only on the heathen, who is referred to as a wise and a good man, but also on the Jew and the Saracen. They may not have the truth, but Llull has not a moment's doubt that they have goodness—and the Mallorcan philosopher constantly repeats that you cannot have one without the other. One of his basic arguments, in fact, consists in the ontological correlation between "right and greatness," "wisdom and love," "love and perfection." This is not, therefore, a fight between enemies. The aim is not to beat an opponent but to convince a companion. Each of them greets the others "in his language and according to his customs." This is more than tolerance. Ramon is telling us that all religions are good because they produce good and wise Men. The time is the end of the thirteenth century, after two centuries of Crusades. And Llull is daring enough not to condemn anyone—and, what is more, not to make anyone win! The heathen does finally convert to God but puts off the choice of joining one of the three great religions. What matters is to come out of oneself (love) and worship God—that is, to enter into the Mystery and take part in it.

Second, the book shows that disagreement among men is a leading evil that must be eradicated, and this is the first task for religion. This lack of brotherhood is a religious crime and not just a political fact. Ramon is well aware that the official religions have for too long ignored harmony between Men, when not in fact promoting themselves through religious wars and fights.

[1] *The Book of the Gentile and the Three Wise Men.*

This is the great scandal of institutionalized religion! The pagan's "woes and torments" echo those of Ramon: "In despair and lamenting was Ramon under a fine tree and he sang his despair to ease his pain." Thus begins his voluminous *Arbre de Ciència.*[2]

We must seek religious harmony among people not through Crusades and inquisitions but through mutual respect and joint research and, especially, through dialogue. Llull conveys his conviction that Men are subjected to a Power that is higher than all of us—which in his writing is not the monotheistic God but Lady Intelligence: the power to *intus-legere* the nature of reality.

Third, the rules of the game laid down by Llull for a dialogue between cultures are prophetically valid for our time:

1. Debate must never be mere intellectual curiosity, and certainly not academic competition, but must arise from an existential yearning; it must spring from the experience of human hardship, from seeing the disastrous results of disunion, and from a realization of its betrayal of history and of the very essence of religion. This is not a luxury! The tears, laments, prayers, and prostrations of our text are not just literary flourishes.

2. The dialogue has to take place on neutral ground, outside the city, in a conducive setting and a pleasant atmosphere: a nice orchard with its wholesome, sweet-smelling fruits. Above all, it must not be carried out in a situation of inequality, with one side owning all the dollars and all the political power, dominating the situation or imposing its language. Religious dialogue is not possible when some ride well shod and others walk barefoot. Geographical serenity is a symbol of historical equanimity. Man is a geological as well as a historical being.

3. The conversation must not only keep to a civil vein; it must also be directed by an impartial, though not indifferent, third party. The heathen will be the arbiter, and the others will not interrupt each other, but will speak in rigorous chronological order and will apologize to one another before and afterward. The act of contrition must be the "introit" for any interreligious dialogue.

4. Arguments of authority—which today we would call arguments of force—must not be used. Paradoxically, quotations from the Holy Scriptures are not suitable to an interreligious discourse. We should not take our own premises as a basis for the others. Neither "*Gott mit uns*" nor "In [our] God we trust" are postulates for the interreligious dialogue. It is in the name of God that some of the greatest crimes on earth have been committed. Dialogue does not presuppose a particular belief, but rather and simply faith in the very act of the encounter—which therefore becomes a religious act.

---

[2] *Tree of Science.*

5. The three wise men do not conceal their opinions, nor do they hesitate to show up "false opinions and errors." The three monotheists make no bones about their belief that the others are on the wrong track. But, in spite of this, they talk and look for an agreement. Each one must be true to his own conscience. Interreligious discourse is not like diplomatic negotiation.

6. The discussion is not a closed dialogue, but it "under-goes" the judgment of one who does not even "have knowledge of God" or believe "in resurrection," at the risk that this stranger might be shocked at the small-mindedness of the established religions. The boldness of Llull's approach sounds like a novelty still nowadays. Let me emphasize that Christians and Muslims, Catholics or atheists, or whoever, will never begin a fruitful dialogue if they just discuss things among themselves—that is, if they don't make a joint effort as the one mirrored in the dialogue of the three wise men and the pagan. Take, for example, the issue of peace in our time. Religion is not an end in itself but rather a means.

7. The effort of religious understanding is constitutively unfinished, in-finite; it will continue as long as it is necessary, because it is in itself the manifestation of our contingency. Perhaps this is the most important and most revealing trait. The dialogue takes place without foreseeable results and independently of human will. No one knows what the outcome of the encounter will be: no one knows on which side the heathen will land. The unity of truth to which the human heart aspires is not uniformity of opinions but perhaps their equivalence, complementarity, or even polarity. Everything suggests that the heathen has found a primordial religiousness that makes him break out with the speech that so strikes "the three wise men," and that all three of them can approve without betraying their respective confessions. This speech speaks of the three theological virtues, the four cardinal virtues, and the seven vices and virtues, so as to "wake the sleeping greats," he says with clear (though hidden) intentions at the end of the book.

All these traits can be summarized in one: the passage from interreligious dialogue to *intrareligious* dialogue—from exteriority to interiority, from the condemnation of others to the examination of one's own conscience, from the problem of political power to personal issues, from dogma to mysticism, if you prefer. Until humanity's religious problem is seen and understood as an intimate, personal problem; until religion is fathomed and discovered as a dimension of the human being—and therefore something affecting all of us; until there is despair and lamenting over the human destiny we all form a part of; until then we will not be able to distinguish doctrinal disputes, political rivalries, and personal ambition from the true religious act—that is, the common search for Man's very purpose and cooperation and accomplishment of the very destiny of the universe. Religion is far more a constitutive dimension of humankind than an institution.

But let's get back to *Llibre del gentil e los tres savis*. As the reader is free to enjoy the text for himself, I shall simply retell what I think is one of the most important elements in the myth implicit in the book:

> As the infidels had long taken part . . . as we, the contemporaries of this declining twentieth century, have already been well-acquainted with modern civilization for some centuries and, despite the unquestionable advantages for us (not for everyone) "having understood their false opinions and errors," and being witnesses to the deterioration in human life and the results ensuing from the violation of nature, the acceleration of the rhythms of the cosmos, the monetization of culture, the quantification of existence; realizing, also, that we have now lost even "the words by which" the current situation "is best expressed," we want to speak of a pagan—that is, of the people who make up at least 80 percent of human population—and of her dialogue with the three wise men. . . .

Not by "God's ordainment" but because of particular dynamics in human history, "it happened" that on our planet there are people who weep and search without hope and without comfort. When there aren't famine, exploitation, dictatorship, torture, and war in one place, there are drugs, depression, debauchery, and distress in another. These people, also, met up with the three wise men. . . . One knew all there was to know about *Science*. His forebears were Hebrews and Egyptians. The other said he possessed *Sentiment*. His ancestors separated from the first wise men twenty centuries ago, so as to put love above all else, in the belief that God was love. The third wise man was *Will*. His origins came from the ineffectiveness of the first two, when it came to putting things into practice. These three wise men have been trying to put the world to rights since ancient times.

But the pagan, the people, the man in the street, has lived—lives—joylessly, in spite of the great discoveries of science, sentiment, and will, or perhaps he has just lost hope in these supposed panaceas.

The three wise men held very beautiful dialogues, and the "mass media" of the privileged were responsible for spreading their points of view all over, together with a barrage of ideologies of all sorts. They called this "education," "information," and even "religion": "Science will save the world. Nothing can be done without Love. Ideas are useless unless they become Reality." Our "pagan," who listened attentively to them, remained nevertheless perplexed: "Must we wait for the last discovery before we can be happy? Isn't love very often counterproductive? Doesn't pure praxis often lead to destruction and fanaticism?"

In this story we have avoided grand discussions among science, sentiment, and will. The whole history of humanity is contained in them. But neither peace nor concord seem to arise from all of it. Perhaps a later understanding will be reached, and the problems of the world will be solved, but while the uproar, competition, and consumption continue, how many more generations will have to be sacrificed? Must we keep on waiting for the future, or has the time already come for us to transcend history?

The heathen—that is, the people of three-quarters of the world—no longer believe in either Science, Religion, or Politics, and perhaps it is time to listen to them in their pilgrimage through the forests of this world.

The people went, in fact, to "the great forest," but they did not take pleasure in "the shores and springs and meadows and the many different kinds of birds in the trees that sang so sweetly," because almost everything was contaminated, and only the rich could visit the most distant and "natural" spots. The palfrey on which Lady Intelligence used to ride had died of starvation and because of the stench of petrol, and the Lady was not to be seen anywhere.

But, lo! Our pagan, our people, after much walking, suffering, and brooding, one day saw a damsel coming on foot. She was middle-aged and was not "nobly dressed," but she was "of agreeable countenance," anyway.

"What is your name?" they asked her.

"My name is *Grace*," she answered.

"What does it mean?" they asked.

"It means that I am agreeable, filled with gratitude, graceful, gratifying, and gratuitous. I do everything *gratis* because I like what I do, I am grateful for everything because no one owes me anything, I find everything gratifying because I ask for nothing. They say I behave gracefully because I do not do things for any extrinsic reason, and that is why people find me agreeable, congratulate me, and they are grateful to me because I admit no form of payment, so that no one can be ungrateful to me or fall into disgrace before me."

"And what did the people understand?" I asked, intrigued.

"Personally," said a confidant, "I understood that life is worth living in itself, that worrying over the means distracts us from the ends, that the object is joy, and that this joy surprises us when we know how to live the tempiternal moments (which are not outside time but are not stifled by it, either). Together we understood, also, that if our life is not freed from the exclusive weight of history, if our ideals do not overcome those of self-absorbed people enclosed in prisons they call cities, if our loves do not transcend the crust of things, we are not really living. We also understood that, if we want to reduce everything to quantitative parameters, to the measure of reason, and to a fleeting time through which we pass unnoticed, we shall not grasp the mystery of existence, the beauty of things, the truth of reality, and therefore we shall never achieve that well-being that surpasses all conception, the God that was the symbol of Mystery and who now perhaps takes on other Names. The solution, for the world and for ourselves, does not lie in the models of the Abrahamic traditions. [The pagan was not convinced.] Perhaps the solution does not lie anywhere, because it is not static."

"But," the people said, "we have not yet managed to grasp this Grace business. We heard her coming, we felt her touch, and we were grateful. We saw once more that the world is beautiful, that everything is gratuitous, if we share it graciously. That's why this Joy, which is another name for Grace, does not paralyze our action, but strengthens us in our longing for justice. . . ."

8

Some Observations on Interreligious Dialogue

The Risks of a Western Mindset

An Analysis of the Present Situation

Once upon a time, there was an anguished lover who, over the course of many years, sent passionate love letters to his beloved in a far distant land. At long last, she wrote back and said that she had married the mailman. . . .

Like her, the West has fallen in love with the messenger. It has become infatuated with a rational approach to reality. But reason, the reign of rationality, is only an intermediary. Religion in the West has sacrificed too much to it. It is time to realize that our task is to forget the letter and hold fast to the Lord.

The West has also insisted on the importance of history. We see missionaries trying to convince Hindūs that Christianity is true because Jesus is a historical person, while Kṛṣṇa is only a myth. But for a devout Hindū this way of thinking makes no sense at all. Napoleon too was a historical figure, too—so what? "Kṛṣṇa is alive in my heart!" Different cultures have different understandings of time. In Sanskrit, the same word can mean either "yesterday" or "tomorrow."

In like manner, the West has all but deified law. But a lawmaker God has little meaning for the non-Westerner.

We in the West try to pinpoint what is essential and specific. The advantage of such a reductionist approach to reality is that we can then dominate it. The success of Western culture shows how effective this method is. But does it make sense when monks try to pinpoint "the specificity of monastic interreligious dialogue"?

Finally, we need to point out the risk of always emphasizing the measurable and the quantitative. Does it really make any sense to report on an encounter in terms of percentages? "My thinking is now 50 percent Buddhist!"

From a lecture delivered by Panikkar in Montserrat (Barcelona) in November 2004, according to the notes taken by Pierre-François de Béthune, published in *DIM/MID International Bulletin* (Louvain-la-Neuve) no. 2 (2004): 17–21.

What Is at Stake in This Way of Thinking

We absolutely need to take into account the risks involved in a way of thinking that has been used to justify cultural imperialism, and that excludes the very possibility of dialogue.

To believe that our Western categories make it possible to understand everything is clear evidence of a cultural imperialism, even cultural colonialism. This sort of violence has become widespread; we must constantly ask ourselves whether it still has influence over us or not.

When we say that Brahman is the God of the Hindūs, we imply that we know perfectly well what a god is. However, for the Hindūs, Brahman is not a creator nor does he exert any providence. Brahman is not masculine; he is not transcendent. Will we ever be able to admit that there are limits in the understanding of God we received from the Semitic and Greco-Roman traditions? Can we admit that there are also limits in our understanding of religion (when we wonder whether Buddhism is a religion) and prayer (wondering if we can pray together with those who do not believe that God is a person)?

As it should be clear, the interreligious aspect and the intercultural one are inseparable.

In addition, in spite of all its positive sides, the Western way of thinking has impeded the development of certain features of Christianity. When the "Symbol" of the apostles became the "teaching" of the apostles, Christianity was on its way to becoming an ideology.

A critical reflection on the meaning and the risks of our Western way of thinking is therefore necessary when we take part in an interreligious dialogue.

The Task of Contemplatives in the Third Millennium

Monks have a historic mission. Today their task, like all contemplatives, is to free Christian faith from the bonds of Western culture. This does not mean some new form of iconoclasm but rather the continuation of what was started at the Council of Jerusalem. We will only be able to go beyond Western culture if reason, which has so deeply been dominating it, is put in its own place.

At any rate, interreligious dialogue always takes place within a cultural context. Before giving more specific suggestions about the method for this kind of dialogue, we need to recall some basic issues.

Embracing the Whole of Reality

A "reformation" is not enough; we must commit ourselves to a "transformation"—and even more—to a change of mind and heart. *Metanoia* literally means an overcoming of rationality.

The mystics of the West are fully aware of what is at issue here. The Victorines in the twelfth century already said that, alongside the *oculus sensuum* and the *oculus rationis*, there is the *oculus fidei*. It is true that the word "mysticism" implies some negative connotations. But until we find a better way of expressing this reality, we cannot put it aside. Mysticism is not a substitute for truth or something extra—a luxury for people having plenty of leisure. It is an integral part of reality; without it, reality is deformed.

God is not a monad, a substance, but a Trinity, a relation. That is why we have to go beyond a monotheism that can be expressed by means of a simplistic *reductio ad unum*. Meister Eckhart said that God is at one and the same time *innominabilis* and *omninominabilis*. If the mystical "third eye" is open, one can see God everywhere.

For this reason we can say that pluralism, correctly understood, is one of the best features of mysticism.

If emphasizing and isolating what is specific simply means to detect what distinguishes one thing from another (for example, what distinguishes monastic interreligious dialogue from other kinds of dialogue), there is very little to be gained from it. The essence of something does not consist in what makes it different, but rather in its *aroma*, in what makes it unique—and *that* is ineffable. But if we insist on speaking about the specificity of monks, then I would say that it consists in the fact that monasticism surpasses all specificity!

The unity for which we crave is that of "blessed simplicity" and "new innocence."

Advaita does not mean "non-duality" (a refusal of duality, which would imply that there is still something "out there"), but a-duality (with privative "a").

As a consequence, it does not make much sense to define as a "double belonging" the attitude we can find in certain religious settings, because by so saying we just show that our starting point is still a dualistic one.

Wisdom is attained by transforming destructive tensions into fruitful polarities. But if you feel that your belonging is twofold, then decide for one or the other side. You can't hang out in the middle.

Consenting to Kenōsis

Over the course of two millennia, the Christian tradition in the West has worked out a symbiosis of two or three cultures. We can rightly be proud of this accomplishment. But at the beginning of this third millennium, even if most mankind is barraged by messages promoting the "American way of life," we know that three-quarters of the world's population remains basically alien to our Christian and post-Christian culture.

So, if we believe in the mystery of Christ, then the time has come to become truly "catholic," that is, belonging to the whole world. In order to do that, we do not need to work out new ways of expressing the Mystery, but rather to consent to an "impoverishment," even a "stripping away." Yes, we will have to begin by stripping Christ of all the Western garments with which we have clothed him. We will then be able to bring about a change analogous to that which the Apostles dared to enact when they did away with circumcision at the first Council of Jerusalem. It is time to prepare for Jerusalem II!

But the way of *kenōsis* is extremely demanding. To go beyond deeply rooted convictions requires a harsh spiritual asceticism. You risk losing everything. To be more precise, *kenōsis* demands that one commit oneself to a radical reassessment of one's faith.

At this stage, it is important to distinguish between *faith* and *belief*. Beliefs are many and often incompatible. (We might note, in passing, that even if they are incommensurable—like the radius of a circle with its circumference—they are still related to one another, and therefore a dialogue can be established between them.) As for faith, it lies beyond these incompatibilities, because it does not have any object, properly speaking. It is rather an act of joining.

To become truly free, we have to develop a faithfulness with no limits.

However, a refusal to absolutize our beliefs does not imply any wish to absolutize our doubts! Faith and doubt are not incompatible, as are fire and water. Both are part of life.

Working Out a Method for the Dialogue

So, what kind of dialogue are monks called to? It would be good to recall the way of dialogue in which many monastic communities have already been involved.

First of all, one has to accept an *aut-aut* conversion in order to really accept the otherness of the other. The other is not just "another," one specimen in a series, but "an other," someone who is different, unique.

In these times we can no longer claim that we know our own religion if we do not know another religion. As it is so often said today, in order to be religious, one has to be interreligious.

Words can deceive us. Translations are often approximations, and terms evolve over the course of history. The teaching of Confucius on "word politics" is still valid today. We know how often our misunderstandings—and, even worse, our caricatures—disfigured other religions. The first thing we have to do is to remedy this situation and avoid every sort of distortion.

While it is obvious that we have to study other religions, it is especially important to remember that the essence of dialogue is a meeting of persons. In order to "under-stand" the other, we have to listen with humility. A meeting happens when people are vulnerable. Such meetings lead to friendship. More correctly: Without friendly and trusting interpersonal contacts, dialogue cannot even begin.

The specific feature of an interreligious dialogue taking place among monastic men and women is that it is a "dialogue of experience." Coming together in silence, working together without expecting any personal gain, engaging in *intrareligious* dialogue—every form of dialogue that is not exclusively intellectual is an experience, a common experience. Although there is no such thing as a mere experience *in se*, it is sometimes possible to perceive a deep communion in silence. What is the meaning of such experiences? There comes a time when we have to try to explain them, but we know that the core of such events cannot be expressed by words. In brief, we can say that those experiences bind us together more closely. This kind of dialogue needs a special "methodology" that, however, still has to be worked out.

Finally, it must be said that this kind of dialogue takes time, maybe many years. Those who feel that they are called to become more deeply involved in the work of interreligious dialogue will need a full immersion in another religion. Lest this immersion simply become a form of spiritual tourism—or, worse than that, a form of colonialist "inculturation"—at least one year would be required.

Not many would be able to make such a commitment. But let us not give in to the tyranny of numbers. History shows us that a few pioneers can do wonders.

Recollections of Père Henri Le Saux—Swami Abhiṣiktānanda

I am reluctant to talk about my friend Abhiṣiktānanda, because it leads to talk about myself as well. I will try to be discreet.

Together we made two major pilgrimages: to Aruṇāchala (Tiruvanamalai) and to Gaṅgotrī, by the sources of the Ganges. These common experiences drew us very close to each other.

We used to talk for a long time (he loved to). During those conversations I had the opportunity to help him become reconciled with himself. He needed to bounce his doubts and questions off someone else, especially since he tended to be a little scrupulous. As a theologian I helped him relate our experience to the Christian tradition. This way he could recollect his first insights, which were often at odds with those of Père Monchanin and his own later ideas.

I think we can say that a great transformation took place in the cave of Aruṇāchala in 1952. There he understood that what was demanded of him was not simply being "open to the other"—something he had control over—but letting the other convert him.

When he finally had two disciples, he realized what it means to be a father. It was moving to see him recognize that he was a man capable of forming intense and transformative relationships.

In spite of all the progress he made, I sensed that he remained torn inside, right up to the very end of his life, at least until his heart attack in July 1973. It was then that he "found the Grail," as he put it in a letter. The image of the Grail reveals much about his inculturation in Indian religion. In order to describe his discovery of the interior unity within the Indian tradition of *advaita*, he used an expression coming from the culture of his childhood in Brittany. He was no longer alienated from himself.

When he died, he thought that his life had been a failure. In fact, he was a genius without knowing it.

Part Two

The Encounter of Religions

The Unavoidable Dialogue

mê phylax tou adelphou mou eimi ego?
Are we perchance responsible for our brethren?

—*Gen 4:9*

Tat tu samamvayât.
Yes! Due to the mysterious and all-embracing harmony.[1]

—*BS I.1.4*

This essay is a brief summary outlining my main views, or rather my life experiences; it offers sort of a manifesto for the dialogue of religions, stressing its importance, its contents, its method. That explains the conciseness of the text.

Although the name "religion" comes from Latin culture, and its current concept is relatively modern and one-sided, human beings have always known something like religion. Man is *homo religiosus*, insofar as the human race has always posed ultimate questions to itself. Such questions bring about the deepest communication between people—questions always aim for dialogue—and are the fruits of a calling that precedes them.

A typology of the encounters between religions would point up the following kairological moments:[2]

---

[1] The reader will observe that these translations are already interpretations.

[2] I have set forth a typology of the relationships between religions in *Religionen und die Religion* (Munich: Hueber, 1965); "Un mythe naissant," Preface to J. Langlais, *Le Bouddha et*

- Isolation and ignorance
- Indifference and contempt
- Rejection and conquest
- Coexistence and communication
- Appropriation and dialogue

To be fruitful, *the dialogue of religions* must be a genuine dialogue.[3] The following *sūtrās*, which portray several qualities of this dialogue, are like nine threads (*sūtra*) woven into a single garland (*mālā*), which ought to be taken as a whole.

les deux bouddhismes (Montreal: Fides, 1975), 9–15; "Autoconciencia cristiana y religiones," in *Fe cristiana y sociedad moderna* (Madrid) vol. 26 (1989): 199–267.

[3] See R. Panikkar, "The Dialogical Dialogue," in F. Whaling (ed.), *The World's Religious Traditions: Essays in Honour of W. C. Smith* (Edinburgh, 1984), 201–21, for the philosophical background of this study.

9

The Encounter of Religions Is a Vital Necessity

Of course the religions of the world do encounter one another, sometimes even peaceably, though more often in confrontation and conflict. This kind of encounter is generally due to political activities. Wars, migrations, trade—as well as the personal encounters of travelers, slaves, merchants, and missionaries—have all contributed to the reciprocal influences of religions upon one another. The meeting of religions is so vital that, in fact, nearly all of today's great religions are the fruits of such encounters. What would Christianity today be without the deep syncretism stemming from its Jewish, Greek, Roman, and Germanic religious roots? What would what we call "Hinduism" be without the contributions of the numerous religions of the Indic subcontinent?

But what formerly took place though slow assimilation, through osmosis and reactions to encounters either spontaneous or consciously sought, has in our times radically accelerated and widened. In some cases, discerning minds have guided the dialogue. But today dialogue is not a luxury or a side issue. The ubiquity of modern science and technology, of world markets and international organizations and transnational corporations, plus the countless migrations of workers, along with millions of refugees—not to mention tourists!—renders the meeting among cultures and religions unavoidable, as well as indispensable. Our current problems of justice, ecology, and peacekeeping require mutual understanding among human peoples. But understanding is impossible without dialogue.

This vital necessity may be expressed at three distinct levels.

At the Personal Level

Modern individualism, which, mainly in Western countries, has seeped slowly and surreptitiously into human consciousness to become an essential ingredient of the modern myth, is gradually giving way, in the West itself, to what has been called dialogical philosophy: "*Esse est co-esse*," "*Sein ist Dasein*" and "*Dasein ist Mitsein*," "The I and the You are essentially interrelated," "*Mensch ist Mitmensch*," "*Welt ist Umwelt*," "*Yo soy yo y mi circunstancia*," "Ecology is ecosophy," "Thinking is dialogical thinking," "Man is androgynous," "Freedom grows with the recognition of responsibility," "There is no private language," "Reality is cosmotheandric"—

these are just some brief formulations that point to the recovery of an ancient consciousness, although on a new level indeed.[1]

Perhaps we could summarize our problem in a phrase: Man is not an individual, a monad. Man is rather a person, a bundle of relationships. And human relationships require dialogue.

In other words, without dialogue, without a dialogical life, Man cannot attain a fully human condition. Man is *animal loquens.* But linguisticality is not only external communication; it is most of all inner communion.

Dialogue cannot be confined to an exchange of ideas with one's neighbors. Man cannot be reduced to an individual. The principle of individuation must be distinguished from the principle of singularity.[2] An unfragmented anthropology would show that Man *is* (and not only *has*) body (*sōma*), soul (*psychē*), community (*polis*), and world (*aiōn*), to which spirit (*pneuma*) should always be added as well.[3]

Nor can dialogue be limited to minor topics. The ultimate questions of human existence demand more than polling the opinions of others; they require us to enter deeply into the very mystery of reality. Meditation includes listening, and—as such—it implies dialogue. In a word: Man is a dialogical being. Dialogue is a necessity for being human. To be sure, this does not mean just empty chatter, but genuine religious dialogue, which is, however, difficult without a genuine liturgical life.

At the Level of Religious Traditions

Today all the "Berlin walls" of individualistic religious postures are—however slowly—collapsing, along with the apartheid of exclusivistic belief systems. Not only from a sociological point of view are people living in a "supermarket" of ethnic "groups," religious "ways," and lifestyle "options." From an anthropological viewpoint as well, people can no longer lock themselves up behind safe pillars of "orthodoxy." In the school, at the office, in the family, even on the Internet, the most divergent religious (and also antireligious) positions come into close contact—which can be puzzling.

We might prefer things to be otherwise, but modern life challenges each of us in the very religious depths of our being. To maintain an obviously superficial peace of mind, religious questions are often banished, and religion excluded from the school, the office, the Parliament, the marketplace—in a word, from public

---

[1] See H. H. Schrey, *Dialogisches Denken* (Stuttgart, 1983), for an overview of some of these currents.

[2] See R. Panikkar, "Singularity and Individuality: The Double Principle of Individuation," *Revue Internationale de Philosophie* 29, no. 1–2 (1975): 141–66.

[3] See R. Panikkar, "Der Mensch—Ein trinitarisches Mysterium," in R. Panikkar and W. Strolz (eds.), *Die Verantwortung des Menschen für eine bewohnbare Welt in Christentum, Hinduismus und Buddhismus* (Freiburg, 1985), 147–90.

life. The religious urge then seeks for a satisfaction somewhere else, and not always along the best paths.

But this is never enough, never satisfactory. We must learn to better handle our religious impulse in other ways.

Has the desacralized West not yet understood from the sustained protest of Islam anything at all about the price of obliging everybody to fit into the same banal pattern of modern life?

Religions as institutions, no matter how loose and flexible their structures, simply cannot escape the unrestrainable winds of ecumenism.

There arise on every level all sorts of mutual influences, bound up with the resulting eclecticisms, syncretisms, inculturations, and also fundamentalisms of every stripe. All such phenomena stem from these unavoidable, indispensable encounters.

There have always been mutual influences. But now the winds are blowing not only from the most diverse corners, and often in opposing directions, but they are redoubling their force to the extent that no single compass can be relied upon to guide us safely. Absolute criteria have been lost. We find ourselves in the open sea.

In short: Traditional religions are headed for shipwreck if they batten down their hatches and try to ride out the storm alone in these conflicting currents. Yet by the same token, they will lose their anchors, their very identity, if they try to avoid the dangers of life on the open sea by seeking safe harbor in the past. One might say that the time of religious "party politics" is gone. But sweeping away all traditions and uprooting every deep-seated custom will not free us from further religious wars—and from that chaos, new, questionable religious forms may emerge.

Dialogue takes the middle way between the old and the new; this makes possible a creative transformation of historical traditions. Without dialogue, religions become tangled up in themselves or slip their moorings altogether. Indeed, one sees more and more clearly today that no tradition has sufficient power within itself to fulfill its own self-acknowledged role. Either they open up to one another, or they degenerate and give rise to every kind of fanatical reaction. Dialogue is really a vital necessity.

At the Historical Level

Man is part and parcel of cosmos. Men cannot live, in the deepest and widest sense of the word, without religion. The destiny of humankind depends on whether a genuine religiousness at once links (*religat*) people with the entire reality and safeguards their freedom (ontonomy). But the fate of the Earth is also at stake. Nowadays human wars kill not only people and cultures but also wreak havoc upon the natural world. Modern warfare is no longer a solely human concern. It is ecologically irresponsible to mobilize armies with thousands of soldiers and their war machines in order to defend some political or economic status quo. The justified alarms of ecology are today audible everywhere on the planet.

But mere *eco-logy* is not enough. A dialogue with the Earth is also required. I have called this dialogical attitude *ecosophy*.[4] The Earth is not just an object, it is also a subject, a You for us, with whom we must also learn to enter a dialogue. Thus we may discover that ecosophy has a certain revelatory role. Our dialogue with the Earth can reveal to us that the Earth is more than an inert mass. If we are able to listen, the Earth herself may reveal, in theistic terms, God's will regarding Man's task on this planet. Or, in history of religions' terminology, the revelation of transcendence today comes to pass not only on Sinai, or Mount Meru, Fuji-san, Kailasā, Kilimanjaro, or Popcatepetl. The whole Earth tells us that our destiny is linked (*religatum*) with hers.

If a truly religious encounter between ourselves and with the Earth does not take place, we shall end by annihilating life on this planet. The dialogue of religions is not merely an academic or an ecclesial or an officially "religious" affair, much less some new vogue because maybe church services have become dull or attendance has fallen off. This dialogue is the field in which the historical destiny of humankind may be played out in a peaceful way.

Without such a dialogue of religions, the world actually will collapse. Here the praxis is decisive, and each of us must contribute to it. But the *urgency* of the task should not make us neglect other *important* aspects of dialogue. Good will alone is absolutely not enough.

Therefore the Dialogue Has to Be

Open

Openness belongs to the essence of dialogue. Dialogue is not instruction or teaching. Every dialogue has two poles, and neither pole can play both roles on its own.

This has a threefold implication.

1. *Nobody can be excluded a priori.*

Not only is every human being allowed to take part in this dialogue, but every ideology, worldview, and philosophy has the right to participate as well. So-called religions have no monopoly on religion.[5] Indeed, what has to be understood by "religion" needs to be spelled out in the dialogue itself. If it is to be a dialogue about the ultimate questions of life and death, then a Marxist, a humanist, or a

---

[4] See R. Pannikar, *The Cosmotheandric Experience*, ed. S. Eastham (Maryknoll, NY: Orbis Books, 1993).

[5] See R. Panikkar, "Have Religions the Monopoly on Religion?" *Journal of Ecumenical Studies* 11, no. 3 (1974): 515–17.

scientist has equal speaking rights with any so-called religious person. If one party wants to end the dialogue, the other party should, however, always stay open to continuing it. Dialogue keeps the doors open.

In this sense, the expression "encounter" or "dialogue" of "religions" should not be mistaken for the undertaking of any special group or closed-door assembly. Religion here must mean *agora*, *kurukṣetra*, the place where human beings—together with the earth below and heaven above—gather to sincerely discuss what matters most to them, their ultimate (and ultimately common) concerns. All are invited, by rights and by their own lights, to the feast of Life.

2. *Nothing should be left out on principle.*

The community of dialogue is not a professional society for experts. It has to do with the most deeply human concerns. Dialogue may implicitly aspire to certain answers but cannot exclude any answer a priori. You have to let all possible questions arise and take shape, whatever shape they will take within the dialogue itself.

Not everybody sees the ultimate questions the same way. Dialogue has no set agenda, still less a hidden one. Everything may be called into question, even the appropriateness of dialogue, and of course the initial standpoints of the partners.

Undoubtedly dialogue represents a real risk. You could lose your own standpoint; you could even reverse your own position. Conversion is possible, but also confusion. Everything is at stake. So dialogue requires an enormous confidence in Man—and in that power, order, or reality that lets Man be Man. One can easily understand, and even approve of, the warnings made by official institutions against the dangers of dialogue. Maybe people were indeed happier before they knew how to read and write, as a pharaoh once upon a time complained and Socrates knew all too well. But once we have eaten from the tree of the knowledge of good and evil, there is no going back. Besides, it would be unfair to keep it only for ourselves.

We want to stress explicitly that neither "God" nor "religion" are necessary assumptions for dialogue. But we have somehow to name this dialogue, and old habits tend to bring such expressions to hand. Their use also hinges on the fact that initiatives for dialogue often come from such sources. But it is all a question, basically, of open dialogue between people concerning the ultimate questions of reality. Whether the language of the dialogue will tend toward a more secular idiom today remains to be seen, and is of course part and parcel of the dialogue itself. These days, genuine religious dialogue more often than not centers on justice, peace, technocracy, and so on, rather than on hell, *nirvāṇa*, or God.

3. *The dialogue remains constitutively open.*

Dialogue is not some emergency device intended to help people reach unanimity. The goal of dialogue is not the removal of diverse opinions, or the uniformity of the world, or the creation of a single world religion—as if reality itself could or should be reduced to a single principle. This might be an unexpected outcome of the dialogue, but it cannot be an assumption. Something would be lost if the pluralistic constitution of truth were to be questioned. Truth can be reduced neither to unity nor to multiplicity—though it accepts, of course, debate on the opposite opinion. Truth is always relation, connection, and admits neither singularity nor plurality.[6]

Dialogue is an expression of this polarity, inherent to Man and reality as such. Truth itself does not have an exclusively objective structure, since the seeker also belongs to it—and there are different seekers. Truth is always relational. Every human being is an *ontonomous* source of self-understanding.[7] The world cannot be completely seen and interpreted through any single window: we are not only *in* a world, we *are* world. Dialogue is a fruit of the human experience of contingency. No individual, no human group, not even all humanity living at any given time can embody the absolute measure of truth. Contingency means that we touch (*tangere*) our limits, and that the limitless touches us tangentially (*cum-tangere*).

In other words, the open character of dialogue belongs to the very nature of reality. The polarity of reality is a feature of its liveliness. Dialogue is not aimed at the victory of one partner over the other; it is essentially a constitutive aspect of human life, of Life as a whole, and of Being itself. Life, I say, not the victory of Good against Evil, nor—even worse—of good people against evil people.

Interior

Dialogue is not mere talk. It comes from a deeper and more internal source than stimulation by others. This source might be called silence, or maybe just the human thirst for truth. Without such thirst, dialogue will be trapped in a superficial exchange of opinions. If dialogue is to be any more than manipulating ideas, it has to issue from the deepest recess of our being. In so many words: the *intra*religious dialogue is a necessary foundation for *inter*religious dialogue.

This interiority also manifests itself at a triple level.

1. Dialogue begins with an innermost questioning.

The Buddhist tradition calls this attitude the Great Doubt; the Christian *compunctio cordis*, *penthos*; and *mumukṣutva* is its Hindū name. A philosophical

---

[6] See my essays in *Invisible Harmony* (Minneapolis: Fortress, 1995); "The Myth of Pluralism: The Tower of Babel," *Cross Currents* 29, no. 2 (1979): 197–230; "Religious Pluralism: The Metaphysical Challenge," in L. S. Rouner, ed., *Religious Pluralism* (Notre Dame, IN: 1984), 97–115; and "The Pluralism of Truth" (the 1989 Sir Francis Younghusband Lecture), *World Faiths' Insight* 10, no. 26 (1990): 7–16.

[7] By *ontonomy* I mean the intrinsic connection of any entity to the whole of Being, the constituent order (*nomos*) of any being qua Being (*on*), that harmony that makes the *interindependence* among all things possible. See R. Pannikar, "Le concept d'ontonomie," in *Actes du XI Congrès International de Philosophie* (Louvain: Nauwelaerts, 1953), 3:182–88.

concept that would serve is humility (*De-mut*), that is, the courage (*der Mut*) to be the servant of a truth that does not belong to any of us alone.

If I do not question myself, if I do not feel that *quaestio mihi factus sum* (I have become a question to myself) of an Augustine; or if I lack *mumukṣutva*, Śaṅkara's fervent longing for liberation—that is, if I am not ready to give up my security or lose my life, as the Gospel would say; if I do not cast myself down at the feet of the master, as in *vedānta* and many other traditions; if I am not aware of my contingency or sinfulness, ignorance, or slavery under my own desires, and am not ready to trust, with my whole heart and mind, in a truth that is no private property of mine, then I am not ready for a mature dialogue. Dialogue is nothing to trifle with. It requires discipline, maturity, humility. Our current obsession with certainty, politically translated into "security," is a pathological phenomenon—besides being something impossible to achieve.

Genuine dialogue begins with the sincere questioning of all my certainties—because I have realized, on the one hand, that I am a fragile vessel and, on the other, that there are in this world other vessels at whose contents I can scarcely guess. Dialogue is a basic human attitude. Certainly its ultimate content is not just doctrine. Religion is neither objective doctrine nor merely subjective attitude. Religious dialogue is neither the comparison of two objective states of affairs, nor the confrontation of two subjective opinions; neither scholarly exchange alone, nor solely ecclesial debate. It arises rather from the innermost core of our self, when we discover we are neither absolute nor alone in this world. You begin dialogue with yourself. In a certain sense it requires the loss of innocence, of the first (prereflective) innocence. No wonder dialogue presents itself as a way to salvation, transfiguration, enlightenment. We discover it is not the work of our ego, since it is this very ego that must be called into question.

If you have no doubts, if your opinion is already set, if you presume that you have already grasped the whole truth, then you surely have no need for dialogue. Dialogue requires inner awareness.

2. *Dialogue touches the innermost heart of the partners.*

You can compare ideas much as you might play cards. You can have rewarding conversations much as you might make a profit in business. But none of this is dialogue. Genuine religious dialogue only sets in when one or the other partner feels concerned, threatened, encouraged, stimulated, provoked, deeply stirred. Nicodemus was no coward when he showed himself willing to go to the Master by night for a secret dialogue. Didn't the apostles run away when Jesus began a dialogue with the Samaritan woman? I doubt that such life-transforming dialogues could take place on television. Dialogue is more confession than information, profound trust rather than public action.

Something must happen in dialogue before the *logos* takes center stage. In every genuine dialogue there is a silent moment that lets the dialogue spontaneously emerge. Real dialogue is made possible by this previous mood, this atmosphere that conveys us to where thoughts have their source, where words take their power, where we meet each other as we truly are. All in all, one could say that a certain sympathy must be there. When I am deeply moved by reading a book, I want to get to know the author. Where I am taken only by the thoughts, I might be curious to ask the author something further, but the desire to get to know him better would not arise. Dialogue can produce "under-standing" only when it "stands under" both grounds, as it were, letting the subterranean streams flow freely. Dialogue breaks new ground by journeying into both the background and the underground, the underworld. Not Hermes but Orpheus is its *devatā*.

3. *Dialogue takes place at the heart of reality.*

There is more still. Modern Westernized Man has become so monocultural that we need to be reminded that the Hebrew *nefesh* means at once life, heart, and human nature, as the Japanese *kokoro* means heart, soul, consciousness, and feeling—just to give two wholly independent examples. The *corpus Christi mysticum*, the *buddhakāya*, and the *dharmakāya* could also be adduced here as examples of different cosmologies that both believe, nonetheless, that communication does not require computers, and that the transformation and renovation of reality follow laws other than those solely of advertising and data processing.

A true contemplative, whether in his forest hut or in the midst of a big city, can undertake a dialogue with wider consequences than any item of news, however exciting, which will probably be replaced tomorrow by a more exciting one. Śāntideva[8] is still alive today and engages us in dialogue not just by his dialectical power but because he was a holy man living at the heart of reality. Holy and wise people, seen phenomenologically, are precisely those human beings who hold open the possibility of dialogue with us despite all the barriers of space and time. We meet many holy people in dialogue with nature and animals. Were they so idiotic as not to know what we all "know," that such beings have no human intelligence? Or have we, perhaps, forgotten that dialogue is more than an exchange of what has already been thought? Are *kāma*, *agapē*, *karuṇā*, love . . . only metaphors?

Dialogue has a mystical core not visible on the surface of human relationships. Something happens to the heart of each partner in dialogue, and something also happens at the inner core of the world. Dialogue lets loose a special *karman*, reaching into the mystical heart of reality. When two wise people are talking, the world holds its breath, as the saying goes, catching the spirit of this ancient truth.

---

[8] Śāntideva (eighth–seventh century BC) was one of the great masters of *Mahāyāna* Buddhism (n.d.t.).

Linguistic

Man is nonetheless *homo loquens.* Language is our gift, and speaking our task. But human words are more than signals for our feelings, or signs expressing our concepts. This world is a symbolic universe, and language is the main human organ for participating in the living symbolic reality of that universe.

Here also we may make a threefold distinction.

1. Dialogue is logos-freighted.

There is no true word without the *quaternitas* of speaker, spoken to, spoken about, and spoken through—that is, without sender, receiver, message, and medium. A word is a sound uttered to a listener by somebody about something. One could also say: subject, object, content, and means, or Man, consciousness, idea, and matter.[9] Here we want to concentrate on the intellectual side of the *logos.*

Dialogue is an activity of the human *logos.* It has to do with ideas, thoughts, interpretations, doctrines, views, and insights. Each of us is, consciously or unconsciously, the carrier of a whole tradition, conveying an entire world. Dialogue makes this explicit, to those at least who can grasp it. We do not say only what we guess or what occurs to us. Genuine dialogue is freighted with the burden and the dignity of the speaker's tradition. In dialogue I express my thoughts; but these thoughts, though thought by me, reveal a past and an environment of which I am scarcely even aware. The partner discovers that I live and speak with tacit presuppositions. And our speech also reveals the unspoken. When the village elder closes his address in the *palaver* of an African village, the headman says, "We understand both what you have said and what you have not said!" Here we should emphasize that in no genuine religious dialogue can Hegel's *Anstrengung des Begriffes* (struggle with concepts) be avoided. We are dealing with a human activity whose need for intelligibility cannot be sacrificed. It would be irresponsible to involve oneself in dialogue about some religious view or other without being versed enough in it. There cannot, for instance, be much fruitful dialogue about God, hell, *karman*, or *śūnyatā* if we only know ridiculous caricatures of such notions. We speak words, but words have their own sense—and even their own power. No responsible speaker can ignore this sense or neglect this power. Awe before the word is the gateway to its contents.

Man speaks about something, but what is said does not completely "cover" this something. The "something" itself is more than a mere rational core. Man is not only reason, or only reasonable, but without reason humanness is not possible. Reason itself is participation in a supra-individual *nomos.*

---

[9] See R. Pannikar, "Words and Terms," in M. M. Olivetti, ed., *Esistenza, mito, ermeneutica*, in *Archivo de Filosofia* 2 (1980): 117–33.

2. *Dialogue is also duologue.*

Dialogue requires the encounter, and may even demand the confrontation, of two *logoi.* "Duologue" does not mean two monologues, but entrusting (without talking down) to the other ideas, thoughts, insights, experiences—lives—which really meet, although they derive from distant sources and may even clash. This requires that the dialogue goes both ways from the outset. Wanting to understand the other makes up only half the platform for a genuine dialogue. I myself have to be ready *to be understood* by the partner, and also prepared for possible misunderstanding. And the same goes for the other side. The other "side" is neither a wall nor a projection of myself. It is a real "I," that is, an autonomous source of self-consciousness, which reacts simultaneously to me in a mutual I-You and You-I relationship. But in order to recognize the other as a You, something much more vital than a bare exchange of concepts must pass *between* us. "True dialogue is not a monologue of the lonely thinker with himself," wrote Feuerbach, in forging a place for the You.[10]

The Vedantic tradition speaks of *śravaṇa* (listening), *manana* (reflection), and *nididhyāsana* (active contemplation) as a threefold method for duologue. The Christian may ask the Buddhist why he does not acknowledge any God, but should also let himself be asked why he does not acknowledge any *śūnyatā* (emptiness). The Hindū may ask the Muslim how he can avoid theocracy, but she in turn must allow herself to be asked how she can overcome anarchy, especially moral anarchy. In other words, dialogue actually has to run in two directions. It has to be intercultural and interreligious. Duologue is not aimed at eliciting correct answers to a given set of questions. Questions are also addressed to us, although they may not be our own original queries.

The word "duologue" also contains another important and often forgotten meaning. We say duologue and not multilogue. A duologue is possible when a common field can be established in which the discussion has a meaning. Each language is dialogical, because it is directed to a listener—or to those who understand that language. The Hindū-Christian dialogue, for instance, builds a language that is not suitable for a Jewish-Christian dialogue. Here we have to withstand the modern temptation, originating in the natural sciences, of wanting to arrive at universal laws by reducing all phenomena to fit scientific parameters. Peoples and cultures are qualitatively different and simply do not allow themselves to be reduced to any common (even if qualitative) denominator.

3. *Dialogue means bilingualism.*

To believe that through a single language we should have access to universal thinking and to human experience as a whole is yet one more remnant of a (generally unconscious) colonialist attitude. A genuine dialogue not only requires

10 Ludwig Feuerbach, *Sämtliche Werke*, ed. W. Bolin and F. Jodl (Stuttgart: 1959), 2:319.

that partners express themselves but that they speak their own language. Not everything can be said in English—leaving aside the fact that only 10 percent of humankind thinks in this language. Not even Indo-European languages are the measure of all things. Syntax belongs to the human ways of attaining intelligibility. The simple fact of changing the disposition of a sentence already betrays another structure of thinking. The word "religion" has a dozen homeomorphic equivalents in the Indic languages, just as in turn the word *dharma* has scores of English equivalents.

Languages do not easily let themselves be dismembered into words. Each language is a way of living, a way of being in the world, and reflects an entire cosmology. If all people were to speak only a so-called *lingua universalis*, this would be a devastating cultural and human impoverishment. It is upsetting to notice that the world is losing about a hundred languages a year: these are cultural genocides! Dialogue, I repeat, requires at least two languages to take part. No authentic dialogue can come about if the You is not shown in it. Dialogue happens between people and not between ideas, still less between answering machines. But to discover the You one has to go to the very source of the dialogue. One has to really know the partner, not just hear what she says. Textual hermeneutics is not enough. Rather, one has to understand, which implies real communication, sympathy, and also love. One has to know the "con-text" and be aware of the "pre-text" that are being expressed in the text.

That each man speaks his own language does not mean merely that each uses his own grammar or brings in his own feelings about the world. It also means that each man is to be considered a unique source of self-understanding. Exactly between sheer subjectivity and pure objectivity lies the vital space for human dialogue and encounter. Man is man in encounter.

Political

In many countries of the world today, academies and churches enjoy freedom, provided that they do not threaten the status quo of the state. Institutionalized religions can go on relatively undisturbed, as long as they acknowledge the unquestionable sovereignty of the state—although, depending on the state, the scope of their freedom may vary drastically. Nevertheless, real religious dialogue cannot be satisfied with this. It cannot acknowledge the political status quo as something absolutely untouchable. Paradoxically enough, nothing enmeshed in space and time can be ultimate for the religious spirit. Religious dialogue is also political, and therefore neither politically neutral nor universal. Socrates was a religious sage, Jesus a religious man, Al-Hallaj a religious mystic. All three were engaged in dialogue. And all three were (politically) sentenced to death.

Here also we may stress three points.

1. Dialogue is not a private affair.

Religion cannot be a private matter, because Man is not a mere individual and religion is a global human affair. Religion cannot be separated from politics. This refers not only to religious institutions, necessarily political structures, but also to religion as an anthropological dimension. Even if somebody wants to defend an "intimistic" concept of religion, religious dialogue about it will belong to the community and display a political character. It belongs to the *polis* (meant as public life) in both direct and indirect ways.

Dialogue changes the self-perception of the participants and so of the religions concerned, which in turn (together with other factors) shape the life of the *polis.* But dialogue is also a political activity in more direct ways. Dialogue may have its roots in the human heart, but its fruits are visible and ready to be harvested in the *agora.* We need not think only of India, Northern Ireland, Lebanon, Palestine, Cuba, Ethiopia, the Vatican, and so forth, where the religious dialogue is obviously political. We mean, rather, that in principle every interreligious encounter touches on human issues that directly influence the life of the *polis.* Trinity also implicates social relations; death requires the arrangement of the burial; sacraments have equally to do with initiation, health, and weddings; God implies the authority in society; justification includes justice; and so on. All this belongs to public and political life.

In the final analysis, religion is not a private matter because Man himself is not a private "thing," and indeed not only morally, insofar as we bear social responsibilities, but ontologically, insofar as the human condition is not the private property of any individual. What is whispered in the ear is soon shouted from the rooftops. All the personal pronouns belong to each other: there is no I without You, and without "Him" in the masculine, feminine, neuter, dual, and plural—and also vice versa. Indeed, religious dialogue is an activity of such a kind that it is related to the very foundations of any political action. To bar dialogue on political problems would turn politics into dictatorship, and religion into something void and irrelevant. It would not only mean accepting the political status quo but holding it in higher regard than any religion. States are not only geopolitical entities, they are also multireligious realities. The mistake of Christian missionaries in Asia, for example, was to suppose that they might have a Christian dialogue with Asiatic religions without taking into account the fact of the former colonial domination. By the same token, a Hindū-Muslim dialogue won't bear much fruit if it is uprooted from the current sociopolitical situation.[11]

---

11 See J. D'Arcy May, "Integral Ecumenism," *Journal of Ecumenical Studies* 25, no. 4 (1988): 573–91: "*Any* breakdown of communication between or within communities of faith constitutes an ecumenical problem" (577). I would interpret "communities of faith" in the widest sense as natural human communities, because, in the final analysis, religion is the soul of culture.

2. *Dialogue is a theory-laden praxis that produces new theories.*

The dialectic of theory and praxis is superseded in dialogue. Dialogue is a praxis stemming from a theory and leading to another praxis, which will in turn serve as the basis for a new theory. Theories are tested and appraised on the grounds of dialogical praxis, which in turn lets new theories arise. Dialogue is a praxis that not only deepens and transforms ideas but equally transforms actions and attitudes. The place of dialogue is not the lecture room or the temple, but the *polis.* Every dialogue, as an encounter of real people and not just a confrontation of concepts, has a political character. Every discussion between people engages the power and the life of the *polis.* The religious dialogue is, moreover, political to a higher degree. It calls into question not merely minor means to minor ends, but the very foundations of human existence, on which political life is also based.

Dialogue as a constitutive human activity corrects the Neoplatonic ideal of the purely theoretical life as an end in itself, superior to practical life, which was considered to be merely a means directed toward a goal. The goal then would be pure theory, standing above politics. It goes without saying that such a view of theoretical versus practical life would consider dialogue merely another means for achieving a disembodied truth, which is quite far from what Plato upheld. Dialogue is not a technique in the hands of either partner, for some practical purpose.

This is not to say anything against the primacy of contemplation. To the contrary, it means that contemplation is not pure theory. *Contemplatio* is indeed an action so penetrated by theory that they both, theory as well as praxis, converge in an a-dualistic harmony—namely, the harmony of being what Being itself is: an act.

Dialogue in this sense means, on the one hand, that no single person can possess the whole truth and, on the other hand, that truth itself is not any purely objective "thing."[12] In other words, human confrontation in the search for truth belongs to the human *polis.* Politics does not mean just applying the most effective means, but also the disclosure, realization, conquest, and discussion about the end of human life.

3. *It includes political contents.*

If an uncritical mixing of religion and politics leads to totalitarian structures on either the religious side (theocracy) or the political side (state totalitarianism), their separation leads to otherwordly religion (purely abstract doctrines) and decadent party politics (mere debate over means and power). The solution to the dilemma lies in an a-dualistic view of both.[13]

---

[12] See R. Panikkar, "The Existential Phenomenology of Truth," *Philosophy Today* 2, no. 1/4 (1958): 13–21.

[13] See R. Panikkar, "Non-Dualistic Relation between Religion and Politics," *Religion and Society* (Bangalore) 25, no. 3 (1978): 53–63; and also R. Panikkar, *Il daimôn della politica: agonia e speranza* (Bologna: EDB, 1995).

It is a fact that the most burning religious dilemmas of our day also have political contents. No religious dialogue can bypass the meaning of "salvation" for Man, letting "salvation" stand here for the ultimate meaning of life. No dialogue on justification, for instance, can leave aside the issue of justice, and no consideration of justice can overlook the socio-political-economic problems of the present-day world. To discuss peace without considering the *pax civilis* is no longer acceptable, just as those who talk about *jihād* and "just war" cannot ignore their respective political situations.[14]

It is equally true that the political problems of the world also have a religious character. The dialogue of religions is not solely within the purview of religious institutions. The religious dimension of Man permeates each and every political activity. To claim, for instance, that Catholic priests or Muslim mullahs or Buddhist *bhikkus* should not involve themselves in politics, is already a political decision regarding religion. Health, education, and welfare problems also have a religious character; they never are solely technical issues that bureaucracies have to face. To go back to the controversy between Galileo Galilei and Cardinal Robert Bellarmine: heaven (the existential reality in which both believed) and the heavens (the movements of which Galileo first calculated) cannot be either totally split off from each other, nor can they remain wholly undifferentiated. There is no theology without some cosmological basis, just as there is no entirely untheological cosmology. Autonomy is as unsatisfactory as heteronomy. The healthy connection is *ontonomic*.[15] The relationship is a-dualistic.

It should be obvious, therefore, that the dialogue of religions is not walled up in the enclosures of "religious" institutions. It stands or falls in the midst of life. It is not some special area of competence for so-called theologians or religious leaders, much less for "experts" or academicians. Shutting out religion from the public forum is as lethal as conceding the political dominion to the clergy. The genuine dialogue of religions liberates Man from human fragmentation and hyperspecialization. Expertise in delimited fields is justified and necessary. But in the domain of dialogue, humanness itself is at stake.

Mythical

A *dia-logos* not only means going via the *logos*, dealing with the *logos* alone; it also means breaking through the *logos*—*dia ton logon*, ferrying across the *logos*—to the *mythos*. Maybe the weakest pillar of the so-called Enlightenment, held from Descartes to Kant to the modern natural sciences to Bultmann, is the naive belief

---

[14] See R. Panikkar, *Cultural Disarmament: The Way to Peace* (Louisville, KY: Westminster John Knox Press, 1995).

[15] See the description of this notion in R. Panikkar, "Le concept d'ontonomie," *Actes du XI Congrès International de Philosophie* (Louvain, 1953).

that, in principle, everything can be cleared up through reason, human or divine. Many people still dream of a *mathesis universalis*, holding to the theoretical possibility of grasping reality with mathematical language, as if reality could be apprehended by a supercomputer. Reason is the critical power of Man; it is what lets us be self-conscious. It is quite significant that Kant, in an unconsciously self-defeating way, talked about *pure* reason, which, to begin with, is so pure that it stays above and beyond every critique.[16] Reason is assumed from the start; it stands as a mythical Gestalt. One always forgets or overlooks one's own *mythos*. And, after all, *mythos* and *logos* belong together. The dialogue of religions, if it is at all alive, cannot leave the *mythos* outside the dialogue.[17]

Here also, three aspects of the process may be stressed:

1. Dialogue pierces through the logos and leaves the mythos open.

Concepts are important, even necessary, but never enough to bring about an integral encounter between people or between religious traditions. A dialogue with concepts alone remains merely dialectics. Dialogical dialogue is more—not less—than debate or rational encounter. In a dialogical dialogue we have to be conscious that the concepts we use spring from a deeper source. Not only do I let the other know me, but I come to a better understanding of my own *mythos* through the critiques and disclosures of my partner. Dialogical dialogue strives neither for victory in the contest of ideas, nor for an agreement that would suppress real diversity of opinions. Rather, dialogical dialogue seeks to expand the field of understanding altogether, in which each partner deepens his own field and opens up a place for the not (yet?) comprehended. This is not the scandal that the diversity of opinions was for Descartes, because neither party absolutizes his/her own standpoint.

Every religion lives out of its own *mythos*, the cauldron of magma from which the *logos* bubbles up to congeal in conceptual structures and doctrines. This *mythos* as a starting point is not a logical postulate. It rather surrounds and supports the tacit presuppositions that form each tradition's horizon of intelligibility, over against which its ideas are seen to make sense.

---

16 See the far-reaching critique of M. Tanabe, *Philosophy as Metanoetics* (Berkeley, 1986): "As far as the critique of pure reason is concerned, reason as the criticizing subject always remains in a safety zone where it preserves its own security without having to criticize the possibility of critique itself. Yet precisely because reason cannot thereby avoid self-disruption, the reason that does the criticizing and the reason that is to be criticized must inevitably be separated from each other. . . Reason must recognize that it lacks the capacity for critique; otherwise the criticizing reason can only be distinguished from the reason to be criticized. In either case, there is no avoiding the final self-disruption of reason. In other words, reason that tries to establish its own competence by means of self-criticism must finally, contrary to its own intentions, recognize its absolute self-disruption" (43).

17 See R. Panikkar, *Myth, Faith, and Hermeneutics* (New York: Paulist Press, 1979), as well as R. Panikkar, "Mythos und Logos: Mythologische und rationale Weltsichten," in M. P. Dürr/W. Zimmerli (eds.), *Geist und Natur* (Bern, 1989), 206–20.

A dialogue of religions that doesn't take into account this disparity of horizons would find itself permanently involved in misunderstandings, and would never reach the ground out of which each religion takes its own self-understanding. What this means is that the encounter of religions cannot be reduced to a comparison of doctrines. Each religion is like a galaxy, simultaneously shaping its own patterns of thinking and its own criteria of truth and reality as well. In order, therefore, to draw valid comparisons, one must come to acknowledge what I call *homeomorphic equivalents*.[18]

Strictly speaking, there can be no comparative science of religions, nor even a comparative philosophy.[19] There is no neutral (a-religious or a-philosophical) standpoint.[20] All this opens us to the *mythos*. But myths, in this sense, cannot be compared; they are literally incomparable. They are that which makes every comparison possible, by offering the horizon within which any comparison can be carried out. Of course, concepts and doctrines can be compared, but only over against the backdrop of a previously accepted standpoint.

This is why encounters not directly aimed at scholarly or theological ends are so important. *Satsangs*, festivals, shared meals and meetings of all kinds, collaborations and contributions to joint projects, hospitality, and the simplest acts of sociability often turn out to be most important and powerful instances of dialogue.

2. *It participates in the respective pisteumata.*

The life of religions—whether manifest in articulated dogmas, general insights, interpreted experiences, performed rites, or applied symbols—may be summarized in a single word: belief. Religion is a matter of belief. Belief is the overarching *mythos* that makes possible the various manifestations that constitute religion. The *mythos* could in fact be considered the aggregate of the tacit conditions of possibility (and thus credibility) of any given state of affairs. Consequently, the dialogue of religions must be a *dialogue of beliefs*. To understand a religion, you have to know its beliefs. Dialogue arises from faith, but it develops at the level of beliefs. But how is such a dialogue to be sustained? Can one make sense of belief statements without partaking in the belief?

Stimulated by Husserl's phenomenology, which speaks of the *noēma* as the pure content of an eidetic consciousness, I have ventured to introduce the notion of *pisteuma*. We think (*noein*) the thought (*noēma*) through the act of thinking (*noēsis*)—that is, through the operation of *noēsis* we reach the *noēma* as the pure

---

[18] By *homeomorphic equivalent* (see above), I understand a third-degree analogy that reveals a similar and corresponding function in the respective systems.

[19] See R. Panikkar, "What Is Comparative Religion Comparing?" in *Interpreting across Boundaries: New Essays in Comparative Philosophy*, ed. G. J. Larson and E. Deutsch (Princeton, 1988), 116–36.

[20] R. Panikkar, "Aporias in the Comparative Philosophy of Religion," *Man and World* 13, no. 34 (1980): 357–83.

intentional content of our consciousness—but the *noēma* does not allow us to attribute any objective truth or existential reality to itself. Paralleling this, the faith-belief (*pistis*) is also really a sui generis awareness, which manifests itself in the *pisteuma* of the believer, in what the believer assumes as true. But the *pisteuma* of the believer will appear to the outsider as a *noēma*. In other words, the nonbeliever can perceive what the believer says (for instance, "Tara is the merciful divine mother who should be worshiped"), but he cannot share that belief. He will, in any case, get a certain *noēma*, different anyway from the partner's *pisteuma*. But one cannot speak meaningfully about a *pisteuma* without participating in it. What can be described is the contents of one's own consciousness, namely the *noēma*, but not the believer's *pisteuma*.

What the believer believes is not a rational *noēma* that could be mediated (by my outsider's understanding), but his own *pisteuma*, which is what he believes. If I do not penetrate to this *pisteuma*, I cannot describe what he believes but only what I, from my viewpoint, suppose he holds to be true. But I cannot reach the *pisteuma* qua *pisteuma* if I do not believe what the believer believes.

Does this mean that every treasure of belief (*thesaurum fidei*), as some religions themselves express it, will remain unmediated and incomprehensible? Not at all! It means only that without dialogue the way will be blocked. To reach the *pisteuma* of the other, I must *somehow* hold that *pisteuma* to be true, that is, I must have some access to the mythical universe in which the other believes. In other words, the faith of the believer, expressing itself in his belief, belongs essentially to that which the believer believes. If I do not partake in this belief, we shall end up speaking at cross purposes from two incompatible platforms: my belief and his belief, my *noēma* and his *pisteuma*. The *noēmata* of religious phenomenology are in fact *pisteumata*.

We have said that I must *somehow* partake in the belief of the partner if I really wish to meet him. This "somehow" means that I have to have access to his *mythos*.[21] Dialogue is the path toward a new phenomenology, a truly religious one. Only in this way can many of the misunderstandings that have so often vexed the history of religions be cleared away. From this follows not only religious tolerance but a new interpretation of religion altogether.

Here the distinction between faith and belief becomes paramount. Belief expresses itself in dogmatic statements. Faith manifests itself in life. Faith is a constitutive human dimension. Belief, expressed through a creed, is a particular formulation of that faith. In this sense, the fact that people can honestly express their faith in different statements of belief is but a natural manifestation of the diversity of cultures and religions. Faith does not lie in propositions, as Saint Thomas Aquinas said.

---

21 See R. Panikkar, "Verstehen als Überzeugtsein," in *Neue Anthropologie*, no. 7, *Philosophische Anthropologie*, ed. H. P. Gadamer / P. Vogler, Teil II (Stuttgart, 1975), 132–67.

3. *The mythos sets the limits of dialogue.*

Genuine and deep dialogue with one another is not always possible. The partners have to share the same myth, they have to stand at least partially under the same horizon of intelligibility. Certainly, this common myth must emerge slowly in the encounter itself, but, as long as we do not share it, religious communication will not be possible. A tree is always a tree as long as people find it in the field of their sensory perception, but no deep understanding will come about if for one person the tree is just a vegetable mechanism and for the other it is a body inhabited by a spirit. If they were to say they do not understand one another, they would come far closer to communicating than when one stigmatizes the other for "talking nonsense," or reduces him to his own categories. When they are aware that they do not understand each other, and then go at it again to find a new basis for possible understanding, this is a dialogical lesson. Success is never guaranteed, but the *attempt* itself is dialogue.

Modernity generates intercultural myths. For instance, the *humanum*, democracy, peace, secularity, and so forth are myths that have a certain interreligious validity. Only insofar as we share such myths can we really communicate with one another. On the other hand, a common myth tends to make doctrinal differences all the more acute. Neighboring religions, for instance, have often developed opposing attitudes that—despite similarities at the mythic level—make understanding particularly difficult. This sometimes comes more easily for distant religions, when a certain reciprocal sympathy has been cultivated. As a single example, Christians and Jews are often the victims of mutual antipathies, in spite of the basic similarities of many of their beliefs.

Religious

The spirit of dialogue, today blowing stronger and stronger even as new and higher walls are erected against it, represents far more than a new fashion or a new strategy on the part of some old religious traditions to pull themselves out of a certain stagnation. It has itself a religious spirit. Dialogue in and of itself is an authentic manifestation of religiosity. Even the ultra-conservatives who see in the dialogue only a danger for the established religions, are bearing witness to the destabilizing character of dialogue. The dialogue of religions in fact pulls down the walls of religious "nationalisms," behind which some people feel safe and sound. In spite of latter-day changes, the old saying "Cuius regio eius religio" is still all too often valid: religion goes along with whoever holds the power. Not much time ago, in some milieus, it was cool to show up as "Marxists," although with reticence—like now as "liberals," with some reserve. The dialogue of religions frees spiritualities from rigid doctrinal frames and creates new connections that vault over all these boundaries so finely drawn between religions. For too long religions, while claiming to connect (*religare*) us to the divine (infinite, transcendence, or mystery), have tended to neglect the human connections. One all too easily forgets the "religion of Man."[22] Religion has to do not only with God, but also and preeminently with Man.

This opens up the way for a new religiosity, whose forms are yet to be found. By no means does this demean the genuine religious spirit,[23] as the three following remarks should show.

1. *The ultimate source of dialogue is the experience of one's own inadequacy.*

We have already mentioned the experience of contingency, that is, our touching (*cum-tangere*) of the boundaries, the experience of our own inability to know the human condition fully. This does not mean that a person cannot find his or her own salvation in their own, relatively isolated tradition. Not everybody is obliged to explicitly cultivate dialogue. But since the traditions themselves are the fruits of past dialogues, the roots of religious dialogue grip down to the very origins of humankind itself.

What we mean is that the mature or contemplative person renounces any absolute claims. The religion of one's neighbor becomes a personal matter, the diversity of religions a philosophical (or theological) problem, the world situation something that deeply concerns us all. Salvation, liberation, happiness, realization, enlightenment, redemption—as well as justice, peace, human fulfillment, or whatever—are not just individual problems. They require collaboration, solidarity, a growing awareness of human and cosmic *inter-in-dependence*. Dialogue is the way to overcome solipsisms and egoisms of every kind. We realize our own selves insofar as we actively participate in the fate of the entire cosmos. Is this not a religious matter?

2. *The new dialogue contributes to the purification of religions.*

The history of religions shows, without exception to my knowledge, that not only have the most sublime achievements of the human spirit been accomplished in the name of religion, but the darkest deviations from human dignity as well. Fanaticism is a well-known religious weed. The dialogue of religions today offers a medication and represents a purification. Institutionalized religions have too often been hindrances to peace and given their blessings to wars—even in our times. The dialogue of religions does not seek to abolish religions by reducing them to the lowest common denominator of a generalized and superficial religiosity. The new dialogue opens up a middle way between, on the one side, all the well-guarded religious fortresses waging war with one another from their high hills—where every castle claims that salvation lies solely within its walls—and, on the other side, a tedious stay in the shallow valleys of human indolence and indecision,

---

22 See Rabindranath Tagore, *The Religions of Man* (London, 1931).

23 See R. Panikkar, "El futuro de la religión," in *Civiltà delle machine* 27, no. 4–6 (1979): 82–89. English and French translations in *INTERculture* 23, no. 2 (Cahier 107; 1990): 3–21.

where every religion loses its identity and specific value. This middle way avoids war, hot or cold, open or treacherous, and at the same time avoids indifference, as if all religions amounted to the same or said the same things. Dialogue opens wide the way of conversation—precisely because religions are different and often seem to be opposed and incompatible. Dialogue smoothes out the ways, and may also build bridges over the trenches that separate the various religious castles. It invites new people into the common life of the human family, without uprooting them from the native soil of their own traditions. It weaves a net of connections that relates and transforms the world of religions. And this open character of the dialogue belongs to the dynamic of the religious spirit altogether.

3. *Dialogue is itself a religious act.*

When we engage ourselves in the dialogue of religions we are also undoubtedly cooperating with the salvation—the healing and making whole—of the entire world. Love for one's fellows, patience, humility, gentleness, forgiveness, asceticism, renunciation, belief, trust, honesty—the list is endless—are essential virtues for performing an authentic religious dialogue. Is this in itself not enough to demonstrate the religious character of dialogue?

In this sense, the dialogue has its own meaning in itself, and it is impossible to turn it awry or misuse it as some sort of strategy for proselytism. Dialogue as such requires a kind of inner conversion, so that it cannot become a means for winning the other over to our point of view. I look for truth and am even inclined to believe that I have found the truth in my religion. But I am not the only seeker of truth. If in my seeking I am humble, that is to say honest, I will not only feel respect for the others' search, but would even like to join them—not just because more eyes see better than two, but for a deeper reason: the others are not only seekers of truth but sources of knowledge. Man is not only an object or a bare subject looking for objectivity; Man is also a microcosm and a *mikrotheos*, a potential *brahman*, a temple of the Holy Spirit, a precious jug able to fill and to be filled up, a contributor to the shaping of reality. The nature of Man implies self-consciousness, and this self-consciousness is not a privilege of mine. Therefore I will not be able to understand myself fully if I do not understand the others, some way or another; that is impossible without a certain dialogue. I am not, then, interested in the others out of idle curiosity: the pilgrimage of the others crosses my own path; it involves me. The search for truth is not about stalking it as an object, it is about letting oneself be conquered by it and, as far as possible, partaking in the fate of all the others. This is undoubtedly a religious activity.

For many people, especially nowadays, bringing about peace among religions and promoting mutual trust amounts to a genuine religious activity, undisturbed by the fact of one's belonging to a particular tradition. To be sure, it is not insignificant whether the highest name is *dao*, *kami*, *śūnyatā*, God, Śiva, Allah, YHWH,

Truth, Justice, Freedom, or Humanity: it is important and helps us keep our identity. But it is no less important to avoid that invoking those names may bring people to hate, to fight, and to slaughter one another. Nor is it less important to "relativize" our respective Absolutes—though that does not mean that they stop being absolute *for us*. Relativity is not relativism. Moreover, many people today tend to leave all those names undistinguished, and may fall prey to an indifference that is not always healthy. But one thing is sure: all this bickering between religions is not salutary, and peace and harmony are human imperatives of a higher order. Maybe we have here a new myth *in statu nascenti*, the myth letting us see religions as peacemaking factors, and the engagement in the peacemaking process as an eminently religious activity.

Whole

From what we have said so far, it should be clear that the encounter of religions is not only a task for specialists. The praxis of dialogue is a way of being religious, it is a religious activity, and this also applies to reflections on the theory of dialogue. In our day, when so many human concerns have been hyperspecialized, this ought to be properly stressed.

Here again, three headings will suffice:

1. *Dialogue is a holistic activity.*

Nobody is an expert at dialogue, because each dialogue is unique. You cannot specialize in religious dialogue. It belongs to religious life in the present. It is the whole Man, precisely as Man (*anthrōpos*), who is engaged in dialogue. In a genuine dialogue, you do not defend ideologies or orthodoxies. You stand there, as you are—naked, vulnerable, without preconditions or hidden agendas. To truly love our neighbor requires us to truly know him. As people encountering other people, we express our deepest convictions and try to adapt ourselves to the worldview of the other, so as to make us understand and overcome our own solipsism. We may even tremble at the prospect of such a dialogue, or maybe bow out, if the challenge seems too great or too risky for us—just as some prophets were frightened of their own calling. The dialogue of religions is not a Parliament where party discipline is the rule and each member speaks for his own party or coalition. It is something more important: here, as we said, everything is at stake. The stage of dialogue is life—life with its risks and surprises. All the rest is play-acting, psychological or sociological role-playing—if not mere careerism. Whoever balks before these dangers should not be entering the agora of dialogue.

Of course, none of these considerations preclude establishing a certain order, or setting a topic for a given dialogue. But the business of sticking to the topic should be voluntary on both sides, so that a partner might well depart from the topic if it seems appropriate to do so. Besides, although the topic may be very specific, every participant comes to the dialogue as a whole person. How often one embarks on a purely scholarly dialogue and ends up in politics or in the personal! And this is all to the good. It demonstrates that the dialogue cannot be artificially limited. The preparation for a dialogue must be both practical and theoretical, but also personal. Dialogue involves the whole Man.

2. *Dialogue has a liturgical nature.*

Modern Western desacralized languages do not have a suitable word for this. If I were to say that dialogue should be a rite or represent a cultic act, I should still have to explain what I mean by "rite" or "cult." I prefer therefore to speak of a liturgical act, fully aware that this word also requires explanation.[24] Liturgy, properly understood, means the work (*ergon*) of the people (*laos*), where this work is inspired by the Spirit. It is a synergy that gathers all the "three worlds": cosmic, human, and divine.

The dialogue of religions as a liturgical act manifests the a-duality of theory and praxis, of individual and community, politics and religion, the divine and the human. Dialogue is not a new religion. It is a liturgy to which everyone and—I would say—everything is invited, and which aims at transforming all things while retaining the identity of all the parts and participants. Every liturgy is a process of transformation, a transfiguration.

Religions enter dialogue as they would a liturgy, to celebrate—each in its own way—the wonder of life (or whatever each religion would call it). Each religion may believe itself to represent the highest truth and to play the leading role, but each is also ready to listen to the others and to let the play of life play itself out, without violence or cunning. Something happens in dialogue that is not controllable from either side. The risk is endured because there is confidence. Many slanders and suspicions are extinguished by themselves.

I have often been stressing that every dialogue is a *communicatio in sacris*, a holy communion, without which no human community can truly be.[25]

3. *It takes on a cosmic role.*

What is the encounter of religions really all about? Is it about my encounter, as an individual Hindū, with Islam? About all our beautifully printed books on the various religious worldviews? About a fad for young people or a crisis for their elders? It is much more—not less—than that.

---

[24] I have made an attempt at this explanation in *Kultmysterium in Hinduismus und Christentum* (Freiburg: Karl Alber, 1964), which later appeared, substantially revised, in French as *Le mystère du culte dans l'hindouisme et christianisme* (Paris: Les Editions du Cerf, 1970).

[25] See P. Puthanangady, ed., *Sharing Worship: Communicatio in sacris* (Bangalore, 1988).

The recent divorce of epistemology and ontology, stemming from the so-called Enlightenment, makes it difficult to the modern Westernized Man to understand that the encounter of religions means something more than merely an encounter of ideas, systems, or, at most, individuals. It is all of this, of course, but it is also an encounter *of* religions, in the sense of the subjective genitive. Religions themselves encounter one another as historical and cosmic forms. The encounter belongs essentially to religion. Each religion is an encounter. Religions are powerful forces in human history and the cosmos at large. The encounter of religions is like the encounter of galaxies, and it represents, likewise, an "astrological" event. The history of the world is touched by it; the very destiny of the world may be influenced by this encounter. Otherwise, a disaster occurs . . . a *dis-astrum*, a collision of stars!

If we take religions seriously, as they took themselves in their heydays; if we consider that every religion brings along its corresponding worldview; if we do not take the myth of history for the only valid myth, then the encounter of religions is also a cosmic act for our times; it is an event that occurs with our cooperation—but only *co*-operation. It belongs to the *kairos* of our world, to the destiny of this *kalpa*, to the challenge of contemporary history. It is not just that some clever guys have discovered that we cannot go on like this. It is rather that some people have uncovered something already written in the stars, felt the freshening spirit of a new dawn about to shine, discovered that the growth of Man demands something like a turning point, that religions themselves are opening up and wishing to take together this new step into the depths and heights of reality. Indeed, something is moving in those spheres, something that belongs to the very dynamism of Being. After all, human history and the life story of the Earth are both incomprehensible without religions. What an array of changes have come about in the Islamic world, the Christian world, and the world of animistic traditions! And this is not the work of any single caliph or pope or chieftain; it is the achievement of what we call religion. I anyway insist on stressing that religion is not archaeology.

Each culture will use different ways of speaking. The main thing is not to absolutize any single cosmology. As we already said, the encounter of religions is more than small talk here and there, or a gratifying increase of tolerance between this or that group. It may sound hard to believe, but what is happening before our eyes has cosmic proportions. Do we need to cite here the metaphor of the "butterfly effect," so widely reported by modern chaos theory in the sciences?

Unfinished

The encounter of religions is an ongoing process. It is always on the way. Its goal is not to arrive at a complete unanimity, or to mix up all the religions, but rather communication, sympathy, love, polar complementarity. Life wants to live, and not slip away into death. *Being* is a verb. Reality is polar, dynamic—Trinitarian, I would add. The strongest harmony, as Heraclitus said, is the hidden one: *harmonia aphanês phanerês kreittôn.*

Here again I follow a *triloka.*

1. *Dialogue remains a continuous process.*

Since dialogue represents an end in itself, the goal is not to complete it—and therefore render it, at some time or other, superfluous. The completion of dialogue is not a finale, but a continuous performance. This constitutive provisionality does not imply relativism, but relativity; nor does it mean that dialogue does not or cannot provide specific answers to particular questions. What it means is that every answer is relative to its question, and that the question itself only appears as a question in relation to a given state of affairs. Dialogue does not give definitive answers, because there are no definitive questions.

Dialogue is also provisional in the sense that there never exists a completed dialogue. Not only does dialogue never finish, but it is never exhausted. This openness not only vouches for its dynamism, its tolerance and novelty, but also reveals the impossibility of absolutes. Answers are never definitive; there is always room for supplements, corrections, continuations. Dialogue is continuous. It remains ever incomplete, but at the same time, it has in itself a genuine completeness, an end in itself. It may be useful to recall here the scientific metaphor of a self-expanding and self-organizing universe.

2. *Dialogue is Trinitarian.*

Provisionality reflects the human situation. It is not properly a weakness of dialogue as such. The dialogue we are dealing with is not a dialectic but a dialogical one, as it has already been stressed. Dialectic dialogue puts thesis versus antithesis, and tends to a synthesis. It is dualistic. Dialogical dialogue is a never-ending process, belonging to the very life of Man. The relationship remains constitutively open, properly displaying a triadic structure. This is not because there may be three *logoi*, but because the process itself brings two participating *logoi* into an open space that will not permit the dialogue to collapse entirely or be utterly extinguished. There is *pneuma*, spirit, behind every *logos*. The classical word for this openness is transcendence—a transcendence that is experienced in the ordinary course of dialogue. No single participant, nor even all the participants together, have the whole of reality at their disposal. We dialogue about something that transcends us, something we cannot dispose of at will. There is always something that lets the dialogue arise. This "something" lies beyond the power of any participant. One could say that both partners are transcended by a third, whether called God, Truth, *logos*, *karma*, providence, compassion, or whatever. This "third," around which the dialogue flares up, thwarts any manipulation from either side. We are not the absolute rulers of religious dialogue, and the situation is all the more striking in that any judge coming from the outside is out of the question. The dialogue is not a formal disputation before any judges.

A scientific discussion can, and properly should, clarify whatever postulates it requires. We can speak about speed, spin, entropy, or whatever, once we have defined our terms. We may then discuss laws, relationships and mathematical structures, or empirical confirmations of hypotheses. But when our dialogue turns to the Good, God, human destiny, justice, or liberation, then my opinion is no more than an invitation to hear a corresponding opinion from the other side. And this makes it possible to begin the dialogue without having in hand the positive criterion of an independent judge. Logical contradiction may be a negative criterion: in a rational dialogue we cannot allow anything totally contradictory in itself. But religious dialogue is not bound to be simply rational, even though it cannot be irrational, if it is to be truly *dia-logos.*

This "third" dimension may be really inaccessible to our thoughts, because we cannot, by our thought, break the very laws of thought. The "third" element is not bound by our ways of thinking. Nevertheless, we raise the claim to have this "third" in the dialogue just as we are aware of our limits, of our contingency. Some partners may claim, though only through their reason, to have access to a revelation, but everyone must stop before the ultimate horizon over against which our words make sense. *Anagkê stênai*, said the Greeks: "We have to stop somewhere." This "somewhere" is the mystery, the myth. In other words, heaven and Earth also take part in the dialogue, and bear witness to all that we human beings have to say to one another.

It is this Trinitarian structure that vouches for the openness and unending process of dialogue. The invisible third partner is not necessarily a self-subsistent, unchangeable Essence or an all-knowing "God." The partners should not be bound to Platonic or theistic foundations. But this third element of dialogue is nonetheless there: the Spirit blowing where, when, and how she will.

3. *The ultimate character of dialogue is its incompleteness.*

The human constitution is dialogical. Polarity belongs to the essence of Man, and reality alike. Religious dialogue brings up our deepest humanness.

Of course, we are speaking about the ultimate structure of dialogue, since at other levels dialogue may well dispel very many human errors, deepen all sorts of insights, and replace unconvincing opinions with better ones. Religions may purify themselves and discard unpleasant rites, moribund symbols, outdated dogmas, and so forth. Through dialogue, insights are deepened and convictions transformed.

But I would like to go even further. Every true dialogue is complete in itself because it is not a means in order to attain something else than dialogue itself. And yet, paradoxically, it is not "perfect" (in the sense of the Latin *perficere*), "ended"

(Greek: *teleios*), as if nothing could be added to it. Dialogue belongs to human life, and life is constant novelty. We proceed in our engagement for dialogue as we do in our lives, in a symbiosis with heaven and earth, without ever exhausting the fullness of Life. The activity of dialogue belongs to this very level.

Here does the deepest anthropological and cosmic structure of dialogue lie. Its foundation lies in the fact that no human being can properly claim to have access to the whole truth of the human race. An angel, as the only individual of its species, might not need any interangelic dialogue. Not so with Man. Even though *a* man or *a* people may receive a particular divine revelation, the human vessel of this revelation will always be bound by human contingency: the echo of the Absolute is no longer absolute.

We have to not only maintain a sense of (human) proportion but also think realistically. We may have the best of intentions, we may welcome all the positive steps toward tolerance and understanding made in dialogue; but human nature, though not immutable, has never shown itself to be particularly peaceful or pure of heart. Dialogue is Man's fixed way, but it can be blocked or deliberately obstructed. And there can also be deserts, seas, and mountains standing in the way. Sometimes dialogue falls apart, or just does not come about.

Another word appropriate to the ultimate dialogical constitution of Man is pluralism. Pluralism is the human attitude we adopt when it dawns upon us that it is impossible, without lethal reductionisms, to bring the whole of human experience into an unqualified unity. In other words, through dialogue we cultivate our humanness. Religious dialogue is the expression of this search. Here, we partake so deeply of the *logos*, in the Spirit, that we come to drink from the same source as that very *logos*: Silence.

Dialogue, so unavoidable and so indispensable, is not only a social imperative, a historical duty: it is the awareness that in order to be ourselves, or simply to *be*, we must go into communion with the earth below us, the Men beside us, the heavens above us.

10

Human Dialogue and Religious Interindependence

I do not intend to succumb to the temptation to speak in terms of concepts, which is both the greatness and the weakness of Western thought. I will speak, then, in terms of symbols, making it plain immediately that every symbol has numerous different meanings and can therefore be interpreted in several different ways.[1]

The first symbol is September 11. For more than two centuries, the citizens of a small nation, Catalonia, which is part of the Spanish state, have celebrated with all kinds of festivities not a victory but a defeat. The Catalans were defeated by the Bourbons, but this humiliation has turned into a national festival that confers cohesion and a sense of dignity on the people.

Will we have the wisdom to transform the criminal attack of September 11 in the United States into a victory that makes us reflect not only on other peoples' guilt but also on our own shortcomings? This would be a reaction that would furnish proof of the true greatness of a people, and would be the best policy in order to avoid triggering endless acts of violence on one side and the other.

The second symbol is the fire in the perfection of the crystal. Fire—Agni, in the Indic tradition—is the father of the Gods; fire is the primordial force that lies in the male seed, in energy, and basically everywhere; it is the vital force of reality. We talk about the force of fire and the perfection of the crystal, a perfect symbol, but which lacks a third component: time. For a crystal to come into being, you not only need fire, you also need time, you need to be patient, to respect the rhythms of nature, of Man, and the whole of reality. Is not the lack of time one of the main plagues of modern life? This lack is a disease that cannot be healed either with haste or by accelerating the pace of events.

The third symbol is the need for time. The respect for time, the realization that time also belongs to reality is an essential factor not only for living well but also for living in peace. Will the world be able to respect the rhythms of time before hastening to avenge the recent events that have so outraged everyone? With this introduction, we are not straying off our subject, but rather entering into the very heart of it: namely, we are all interindependent.

---

[1] Speech held at the Pio Manzù Research Centre, Rimini, Italy, originally published in *Il fuoco nel cristallo* [Fire in the crystal], no 21 (Rimini, 2001), 136–41.

The original title of this lecture was not "Human Dialogue and Religious Interdependence," but "Human Dialogue and Religious 'Interindependence.'" This spontaneous correction made by the editors constitutes the fourth symbol. We believe that we are interdependent, and indeed it is true that we are not alone and that everything is interrelated, but is equally true that it is the weaker or poorer or less intelligent people who depend on the stronger, richer, and more intelligent ones. In southern India we say that when an ant is tied by a rope to an elephant, it is hardly the elephant that moves in the direction of the ant, but exactly the contrary. Interdependence makes sense only if it can be interindependence, and this is possible only if we admit a religious fact above all of us, a bond that confers on each and every one of us a measure of freedom that enables us to be independent while remaining bound up with one another.

When I say "religion," I am not thinking of religion as an aspirin, as a cure for our headaches, of whatever nature they may be. Religion is not an aspirin: either it is the food of life or it is only palliative remedy.

If we consider the history of the times of the duke of Modena, to mention but an example, the townspeople and peasants depended on the duke—that is to say, a regime of dependence held sway that religion sometimes, like an aspirin, attempted to justify, which explains why many have turned their backs on a certain artificial pseudo-religiosity.

We can be proud of taking a step forward, which, however, I would not call development, because that is an excessively mechanistic, excessively antihuman term: Man does not develop but grows and matures; we are not machines.

Clearly, we have grown up in a setting that acknowledges interdependence. Democracy is properly a step ahead in acknowledging this interdependence. But if one person possesses atom bombs, a thousand allies, or a thousand dollars, and the other person has only a sword and is alone and poor, interdependence is merely a euphemism. Nicaragua, for instance, dare not go against the United States, which is its neighbor. Though recognizing interdependence with others, at least theoretically, is admittedly a positive step, we cannot for this reason alone claim to have achieved our goal. Human beings are abstractly equal as numerical entities, but, in actual fact, they are all different—and unique.

This uniqueness is the basis of interindependence. If we are unique, we cannot be reduced to any single common denominator, we are not quantifiable. Interindependence is the recognition that, from the tiniest elementary particle to the maximum expression of reality, but above all in the human sphere, there exists an interindependence within a mutual dependence on the universal *karma*, on the Mystical Body of Christ, on the *buddhakāya*, and so on. Every being, as well as every atom, has its own degree of freedom. Every man is not only dependent on the others, on fate or on an objective reality, but is also bound through a relationship of interindependence with humankind and the entire cosmos, which is what constitutes our dignity and is the source of our responsibility.

Interindependence recognizes the dimension of freedom of all reality, and thus the fact that none of us is an absolute arbiter of anything. We can perhaps manipulate the gene, but we cannot manipulate reality. Even a so-called divine omnipotence would mean an attack against human freedom.

The recognition of interindependence clearly implies a new cosmology and even a new vision of the true sense of religion. If religion means an openness to the Mystery, it follows that no one has a monopoly on it, because the Mystery is infinite. I cannot believe, then, by virtue of my faith, that only my own truth is valid, consigning others to the sphere of error or of evil.

If terrorism is an evil, it cannot be combated with bombs. Combating evil with evil leads to no kind of solution.

At the beginning of this year, in India, which has a population greater than that of North America, Europe, and Russia put together, and which is struggling against the national plague of terrorism, the president of the Supreme Court has stated that there is something worse than terrorism: antiterrorism. Terrorism and antiterrorism are on the same plane inasmuch as, if the latter were on a higher plane, it would not abase itself to fighting with the same weapons as the enemy.

For this reason, a new type of anthropology is needed, as all the speakers who have preceded me have stressed; because, if Man is only a well-developed monkey, then the law of the jungle applies, and the strongest will carry the day. In that case, however, there will be neither peace nor joy.

To put it metaphorically, the devil, as a fallen angel, is more intelligent and astute than Man.

To cultivate religious dialogue, the interindependence of all cultures and all men must be recognized; otherwise there is no human dialogue, but only dialectic or armed strife. This dialogue is much more demanding than annihilating those who think differently from ourselves, however wicked they may be. Evil belongs to reality, but evil, I repeat, cannot be defeated by a new form of evil. The textbooks in our schools quote a phrase that I do not believe was coined by Niccolò Machiavelli, whom I regard as being too intelligent for such a simple-minded statement, but which precisely for this reason, perhaps, has captured the popular imagination, and unfortunately also that of the politicians: "The end justifies the means."

This statement, in addition to being a moral aberration, is a wrongheaded idea: if the end is what justifies the means, that implies that the means are (turn out to be) good if the end is good. This is plainly a straightforward tautology. Means that turn out to be good, because they are justified by a good end, serve then to achieve the end that one supposes to be good. If the means depend on the end, there can be no bad means, if the end is good. Here is the dependence that makes the means depend on the end. If the end is to defend one's home or fatherland or eliminate terrorism, that is, a good end, then any means conducive to achieving this end is automatically good. What remains to be seen is whether the means are real means, that is, if they achieve the end, and thus we have a situation whereby only effective means are justified, which plunges us into the most savage form of pragmatism: "God is on the side of the hardest hitters!"

Interdependence is not a tautology but a vicious circle. If the means and the ends are interdependent, everything that refers to the means is related to the ends and vice versa. The ends are good because the means are good, and the means are good because the end is good, and are true means when they serve the purpose.

Interindependence is quite different. The means do not depend solely on the end, but also possess a measure of independence in relation to the end, which enables them to be defined as good or bad. They are therefore not merely means, but have their own *ontonomy*. The independence of interindependence implies the fact that the fabric of reality is not a rigid grid in which everything is predetermined and mechanical, but a relationship between beings that are not entirely predetermined. This field of freedom is the field of relationship in its deepest sense.

The great challenge of this third millennium is that we cannot continue to live and think in terms of the old categories: what is at stake is the destruction of Man and nature.

President Mikhail Gorbachev, in a speech delivered in New York during the World Forum Millennium 2000, says quite literally, "We still use outdated tools and old-fashioned approaches. . . . This is the drama of global politics." Many decades earlier, Einstein had already said something similar.

This is the challenge of the religious dimension, inherent in every man or woman, whether a believer or not, because faith is not the legacy only of a few. Beliefs may differ, but faith is a constituent part of the human being. Every man is open to the unknown; to the Mystery; to what he does not know; to what he cannot manipulate; to what he believes to be beautiful, true, and good; and by which he feels attracted though he is unable to say what it is. We know how to use things, but we do not know the mystery of reality; we must be humble.

Religion—and I understand perfectly that there is an allergy to the term, considering the uses and abuses that have been perpetrated in its name—is a dimension of Man. True religiosity leads us to listen to others, because no one is self-sufficient. Thus arises the religious dialogue, which is an in-depth exchange of Man's experience qua Man, and not so much as an expert in any particular specialized field. Therefore, many religions (including Islam) tell us that knowing oneself is to know Man, and that knowing Man is to know God. Yet in order to achieve knowledge, it is not enough simply to calculate, or to *see*.

For the Greek genius, the main metaphor is that of sight: seeing, clarifying, revealing. For an ancient civilization such as the Indic civilization, on the other hand, the main metaphor is not seeing but hearing. Seeing means judging, that is to say, I, in a certain sense, am the master of reality: if I close my eyes, I can no longer see. Closing one's ears, on the other hand, is not as easy a task, and is unquestionably a more artificial exercise.

To know, you also need to be able to listen, which means not judging straight off but being patient and tolerant. Knowing how to listen is an art that can modify our day and age, leading to that major change of mentality that begins in us but ends in our culture as well as in the other peoples'. This change of mentality, or *metanoia*, is neither a technical nor a political problem. Man's profound convictions cannot be changed either by technical manipulation or by political legislation. The transformation that is needed is a religious issue.

Hence the importance of *intra*religious dialogue, which requires the recognition of the interindependence of the entire fabric of reality. The crystal does not burn in any ordinary fire: you need a high temperature. I would hope my words may succeed in kindling this "fire in the crystal."

11

For a Dialogue among Civilizations

If we do not manage to decentralize "culture," and to stop thinking that every little village, every little town, and ultimately every person is the very center of the whole universe; if we do not overcome the complex of feeling marginalized because we do not live in New York, or we do not speak Chinese or English or Russian, we will never find a solution to the problem of dialogue between civilizations.[1]

Intercultural dialogue, in my opinion, has not yet begun as it should, but it has begun. We feel the inescapable need for dialogue with a world different from ours. That said, in a more academic form I would say: today it may be stated that no culture, no religion, no civilization is self-sufficient. And this has a double meaning: it cannot solve the problems that the man of that culture, civilization, or religion poses; nor can it solve the problems of the world. No civilization, culture, religion, or form of life is self-sufficient: it no longer manages to provide answers to Man's questions, and it no longer manages to provide answers to the questions of others.

I would say that not only is no civilization self-sufficient, but it is not even sufficient. . . . I believe it can be claimed that today, even theoretically, the problem of the type of life, forms of belief, the image of a common life, and the organization of the ideal society does not find an adequate solution anywhere. The West is now all too aware of not having a solution for the world, neither for itself nor for others. Other traditions are equally aware of their shortcomings on the one hand, and on the other they know they cannot be a paradigm or a model for the rest of the world.

What remains, in my opinion, is mutual fertilization, real, live dialogue, not dialectic but dialogal between cultures. If nobody has the solution, perhaps we can seek together, we must seek together; and, perhaps, together we can find.

So how is this dialogue happening? It is happening because we cannot do without it. It is absolutely necessary to live. What are the conditions for this dialogue? The first has already been stated: we need to be aware that nobody has the answer, the solution. On the other hand, if we must meet, we cannot meet in a situation of inequality: one cannot have dialogue with conditions of inferiority on one side and superiority on the other. It is written somewhere that the last shall be the first. To achieve dialogue we must understand the other.

---

[1] Reworking of a talk from a conference at Città di Castello, Italy, in August 1983.

Native Americans say, "You cannot speak to your neighbor, nor to your enemy, until you have walked a mile in his moccasins." That is, one cannot understand the other from the outside. One cannot understand the other if one does not believe in what the other believes. This is fundamental.

We cannot say, "I respect your things, I do not understand them at all, but I respect them." Respect is a necessary condition, but it is not a sufficient condition. We cannot think that the problem can be solved with a sort of coexistence: "You think about your own affairs.... I am a Westerner, I am a Christian, I am Hindū, I am this or that. I respect your things, which I do not understand, but...." Here the preconditions for dialogue are missing, because it is not a question of prerequisites for roundtable talks; they are not conditions of equality.

I cannot understand the other if, in a certain way (and this certain way is important), I do not believe in what the other says or does. On the other hand, I cannot believe in it if I do not believe in it: there are no two ways about it. This renders the problem enormously difficult. Here is the profound change required of the immense majority of men of our time.

Perhaps not all, but the majority of the cultural phenomena of our times have a certain claim to universality. Christians have thought for centuries that they could supply the absolute solution to all the problems of the world. Marxists similarly thought, for at least a century, that they were bringing to the world the good news of justice, solidarity, and fraternity. Modern technocrats or scientists think that science is neutral and universal, and that with a bit of science everywhere and a bit of applied technology everywhere—at least in theory—we would obtain solutions to the most agonizing problems of mankind.

These claims of absoluteness are the greatest obstacles to true dialogue, to a mutual fertilization between cultures, and therefore to a solution of the human problem.

There is a current called phenomenology, which claims it wishes to say nothing about what things are (essence), but wishes to describe them in a universal form, in a form that can have absolute value for all men. A great philosopher, Husserl to be precise, theorized phenomenology at the beginning of the twentieth century, describing it as a truly universal form. This model does not take a position regarding the truth or reality of the phenomenon but describes it in a form that all can accept. It speaks of "*noēma*." *Noēma* is the manifestation to the human conscience of the "thing" in its universal and phenomenal appearance, so that all can take it as a starting point to draw consequences at a level of praxis, degrees of reality, and so on.

The philosophical thesis I would like to defend is that, when we are dealing with Man, when we are dealing with human phenomena, the *noēma* is not enough. When it is a matter of understanding the cultural problems or the religious problems of men of our time, or of men of all times, a phenomenological description in this sense is not sufficient. We need the *pisteuma*. "*Noēma*" derives from a Greek word that modern philosophy has basically taken from Aristotle, and it means "that which is thought" (cf. *nous*, *noēsis*). In opposition or comparison, or as a supplement to the *noēma*, I would like to introduce the *pisteuma*. If *noēma* indicates thinking, *pisteuma* (from *pisteuō*, *pistis*) indicates "that which is believed."

Therefore, I cannot understand the other if I do not believe in what the other thinks and believes. To think that I can understand the Hindū, or that the Hindū can understand the Christian, or that the communist can understand the bourgeois, or that the bourgeois can understand the Marxist, or that the Marxist can understand the scientist, or that the scientist can understand the phenomenologist, or that the phenomenologist can understand the sociologist, and so on, without believing in what the Marxist, the scientist, the communist, the Catholic, the Hindū believes in . . . does not allow us to describe the same phenomenon.

If I say: Durgā is the goddess of fertility, or the goddess of serapion (which is more correct), but I do not believe in what I am saying, and at the same time I state, "I understand these things, Durgā is the goddess of fertility, etc., but . . . ," I am not speaking of the same thing as the person who believes that Durgā is the goddess of serapion, of fertility. We utter the same name, but we are not speaking of the same thing. The idea that there exists a goddess who presides over the phenomenon of fertility is for me just an empty phrase. But he who believes sends his daughter to the goddess instead of sending her to the doctor . . . ! The "phenomenon" is not the same; the two people are not thinking the same thing.

So, to understand the other, one must believe in what the other says. And if one does not believe, we are not speaking of the same thing. Expressed in a more philosophical form: the human being is not the object, but the subject, so he cannot be the object of research to understand human phenomena. Self-interpretation of the human phenomenon belongs to the very nature of what Man is. Saying what Man is without introducing in this definition all that human beings think they are is not answering the question; it is only stating what I think Man is. My idea of Man is very respectable, but it is not "what Man is." What Man is, is what all think Man is. So, if I meet someone who thinks he is a certain type of person, and I do not understand his way of thinking, I have not found the solution to the problem of Man, unless I also consider that concept that is different from mine.

The true concept, the true anthropology to understand the human phenomenon cannot forget the interpretation Man gives of himself. Until the last little woman from the last island of the last archipelago has spoken her last word, anthropology (as a science of Man) will not be able to give a satisfactory answer, unlike all the sciences which think they are objective.

Politics

A true and authentic dialogue between cultures cannot take place in the current political conditions. In other words, if we think that there is a possibility of dialogue with the Bantu, with Indios, with the Hindū, or with the Inuit, in the current political conditions, the dialogue will be compromised from the outset. Dialogue is not possible. To assume that one can speak to African tribes accepting the status quo of the postcolonial system—for example, the current borders assigned to African states—is an aberration. The result is that there are more than 17 million absolutely displaced people, twenty-six or twenty-seven declared wars, civil war almost everywhere, and the most appalling corruption among the small élite who want to Westernize their countries.

This situation shows that current Western political dogmas do not offer the conditions for intercultural dialogue. Reducing other cultures to a bit of folklore, such as dance and little things like that, is still colonialism. We are convinced we respect them because we let them dress up in their traditional ways, but they must respect the rules of play of our system of nations, our concept of state, democracy, legal system, and so on. This is not a criticism of the Western legal system, nor of democracy nor of the state; it only means that this is satisfactory (or perhaps unsatisfactory) for the West, but it is not the universal paradigm for dialogue between cultures. If we are interested in intercultural dialogue, we cannot expect one culture to offer us a model.

This requires profound change—a capacity to listen and to take the other really seriously.

Religion

Which changes should be brought about in the religious sphere? Here, too, changes are imperative. I do not want to enter into theological problems that would be complex, but I would like to state clearly, first, that Christianity's claim of absoluteness is a novelty in Christianity, it is not traditional doctrine. In practice, it is in fact a Hegelian formulation.

Second, if Christianity does not renounce this claim of absoluteness, it will not be able to perform any role in interreligious dialogue.

Third, there is a possibility of internal debate in every religious tradition (Christianity, in this case), not in order to diminish its message but so that it presents itself as the unique and absolute religious form of human existence.

Science

One of the greatest obstacles to dialogue between cultures is the popular belief in the scientific means of the West—that is, the belief that science is universal: 2 plus 2 makes 4 everywhere, or on the basis of Newton's physics, things fall with the same rules here as in Patagonia. . . . Blessed are those who believe, and are so naive!

I support a thesis that modern science, the physical-mathematical and chemical sciences, are linked to a determined culture, so they are not at all universal.

Wanting to impose science as a universal fact that can be assimilated and applied in the Hindū world or in Patagonia in a neutral manner, as if it had nothing to do with its own origins, is another legacy of colonialism, Western imperialism—a belief that began in the nineteenth century and must now be left behind.

Not to realize, for example, that physical science has a concept of space, time, and matter that is peculiar to a very concrete, very particular, very defined *forma mentis*, which did not exist even in the West until four or five centuries ago, is simply an error, as well as a historical one. It is enough to see how someone from another culture assumes this mentality, to realize that it is a cultural phenomenon, peculiar to a specific way of seeing and living reality, that cannot pretend to be universal.

If one thing in current reality appears all too evident, it is what was said at the start: none of us, collectively speaking, neither Christians, nor scientists, nor Hindūs, nor Westerners, nor Orientals, seems to have satisfactory solutions.

Let me conclude in a slightly more Oriental way, telling a story, of which a small part is original, and the rest is my interpretation.

First the original story, then the interpretation. We are in the imperial gardens of Kyoto in eighteenth-century Japan. Two Christians are walking and conversing with an aura of great peace, which is firstly Japanese and also Christian. Two figures are coming toward them. Just think: the emperor and Jesus! The two are Christians, and they are Japanese: the emperor is the incarnation of their civilization; Jesus is the savior of the world. They are Christians, they are Japanese, and so . . . whom should they bow to first? Jesus and the emperor are approaching, there is no time to think! Then one of the two, perhaps the older one, says, "Listen, we'll bow to the Emperor, and Jesus will understand."

I am sure that, had they been Shintoists, they would have bowed to Jesus, thinking that the emperor would understand.

The meeting of cultures can be achieved, it seems, only with transgression from one's own culture. Precisely because we are in it, there is something—which can be called "forgiveness," that is, "Jesus will understand"—that permits us to find a solution, a solution that does not emerge by virtue of logic but by virtue of forgiveness, by virtue of a mutation, by virtue of a more profound intelligence.

I am also sure that, if instead of being Shintoists or Christians, they had been two modern scientists . . . hara-kiri. There is no solution, they must kill themselves. The dilemma cannot be solved logically.

There is also a possible cultural solution. If they had been two artists, who take the world as rather a joke, they would have said, "You bow to the emperor, I'll bow to Jesus." That way, everyone is happy.

But maybe we should all bow to something, even if it is an inward bowing. Perhaps we all have to transcend this historical moment that seems to have no way out.

*

[Continuation with comments on points raised by the audience]

A question that would require a whole new close examination would be the explanation of what is intercultural dialogue that is not merely dialectic, not merely between victors and vanquished on a dialectic level. I have called it dialogal dialogue. What does this mean? It is that dialogue that I participate in not so much to win or to convince, but to be seen by the other, so that it is the other that reveals my preconceptions to me. This seems to me of extraordinarily serious importance.

Dialogal dialogue removes my ingenuity whereby I think that what is valid for me is valid for everybody. Thus I discover that I, too—I the Christian, I the Buddhist, I the modern man, I the scientist, I anyone else, have unanalyzed presuppositions, which I cannot see: I need the other because the other reveals them to me before my eyes. For example, all of you here will have realized immediately that my Italian accent is neither Umbrian nor Florentine . . . and maybe not even Italian. But you also speak with a specific accent, pleasanter, more correct, and we reveal our respective presuppositions to each other. When I stated that the presuppositions of science are not universal, this, from the standpoint of Western culture, is not visible.

Another example, the great phrase from Kantian morality: "Act only according to that maxim whereby you can, at the same time, will that it should become a universal law"—the categorical imperative. In opposition to this I would place the "personalistic imperative," and I would say the exact opposite: "Do precisely what nobody else can do." Be aware of your role, without expecting your activity to become the universal norm for all. Instead do what nobody else but you alone can do. Shoulder your own responsibilities. You fulfill yourself morally when you do what you think you should do, and at the same time you do not absolutize, because you think that nobody else can do it.

I have been asked whether, to understand another culture, it is necessary to believe in the other. What does believing mean? This is a legitimate and justified question. I would say believing in the other means being convinced that the other is telling the truth—so, a sort of middle way between sympathy, liking, *Einfühlung*, "shared observation," and all the other anthropological categories. But it is more than this: it is also, if I may play with words, sharing, although not sharing absolutely: being convinced of the truth of the other's words. One comes far closer to comprehension of the other, saying, "My friend, I do not understand how you can say that!" rather than, "Yes, I understand you perfectly, but you know. . . ." The idea that everything must be understood is typical of Western culture. Not everything is to be understood: there exists a form—I would say—that is less aggressively masculine, more passively feminine, of not understanding and, nevertheless, receiving, accepting, embracing.

Believing in what the other believes means sharing his conviction of stating the truth, after which I can make philosophical distinctions: I do not necessarily have to think that this is the whole truth, I can integrate that truth in a truth that I deem greater, more universal, more embracing. That is, if someone believes in the Gods, I can believe in them, too, but interpreting them as more or less divine, or more or less superhuman spirits, which I insert in a (for me) broader framework.

This requires a different epistemology from that which is used in the West today. I have even personally forced myself to construct this epistemology. As a corollary, here is another question: Does that mean that I should sacrifice my identity or my position?

My answer is a categorical "no." I could say, in a philosophical form, that my identity does not imply the exclusion of others; in even more strictly philosophical terms, that intelligibility is not achieved so much by virtue of the principle of noncontradiction as by virtue of the principle of identity. In a less philosophical form, I will use an example. It seems that a very clear position of Judaism is to consider themselves the chosen people; subsequently, also the Christian church, heir to Judaism, thought, "The church is the place of salvation." Now, if I believe that also the Hindū, the Muslim, and so on are the "chosen people," that does not mean that the Jewish people are not. There is no contradiction. In short, to believe in what the other believes, I do not have to—or even need to—sacrifice my position.

There is something more, and this is one of the activities that I have always carried out with great joy: to see that, as I grow to understand the other, I understand myself better, and I even change my interpretation of myself. As Catholics study Protestants better, they understand themselves better; as Scholastic philosophers study Marxism, they understand Scholasticism better and they begin to understand Marxists better, and to realize that perhaps what they thought should be expressed differently—all without abandoning one's own identity.

The question that arises concerns the fact of whether it is contrary to the Christian position to stop thinking that Christianity gives a unique adequate answer. I do not currently identify with this perspective. There are certainly distinctions and contradictions of a doctrinal order, but doctrinal contradictions are not by nature religious contradictions. One thinks of the Dominican and Jesuit orders, of Duns Scotus and Thomas Aquinas, or Bonaventure and Malebranche: all Christians, but doctrinally contradictory, there is no question about it. If the doctrine of the univocity of the being is true, the doctrine of the analogy of the being is false. If one says that, without the doctrine of the analogy of the being, one falls into pantheism, which destroys Christianity; and the other says the being is univocal, in theory the other cannot be Christian. And yet there is no doubt that Duns Scotus is a Christian, and there is no doubt Saint Thomas Aquinas is a Christian.

Contradiction in the doctrinal order does not imply incompatibility in the religious order. So it is not a matter of diluting the message of any culture, of any religion, but of understanding this culture or this religion in a sphere that did not exist before. This is all the problem of the text and the context, the problem of hermeneutics.

I have been asked if there exists a way out of the problem of no culture being self-sufficient. Certainly, the way out is dialogal dialogue, which implies conscience, liking, love, and also a willingness to enter into this dialogue.

What happens in other cultures? Other cultures are suffering from a much greater crisis than that of Western culture. Other cultures find themselves in a threefold crisis. First, an appalling inferiority complex, which very often prevents them from even expressing themselves correctly. Second, they certainly find themselves in a position of inferiority from many standpoints, the economic one, among others. Third, they are going through a period of decline, with all the extremist forms to seek a remedy to this decline.

People often speak of the enormous influence in the West of all these movements coming from Asia, with gurus, sects, and preachers. This is true. But if you go to Africa or Asia, the influence of Western gurus, Western teachers, and Western universities, science, and technology is infinitely superior.

Must the West change its politics? I would say so. I do not intend to dictate solutions to the East or the West, but evidently the West today offers the System, the dominant framework of the political order, and this is what must change.

Let us think of Native Americans. Neither Canada nor the United States have respected the agreements, the international treaties signed with them. Not only have they destroyed them in the bloodiest way but, on a legal level, they have not respected the commitments they freely made. The dialogue between the American Indians and the politicians of Canada—where I had the opportunity to intervene fairly directly—and of the USA is extraordinarily interesting and extraordinarily difficult, because the American Indians do not recognize Western political order. They do not recognize the passport: once an entire delegation arrived in Geneva without passports, other than passports as "the Indian people."

In any case, it is evident that Western politics must change. One of the greatest difficulties is the identification between state and nation that exists in the West. This is an acute problem for some cultures, even in India, and there are many people who are beginning to work on it. Personally, I managed to present UNESCO with a project relating to this problem. The world is beginning to be aware that the situation must change.

Is there a Utopian dimension to all this? Of course! Just as it was Utopian 150 years ago to claim that slavery should be abolished. If you read the documents of the time, especially those from North America, you will find that the Christians said, "You must treat the slaves as children of God, benevolently, without exploiting the women . . . ," but without questioning the institution of slavery as such, because without it there would be no coffee, no cocoa, no nothing; the economy would be in ruins. Nowadays we are beginning to think that that Utopia was legitimate. So, if one believes in an ideal, one works for it and does one's utmost; otherwise, it is just a waste of time.

There remains the danger of losing one's identity, the danger of relativism, and also of an irenicism of truth. I would say: there are so many dangers, so I agree with those who state that these problems are dangerous and difficult, and that one cannot play about with them or face them unprepared. However, I would like to underline the fundamental distinction between relativism, which in my opinion is the danger, and which I absolutely refute, and relativity.

Relativism means there is no criterion: everything is good, bad, black, or white; there is no distinction; everyone can do what he wants; I am so tolerant that nothing bothers me at all; I have no criterion for anything, so everything is all right. This, in my opinion, is not only a danger: it is false, wrong, it leads nowhere, and it is also self-contradictory. If everything is relative, so is my statement that everything is relative.

Relativity indicates the awareness that any statement, of any kind, has its validity only within a determined sphere, in relation to something else. Every statement has a text, a context, a system of coordinates, a system of axioms, a specific culture, and so on. Relativity means that we cannot absolutize—in the human order, and in any order we can access—any statement or truth or anything: everything is "in relation to." I would say more: any statement, any intelligibility, is in itself a relation.

As for my assessment of the theories of Ivan Illich, this would require a conference all to itself. Apart from my liking for and friendship with him, I rather agree, without identifying myself, with his negative critical position in relation to civilization and the modern Western system. But with some reservations, because in my opinion this iconoclastic attitude may not help a lot, it does not aid a work of construction, which at this moment must in any event be a provisional construction because, as we have said, the dominant culture does not yet permit true dialogue. So the need on the political level is for a very refined order, because first one must dismantle or deconstruct the dominant system, in order to then establish a dialogue. In this sense Illich is very helpful, but as a precondition for a second part, which is what I would attempt to establish as the more important, to offer a way or suggestion of the direction to be taken.

Let me express some almost incoherent sentences: the world economic situation was created by the international market, and not by the real condition of the world. The role of the economy is important in every culture and every civilization, but (look at its etymology) it is not necessarily the order that is today called economic and therefore financial. It is something completely different. It is the *nomos* of the *oikos*, it is the "housekeeping." This is precisely where the role of intercultural dialogue is important, because I think that this pan-economic ideology is one of the most dangerous characteristics of the current system. World monetary unification leads to the law of communicating vessels, so it is in the very nature of things that rich countries become ever richer and poor countries ever poorer. I cannot give you a loan unless this loan has interest; and it has no interest unless it permits me to grow; and in a closed system, I cannot grow unless someone else shrinks. So the current economic problem is one of the greatest obstacles to a dialogue between cultures. This is so important that, if the economics is not questioned, the problems with dialogue will not be solved.

Recently there was a large, very high-level conference in Geneva (which I had to take part in, and for which I still have to write a couple of things). Anderson and all the heavyweights of economics were there, the president of the World Bank, and so on. The subject was "Economy and Social Order." There we saw for the first time that the whole economic problem could not be solved without returning to the problem of "What is the human social order?" To my amazement, more than 50 percent of the participants agreed with the theory that the world economy has no way out, if it does not change radically, if it does not decentralize (but nobody knows how), if it does not bear in mind what is known in current jargon as social order.

On this matter I, too, have very concrete theories. I am in favor of the "demonetization of culture." As there must be demilitarized zones, so should there be demonetarized zones. Current culture has sanctioned that everything, even breathing and drinking, depends on economics. Culture must be demonetized. How? These are the great problems emerging today.

I would like to close with a certain optimism: the very fact—as happened in Geneva—that those who hold the most precise information on the global situation of politics, economics, and so on are convinced that it cannot go on like this opens up to extraordinary hope. The fact remains that unanimity and consensus about the solutions are lacking, and that there is all the strength of the status quo and hidden interests which push toward ever greater wealth, armaments, and so on.

But more or less everywhere in the world, East, West, Africa—an awareness is growing at all levels and in all types of human disciplines that we cannot go on like this. There is also a growing awareness that banal reforms here and there would only prolong the death throes of a dying system. There is not yet consensus on the next step, but it is in any event a sign of the times—a situation that, although it appears in the form of negativity, sets us all, at all levels of human life, on an interdisciplinary, transcultural, interreligious quest: rich and poor, North and South.

This solidarity, which I would like to be not only human but also cosmic, and also divine if you like, is a symptom of hope, which leads us on to the right track. Because, when one opens one's eyes, he sees very clearly that there is nobody at the head of the column, nobody who can say, "We must go this way!"

A father of the church, Gregory of Nyssa, said of the father of all believers of the Semitic faiths, Abraham, as he left the town of Ur, "And then Abraham was sure of taking the right road, because he did not know where it led." We find ourselves faced with a similar act of faith: we do not know where to go, but we go. As long as we walk and give each other a hand, maybe we will be able to move forward joyfully and even reach somewhere!

There is not a mission that relates to one category, one class, one social condition, one people in particular nor, I would say, is there a message or a task within any type of messianism. For this reason, in my opinion, the challenge belongs to each human group, or person, who is capable of taking on this responsibility. This is an appeal—in a certain sense much more profound, and therefore religious and cultural—directed at all those men and women who see the situation and have the courage to take up the flag. This cannot be done alone. However, I do not believe that such groups are "chosen": they are the result of freedom and grace.

SECTION II

EXAMPLES OF DIALOGUE

12

Śūnyatā and *Plērōma*

The Buddhist and Christian Response to the Human Predicament

εκ τού πληρώματος αυτού
ἡμεῖς πάντες ελάβομεν
From his fullness we all have received.

—*Jn 1:16*

pratītiasamutpādaḥ śunyatāṃ
[the] interdependence [of all things is] emptiness

—*Nāgārjuna, Mūlamadhyamaka-kārikā XXIV.18*

The Human Predicament

In spite of the scores of attempts at defining religion, I may venture this simple and brief statement: religion is the path we follow in order to reach the purpose of life, or, by an even shorter phrase, religion is the *way of salvation.*[1] One has to add immediately that here the words "way" and "salvation" do not require any specific content; they rather stand for the existential pilgrimage we undertake in the belief that this enterprise will help us achieve the final purpose or end of life.[2] A *way to fulfillment*—if we prefer.

In other words, under the particular perspective that we may call religion, every human culture presents three elements: (1) a vision of Man as he actually

[1] Text appeared in J. M. Robinson, ed., *Religion and the Humanizing of Man* (Waterloo, Ontario: Council on the Study of Religion, 1972), 67–86.

[2] The nature of this chapter, I hope, justifies the omitting of so-called secondary literature, otherwise so helpful, and the limiting of the quotations to just indicative samples. Most citations are taken from R. Pannikar, *The Silence of God* (Maryknoll, NY: Orbis Books, 1989); *El silencio del Buddha* (Madrid: Siruela, 1996); and *Humanismo y Cruz* (Madrid: Rialp, 1963).

appears to be (*hic et nunc*); (2) a certain, more or less developed notion of the end or final station of each (*illic et postea*); and (3) the means for letting us pass from the former situation to the latter.[3]

The first element can be called the *human predicament*, that is, the particular way in which Man is seen and evaluated. I use this expression rather than the more common "human condition" in order to stress that not all religions understand Man's factual situation as the word "condition" would suggest. Man is not independent from what we take ourselves to be, and the human condition is precisely conditioned by Man's own view on it. By human predicament I mean the factual status of Man as it is evaluated according to a particular conception, being itself part of that very status.

No religion, and much less the ones we will take into account, can be encompassed in a monolithic doctrine, as if a single doctrine could sum up all it stands for. In this chapter we will choose only a pair of notions, one from each tradition, to represent an orthodox view in the respective religions.

The human predicament as seen by the Buddhist tradition could be summarized: (1) in a philosophical presupposition, the *anātmavāda*;[4] (2) in a theological statement, the *āryasatyāni*,[5] which expands the anthropocosmic intuition of *sarva duḥkha*;[6] and (3) in a moral injunction, best rendered by the last words of the Buddha: "Work out your salvation with diligence."[7]

The human predicament seen by the Christian tradition could be summarized: (1) in a philosophical presupposition, the creation of the world;[8] (2) in a theological statement, the redeeming or saving power of Christ,[9] which expands the cosmotheandric intuition of the Incarnation;[10] and (3) in a moral injunction, best rendered by the words of Christ summing up the Law and the Prophets: "You

---

[3] See R. Panikkar, "Have 'Religions' the Monopoly on *Religion*?" *Journal of Ecumenical Studies* 11, no. 3 (Summer 1974): 515–17.

[4] That is, the doctrine of the non-self or of the ultimate unsubstantiality of the being. See, for example, *Saṁyutta-nikāya* III.66; *Dīgha-nikāya* II.64ff.; *Milindapañha* II.1.1 (or 251); II.2.1; III.5.6; et al.

[5] The Four Noble Truths or *aryasaccāni* (in Sanskrit, *āryasatyāni*), namely: the universal fact of sorrow, the different cravings as the cause of sorrow, the stopping of all cravings as the stopping of sorrow, and the eightfold path leading out of sorrow: right vision, right intention, right discourse, right behavior, right livelihood, right effort, right memory, and right concentration. See *Saṁyutta-nikāya* V.420ff.

[6] That is, all conditioned things (*samkhāra*) are sorrow. See *Dhammapada* XX.6 (N. 278). Suffering, uneasiness, and turmoil are other versions of *duḥkha* (from the root *duṣ*, to deteriorate).

[7] See *Mahāparinibbāna-sutta* VI.10; III.66; et al. See, incidentally, Phil 2:12: "You must work out your own salvation in fear and trembling."

[8] Gen 1:1ff.; 1:31; et al.

[9] See Lk 2:11; Acts 13:23; et al.

[10] See Jn 1:14, et al.

shall love the Lord your God with all your heart, and all your soul, and all your might. . . .[11] You shall love your neighbor as yourself."[12]

We may try to express in our own words the gist of this double vision. It should be remembered that, until recent times, these two traditions agreed about the human predicament. Rightly or wrongly, they seemed to concur in saying that we are endowed with a craving—literally, a thirst[13]—or with a lust—literally, a desire[14]—that is the cause of our unhappiness. The two religions will elaborate this as Ignorance or Fall, so that enlightenment or redemption is required to overcome it. At any rate, the human predicament is neither as it should be, nor as it could be. The Buddha[15] and the Christ[16] claim to be able to remedy this situation. A human being has to transcend Man's present condition in order to be freed, that is, disentangled from the wheel of *saṁsāra*,[17] from this *kosmos*.[18] Both Buddhism and Christianity stand for human liberation.[19]

Here both traditions express an almost universal human experience. Both are convinced that Man is a not yet finished being, a reality that looks unachieved, growing, becoming, on the way, a pilgrim. This is the human predicament. The real problem lies in the response that each of these two world religions gives to it.

The Buddhist and Christian Responses

Nirvāṇa *and* Sōtēria

As we have said, the second element in all religions is the notion that there is an end or a final station of Man. We, these unfinished beings, are not to remain as we are, but we have to undergo a more or less radical transformation, a change, in

---

11 See Deut 6:5.

12 See Mt 22:37–40.

13 The Pali *taṇhā* corresponds to the Sanskrit *tṛṣṇā*, meaning thirst. Besides the text already quoted, See *Anguttara-nikāya* III.416; IV.400; *Saṁyutta-nikāya* I.1; I.8; *Majjhima-nikāya* I.6; II.256; *Itivuttaka* 30; 50; 58; 105; et al.

14 The New Testament term is *epithymia*, which Latin theologians translated as *concupiscentia*. See 1 Jn 2:16–17; 2 Pet 2:18; Gal 5:16; Rom 6:12; 2 Tim 3:6; et al.

15 See *Majjhima-nikāya* III.6, et al.: "The Tathāgata limits himself to show the path," et al. (see also *Majjhima-nikāya* I.83).

16 See Jn 10:9; 14:6; et al.

17 See *Milindapañha* 326, et al.

18 See Jn 16:8ff.; 17:9ff.; et al.

19 See *Udāna* V.5: "As, O *bhikkhus*, the great ocean has but one single taste, the salty taste, even so, O *bhikkhus*, the discipline of the teaching has but one single taste, the taste of liberation. That the discipline of the teaching, O *bhikkhus*, has a single taste, the taste of liberation, this is, O *bhikkhus*, the sixth marvelous and extraordinary thing of the discipline of the teaching." See the same metaphor in *CU* VI.13 for a different, but related, teaching. See also Jn 8:36; 1 Pet 2:16; Rom 8:21; et al. for the Christian side.

order to reach that state that Buddhism calls *nirvāṇa*[20] and Christianity *sōtēria.*[21] Religion is the dynamism toward a *terminus ad quem*, originating in a disconformity with the status quo.

Significantly enough, the canonical writings of both traditions do not seem inclined to limit the nature of these two terms. *Nirvāṇa* is simply the cessation of becoming,[22] of all *saṁsāra*,[23] of all links,[24] of every thirst.[25] It is the blowing out of all the *karma*,[26] the indescribable term of which not even "being" can be predicated,[27] the radical originating power of everything,[28] and the end with neither a way in nor out.[29] It is beyond all dialectic[30] and thinking,[31] without subject or object.[32] The whole effort lies in reaching it, not in describing or understanding it.[33] But this sentence is false, if it is taken to link *nirvāṇa* in any way with our will or imagination.[34] *Nirvāṇa* is "unborn, unbecome, unmade, unaggregated."[35] *Nirvāṇa* is not transcendent in the usual sense of the word; were it to transcend anything, it would already be transcendentally linked with what it transcends.[36] *Nirvāṇa* is the mere destruction, or rather the unmaking,[37] of all that is and that, by the very

[20] The word is not exclusively Buddhist, as is proved by *BG* II.72; VI.15; *MB* XIV.543, et al.; and confirmed by the discussions on the non-Buddhist meanings of the term in *Dīgha-nikāya* I.3; 19; etc.

[21] The word is, on the one hand, the Greek rendering of the Hebrew *yeshuah*, *yesha*, and *yoshuah*, and, on the other hand, the Christian reuse of the classical term *sōtēria*, which was often ambivalent, i.e., applied to Gods and men alike.

[22] See *Saṁyutta-nikāya* II.68.

[23] That is, "of all this-worldly elements," "of all creatureliness," one could venture to translate. See ibid., I.136.

[24] See ibid., I.210.

[25] See ibid., I.39.

[26] See the etymology of *nirvāṇa:* from the intransitive verb *nirvā*, to be extinct, consumed. The root *vā* means blow, *vāta* means wind (see *spiritus*, *pneuma*). *Nirvāṇa* is the extinction of all combustible (mortal, contingent, temporal) material.

[27] See *Kathavatthu* XIX.6.

[28] See *Itivuttaka* II.6 (or 43); *Udāna* VIII.3.

[29] See *Udāna* VIII.1.

[30] See Nāgārjuna, *Mūlamādhyamakakārikā* XXV.1ff.

[31] See Candrakīrti, *Prasannapadā* XXIV, *passim.*

[32] See the entire chapter 3 or *suññatavagga* of *Majjhima-nikāya.*

[33] See the famous parable of the man wounded by the arrow who dies, having wasted his time inquiring after such unnecessary details as who shot it and why, in *Majjhima-nikāya* I.426ff.; *Anguttara-nikāya* IV.67ff.

[34] See *Majjhima-nikāya* III.254, where concentration is defined as void, signless, and aimless.

[35] *Udāna* VIII.3. See also Candrakirti, *Prasannapada* XXV.3 (ed. La Vallee Poussin; tr. R. H. Robinson, p. 521): "*Nirvāṇa* is defined as unabandoned, unattained, unannihilated, noneternal, unextinguished, unarisen."

[36] This could be considered the quintessence of Nāgārjuna's insight.

[37] See the important concept of *asaṁskṛta*, the nonconstructed. The notion of *akata* (*akṛta*), the not-done, not-made, not-created, stands in contraposition to the *saṁskṛta*, the constructed, of the Indic tradition. See *Dhammapada* VII.8 (97).

fact that it can be undone, destroyed, and negated, proves its nonreality, so that *nirvāṇa* is the most positive "thing" because it destroys nothingness.

The same vagueness seems to mark the Christian scriptural idea of *sōtēria.* It is salvation from perdition,[38] from death,[39] through Christ,[40] who leads to salvation.[41] It seems to be eternal,[42] for it is the salvation of our lives.[43] Often the word "salvation" is used without any further qualification, apparently accepting its common meaning.[44] There is a way,[45] a word,[46] and a knowledge[47] of salvation. Jesus is the savior;[48] he saves the people from their sins,[49] and there is salvation in no one else.[50]

In other words, neither *nirvāṇa* nor *sōtēria* developed cosmological or metaphysical underpinnings. *Nirvāṇa*, or rather *pari nirvāṇa*, is the extinction of the human condition, and *sōtēria* the freeing from sin.

Śūnyatā *and* Plērōma

It would require a thick volume to present even cursorily the different interpretations of these central notions. As already indicated, we will alleviate the difficulty by choosing two significant examples and offering only the bare sketch of their doctrines. The two keywords are *śūnyatā*[51] and *plērōma*,[52] emptiness and fullness. Both are radical terms, and could both be said to represent most emphatically the quintessence of their respective traditions. Furthermore, as the prima facie meaning of the words themselves suggests, both terms seem to be at total variance, not only with one another but also with modern humanistic traditions.

---

[38] See Phil 1:28.

[39] See 2 Cor 7:10.

[40] See 1 Thess 5:9, et al.

[41] See Heb 11:10.

[42] See Heb 5:9.

[43] See 1 Pet 1:9–10.

[44] See Jn 4:22.

[45] See Acts 16:17.

[46] See Acts 13:26, et al.

[47] See Lk 1:77.

[48] See Lk 2:11 and the very name Jesus (*Yoshua*), which means "salvation."

[49] See Mt 1:21; Acts 5:31.

[50] See Acts 4:12.

[51] The root *śū* (*svid*) means "to swell." Betty Heimann repeatedly points out that *śūnya* and *śūna*, the void and the swollen (the excessive), both come from the same root *śun. Nirvāṇa* is also called *kṛtsham*, the whole, or *śukla*, the indiscriminate whiteness; see her *Facets of Indian Thoughts* (London: Allen & Unwin, 1964), 100, 110–11. The term *śūnya* (empty or void) exists already in ancient pre-Buddhist and non-Buddhist literature. See *AV* XIV.2.19; *SB* II.3.1.9; *TB* 11.1.2.12; and many *Upaniṣads*. An interesting compound is *śūnyāgāra*, the deserted, empty house (*JabU* VI), signifying the house where the *saṁnyāsīs* or Hindū monks were supposed to live (or a dwelling place of the God, a temple: *devagṛha*). See also *MaitU* VI.10.

[52] There is no need to stress that *plērōma*—i.e., that which fills (up)—is of pre-Christian origin and has its full meaning in Greek literature.

The end of the journey, the goal of Man, is by definition *nirvāṇa* or *sōtēria*, but the nature of this goal is supposed to be *śūnyatā* in the former case and *plērōma* in the latter, according to some schools in the respective traditions.

In complete harmony with the central Buddhist intuition of *nairātmyavāda*, or the doctrine of the ultimate unsubstantiality of all things, the concept of *śūnyatā* (vacuity, voidness, emptiness) tries to express the very essence of the absolute, the ultimate nature or reality of all things.[53]

Śūnyavāda is not philosophical nihilism or metaphysical agnosticism, but a positive and concrete affirmation, one of the deepest human intuitions regarding the ultimate structure of reality.[54] It says that everything, absolutely everything, that falls under the range of our experience—actual or possible—is void of that (superimposed and thus only falsely appearing) consistency with which we tend to embellish our contingency.

All, including the faculty of reason with which we express this very idea, is in the grip of a contingent flux. The "other shore" in the recurring Buddhist metaphor is so totally transcendent that it does not exist; the very thought of it mystifies and negates it.[55] "*Nirvāṇa* is *saṁsāra* and *saṁsāra* is *nirvāṇa*," says one well-known formulation,[56] repeated again and again in different forms.[57] There is no way to go to the other shore because there is no bridge, nor even another shore. This recognition is the highest wisdom, the *advaitic* or a-dualistic intuition, or the *prajñāpāramitā*. To recognize *saṁsāra* as *saṁsāra*, that is, as the flux of existence, and that same existence as being in flux, is already the beginning of enlightenment, not because one transcends it (for there is no "other place" behind or beyond) but because this very recognition sweeps away the veil of ignorance that consists precisely in taking as real or substantial that which is only pure void and vacuity.[58]

This is why only silence is the right attitude—not because the question has no answer, but because we realize the non-sense of the question itself, because there can be no questioning of the unquestionable (it would be a contradiction)

[53] See the beginning of Nāgārjuna's *Mulamadhyamikakārikā* I.1: "Neither out of themselves, nor out of something else, nor out of any cause, do existing things arise."

[54] See the expression *svabhāvaśūnyatā* (emptiness of [in] its own being) as one mode of emptiness described in the *Pañcavimsatiśahāsrikā* (one of the later *Prajñāpāramitā-sūtras*), or the expression *svabhāvaśūnya* as the quintessence of the *prajñāpāramitā*. See also the *dharmaśūnyatā* of Śantideva's *Sikṣāsamuccaya* XIV.242 and the *śūnyabhutaḥ* (void of being) of the *MaitU* VI.23.

[55] The simile of the other shore is recurrent in Buddhist literature. See *Anguttara-nikāya* II.24; IV.13; IV.160; *Itivuttaka* 69; *Saṁyutta-nikāya* IV.175; *Prajñāpāramitā-sūtra* IX; et al.

[56] See Nāgārjuna, *Mūlamādhyamakakārikā* XXV.19.

[57] Were there any difference between the two, this would be *saṃsāra* or *nirvāṇa* of some third thing, each of which is contradictory.

[58] See *Lalitavistara* XIII.175ff. *Majjhima-nikāya* I.297 stresses that the world is empty (in Pāli, *suñña*) of self and of what pertains to the self (*attā* and *attaniya*). See also *Saṁyutta-nikāya* IV.54 and 296, et al.

and there can be no answer when there is no question.[59] Who can question the unquestionable? Certainly not the unquestionable itself, and from this questionable world there can be no question about what cannot be questioned. Anything that can be questioned is certainly not unquestionable. Hence the "ontic silence" of the Buddha.

In complete harmony with the central Christian doctrine of *Incarnation*, the concept of *plērōma* (fullness, fulfillment) expresses the end of Man and of all creation.[60] Not only did the Redeemer come at the fullness of time,[61] but he let all those who believe in him be filled with his own fullness,[62] for of his fullness we have all received,[63] and in him the fullness of the Deity dwells bodily.[64] It is then the fullness of God[65] that fills everything, though there is a dis-tension, a period of expectation and hope until the restoration of all things.[66] Once the whole world is subjected unto him to whom all has been subjected, then he will subject himself fully to God, so that God will be all in all.[67]

Apart from the possible hermetic, Gnostic, and other uses of the word *plērōma*, the Christian tradition has understood this message as meaning our being called to be as perfect as the heavenly Father,[68] being one with Christ[69] as he is one with his Father,[70] and thus becoming not "like God," as the Tempter offered,[71] but God itself,[72] through our union with the Son by the work and grace of the Spirit.[73]

Theōsis, divinization, is the technical term that has been used for long centuries of Christian tradition; the simplest formula was to say that "God has become Man in order that Man might become God."[74] The entire Christian "economy" is the

---

[59] See *Saṁyutta-nikāya* III.189.

[60] See Eph 4:13, et al.

[61] God sent his Son at the fullness of "time" (*chronos*; Gal 4:4), but in the fullness of "[fitting] times" (*kairos*) will He gather all things in Christ (Eph 1:10).

[62] See Eph 1:23.

[63] See Jn 16.

[64] Col 2:9.

[65] See Eph 3:19.

[66] See Acts 3:21.

[67] See 1 Cor 15:28.

[68] See Mt 5:48.

[69] See Jn 15:lff.

[70] See Jn 6:56–57; 17:23; et al.

[71] See Gen 3:5.

[72] See Jn 1:12 (and, with qualifications, 10:34–35), et al.

[73] See Jn 14:17; 15:26; et al.

[74] See Clement of Alexandria, *Proptrepticus* I.9 (here using *theopoieīn*, which generally referred to the making of idols); Gregory of Nazianzus, *Oratio theologica* III.19 (PG 36:100); Athanasius: Αυτός γάρ ενηνθρώπησεν, ίνα ημείς θεοποιήσωμεν; "Ipse siquidem homo factus est, ut nos dii efficeremur" [For he was made Man, that we might be made God], *De Incarnatione Verbi* 54 (PG 25:192); *Oratio 4 contra Arrianos* VI (PG 26.476); Augustine, *Sermo* 128 (PL 39:1997); *Sermo de Nativitate* 3 and 11 (PL 38:99 and 1016); "Propter te factus est temporalis,

transformation of the cosmos until the new heaven and the new earth,[75] which includes the resurrection of the flesh.[76] Our destiny is to become God, to reach the other shore where the Divinity dwells, by means of a transformation that requires a new birth in order to enter the kingdom of heaven.[77] *Metanoia*, change of heart, of life, and ultimately a passage from death to new life, was the central topic of Christ's proclamation,[78] for which John the Baptist, the forerunner, had already prepared the way.[79]

We should try now to understand what these words symbolize within their respective traditions.

Without *śūnyatā*, the thought is bound.[80] The fact is neither that the bound one is released, nor the unbound one unreleased.[81] To realize the emptiness of all things is the culmination of all wisdom (*prajñā*), which leads to the discovery of the radical relativity of all things and their interdependence (*pratītyasamutpāda*), which gives rise to the accomplishment of *nirvāṇa*. In point of fact, there is more a sense of equality than of hierarchy among these four notions.[82] We are not describing four steps, either epistemological or ontological, but four ways of conveying one and the same realization: the realization that there is no-thing definitive in this world, and that any other possibility, even the thought of it, is still linked with our "this-worldly" experience, hence conditioned, dependent, not definitive—in a word, empty. Were it not for this emptiness, things could not move; change would be impossible, because material bodies could not move if there were no space between them. Emptiness is the very condition for the type of existence proper to things, and there is no-thing else, for any-thing else, anything that could be, would be affected by the same emptiness, for the very fact that we consider it possible, and thus an object of our thought.

There neither water nor earth,
neither fire nor air can subsist,
there the stars do not shine nor does the sun illumine,
there the moon does not brighten, nor darkness exist.[83]

---

ut tu fias aeternus," says Augustine in his lapidary style, *Epist. Io.* II.10 (PL 35:1994); "Quod est Christus, erimus christiani," repeats Cyprian, *De idolorum vanitate* XV (PL 4:582); et al.

[75] See Rev 21:1.

[76] See 1 Cor 15:12ff.

[77] See Jn 3:3ff.

[78] See Mt 4:17, et al.

[79] See Mt 3:2, et al.

[80] See Śāntideva, *Bodhicaryāvattāra* IX.49.

[81] See Candrakīrti, *Prasannapadā* XVI.8 (ed. La Vallée Poussin, p. 293).

[82] *Prajña, śūnyatā, pratītyasamutpāda, nirvāṇa.*

[83] *Udāna* I.10.

Without *plērōma* there would be no place for God, and human existence would make no sense. Man is more than Man; when he wants to be merely Man, he degenerates into a beast.[84] He is destined for higher things.[85] Whenever he is disquiet,[86] whenever he searches for something, it is because God is already calling him.[87] Divine transcendence is safeguarded because the Christian divinization is, properly speaking, more a "filiation" than an undiscriminated fusion with the Father. The Christian Trinity is here the warranty for the appropriate distinction without separation.

Man, and with him the entire universe, becomes one with the Son by the power and grace of the Spirit—as the Son as a person is one with the Father, but he never becomes the Father. Even more, orthodox Christian thinking will stress, in one way or another, that, while the Son is God of God, Light of Light, Man *becomes* one with the Son, and therefore reaches the Godhead in and through the Son. Man's temporality remains forever a scar, as it were, in the very heart of his being. Divinization—Christian tradition will stress—does not mean human alienation, precisely because we are of divine nature.[88] We are called upon to share God in a fuller way, to go home to our primordial nature and origin. Divinization reestablishes the image that had been distorted and makes us what we are really called upon to become. Divine sonship is the truly human vocation. What Christ is by nature[89] is what Christ as our brother[90] has enabled us to be and do by adoption (redemption): to share his sonship[91] in a new birth,[92] born again of water and the Spirit.[93]

---

[84] See the famous saying of Pascal, *Pensées*, 358: "L'homme n'est ni ange ni bête, et le malheur veut que qui veut faire l'ange fait la bête."

[85] See the oft-quoted passage, "Agnosce, O christiane, dignitatem tuam, et divinae consors factus naturae, noli in veterem vilitatem degeneri conversatione redire. Memento cuius capitis et cuius corporis sis membrum," Leo I, *Sermo* 21.3 (PL 54:192–93).

[86] See the famous Augustinian saying, "Inquietum est cor nostrum donec requiescat in te," *Confessions* I.1.1.

[87] See Maximus Confessor, *Ambigua*: "God has inserted in the human heart the desire of him" (PG 91:1312); or, accepting the idea that a purified *epithymia* (concupiscence) can become the burning desire of him, *Quaest. ad Thai.* (PG 90:269). See the Christian commentary on Jn 6:44: "Nemo te quaerere valet nisi qui prius invenerit" (Bernard of Clairvaux, *De diligendo Deo* VII.22 [PL 182:987]); also, "Consoletoi, tu ne me chercherais pas, si tu ne m'avais pas trouve" (Pascal, *Pensées*, 553).

[88] See 2 Pet 1:4, et al.

[89] See Rom 8:29, et al.

[90] See Heb 2:11, et al.

[91] See Gal 4:5, et al.

[92] See 1 Jn 2:29, et al.

[93] See Jn 3:5, et al.

Religions and the Humanizing of Man

It was a Greek who said that Man is the measure of all things.[94] But it was another Greek who refuted him[95] and furtherly affirmed that God, not Man, is the measure of all things;[96] so that his own disciple could say that Man, though mortal, should not be satisfied with mortal things, but strive to become immortal.[97] They all might have remembered one of their predecessors saying, "The idiosyncrasy of Man is his *daimon*."[98]

From a Hebrew source of inspiration it was written that God created Man in His own image and likeness,[99] and again from the same source the sentence was often reversed, and considered more a definition of God than a description of Adam: God in the image of Adam.[100]

It was a Jew influenced by Greek culture, and by what his faith regarded as a unique event, who wrote that the divine Word, the one dwelling with God, became flesh;[101] and a Roman who presented that same person as "the Man."[102]

It was a *kṣatriya* from the East who refused to speak about God, nor did he indulge in merely theoretical speculations.[103] This man was directly and exclusively concerned with the task of giving concrete and effective advice about the handling of the human predicament.[104] Reacting against the religious inflation of his time and against the deleterious human condition of his contemporaries, he centered all his life on showing how to get rid of the almost all-pervading human disquiet and anxiety, refusing even to undergird his teachings with any anthropology.[105] In this, he echoes the tradition of his own culture, which had so strongly emphasized:

---

[94] Πάντων χρημάτων μέτρον ἄνθρωπος (Protagora, *Frag.* 1).

[95] See Plato, *Cratylus*, 386a; *Theaetetus*, 152a.

[96] See Plato, *Laws* IV (716c).

[97] See Aristotle, *Nicomachean Ethics* X.7 (1177b.31).

[98] Literally: ἦθος ανθρώπω δαίμων—"The *ethos* to Man (is his) *daimōn*" (Heraclitus, *Frag.* 119).

[99] See Gen 1:26–27.

[100] This could be said to be the theological justification of all humanisms of a biblical origin.

[101] See Jn 1:14.

[102] See Jn 19:5.

[103] See the famous *avyakṛtavastuni*, or unutterable things, which the Buddha refused to answer to. See the *vaccaghotta Saṁyuttam* (*Saṁyuttam-nikāya* III.33), *avyakata Saṁyuttam* (*Saṁyuttam-nikāya* IV.44), *culamālunkya sutta* (*Majjhima-nikāya* 63), the *aggivacchagotta sutta* (*Majjhima-nikāya* 72), etc.

[104] See, for instance, Buddha's refusal to elaborate on the nature of *karma*, because the only thing that matters is getting rid of it. See *Anguttara-nikāya* II.80; *Dīgha-nikāya* III.138; *Saṁyuttam-nikāya* III.103.

[105] That the Buddha "has no theories" (*Majjhima-nikāya* 1.486) is a constant idea in the Buddhist canon, later converted by the *Madhyamika* into the central message of Buddhism.

The Man, indeed, is the All,
What has been and what is to be[106]

because the primordial Man is the supreme reality.[107] No wonder Buddhism was to flourish in the humanistic soil par excellence, the Confucian world, and in the Chinese culture at large.[108]

Following up the functional description of religion we have already given, we may add that religion is the way in which Man handles his human predicament in order to steer it toward a somewhat better situation. Today we are acutely aware of the urgency and difficulty of performing such a task. Here (the sketch of) these two great religious traditions may prove of some value. By this, we are saying that comparative religion, far from being merely a comparison of religions or a historical discipline, is in fact a study on ultimate human issues—that is, of religious situations—with the aid of more than one religious tradition, so that, by illuminating the concrete human predicament with the accumulated experience of humankind, we may be in a better position to understand it.

Buddhism, Christianity, and Humanism

In this light, we may now focus on the contemporary humanistic situation. For some decades "humanism" has been a powerful word.[109] It expresses a valuable myth that, in the traditionally Christian countries, can be understood as a reaction against a certain devaluation of the Human in favor of something supernatural.[110] The twentieth century has seen the birth of all possible humanisms: atheistic,

---

106 *RV* X.90.2.

107 See *SU* III.8 ff., et al.

108 This reference to the Chinese world implies that no complete and valid discourse on humanization can take place today without including what is perhaps the most humane of all cultures, whose ideal has always been the perfect Man. See a single example, which may well be considered representative of more than one tradition: "Therefore the Perfect Man makes his spirit and mind penetrate the limitless, and cannot be impeded by limits; pushes to the utmost the sight and hearing of eye and ear, and cannot be constrained by sound and forms—because he identifies with the self voidness of the myriad things. Thus, things cannot hinder his spirit-intelligence." Seng-Chao, *Emptiness of the Non-Absolute* (Chao-lun III; trans. R. H. Robinson).

109 No point in giving here a bibliography that would cover more pages than our entire chapter.

110 See the well-known *splendida vitia* by which Augustine meant the "virtues" of those who were not reborn in baptism; and again, "Bene currunt; sed in via non currunt. Quanto plus currunt, plus errant; quia a via recedunt," *Sermo* 141, c. 4, n. 4 (PL 38:777); or again, "Maius opus est ut ex impio justus fiat, quam creare caelum et terram," *In Ioh.* tr. 72, n. 3 (PL 35:1823), commented upon by Thomas, "Bonum gratiae unius maius est quam bonum naturae totius universi" (*Sum. theol.* I-II, q. 113, a. 9, c. et ad 2); and again, developed in his own way by Meister Eckhart in his *Serm. lat.* II.2 (*Lateinische Werke* IV.16, n. 10); et al.

scientific, new, classical, modern, medieval, social, and even hyperbolic. Isolated voices have also been raised in favor of Hindū and Buddhist humanisms. It is difficult to decipher what is not a humanism, except some exaggerated and obviously inhuman tendencies in several ideologies. We are weary of certain dehumanizing trends in established religions. Humanism may be a healthy reaction.

Currently, modern ideologies and so-called technocracies of every sort are also seen as dehumanizing forces. Not only are a transcendent heaven and an eternal hell now viewed as dehumanizing, but society, techniques, modern cities, and so forth are seen as deleterious to us as well. In this context, some challenge traditional religions to really serve in this task of humanizing Man. Here we may add some reflections from the Buddhist and Christian viewpoints.

To begin with, religions are very sensitive about being dictated to from the outside, or being told to serve anything, for they suppose themselves to be above any servitude. What matters is not "saving" the human predicament according to our individual opinions, they will say, but seeing the situation as it really is in the light of the religious tradition. Perhaps what is called the "humanizing of Man" is nothing else than his entanglement and damnation.

Avoiding these touchy attitudes, which come only from superficial approaches, we would like to approach the problem from the perspective of comparative religion, or philosophy of religion as we defined it above.

The roughly seven thousand years of historical memory show a common pattern, which can be found almost everywhere: the human desire for immortality. Overcoming death has always been a central religious and human concern. As to the means, religions differ. From the viewpoint of the history of religions, the thrust toward divinization could be interpreted as a means for rescuing the human beings from the clutches of death, as well as from the fear of Nature or the grip of the whole cosmos.

In almost every religious tradition, the fundamental trait of divinization is immortality. The human predicament is that mortal Man must overcome his situation, following the different ways offered by the most diverse religions. One way or another, traditional religions try to overcome the human condition by reaching the Unconditioned. Divinization could appear phenomenologically as the unconditioning of human condition. We reach the Divine (which can be variously interpreted) once we have overcome our mortal condition. Christianity would be a peculiar instance of this attitude. Its doctrine of Trinity lets it state a total divinization (union with the Son) without destroying the "God-Man" difference.

Buddhism shows a different attitude. It does not want to uncondition, but rather to decondition human beings; it is not concerned with the reaching of transcendence, but with the overcoming of immanence; it does not care as much about God as about deconditioning us in a radical and ultimate way. We have to cease being what we *are*, not in order to become another thing, not even God, but in order to negate totally the human and worldly condition. Buddhism shatters the human dream of any imaginable or thinkable survival.

Over against these two attitudes, present-day secularity could represent a new attitude that considers time, that is, the temporal universe, to be real and positive, therefore not to be transcended.[111] Secularity does not mean unconditioning or deconditioning the human predicament, but soberly recognizing it as it appears. There is no escaping it or denying it. The driving force behind any humanism is to make us really ourselves and nothing but ourselves; we, humanism would say, should banish any fear of worldly or superworldly powers. We have come of age; we need not fear being ourselves. But, having overcome our fear of nature, of God and the Gods, we now begin to fear ourselves and our social reality. So the whole problem crops up all over again. We might ask: What are we, that we have to be made ourselves? Who is this being who needs to be made, to become what he is not (yet)?

Homo Viator

An in-depth study of these three answers may perhaps furnish humanity with a more elaborate model than any of the one-sided solutions so far proposed.[112] This would be a task of comparative religion.[113]

We may observe a double assumption: (1) Man is an unachieved being; (2) this achievement is the real Man.

The first part is almost a matter of course. The human status quo is never definitive. There is always room for change, repentance, hope, enlightenment, salvation, betterment, and the like. The human predicament is infinite because it is not finite, not finished. Man is an open being; we "ek-sist" by stretching out our being, along time and space at least.

The second assumption is less obvious, and yet equally common to the three fundamental attitudes at issue. No human tradition, be it religious or secular, endorses our alienation. To convert us radically into an altogether different being would not only be heterodox and foreign to any tradition, but nonsensical too. Any difference has meaning only within and over against an underlying identity. An absolute change is a contradiction in terms, for nothing would remain of what is supposed to have changed.

---

[111] See the etymological hint: *saeculum* is certainly not the *kosmos*, but rather the *aiōn*, the life span (cf. the Sanskrit *ayus*), i.e., the temporal aspect of the world.

[112] We say "one-sided" because it cannot be denied that the traditional answers have not taken into account the whole of the human horizon; in our kairological moment, this is, however, imperative.

[113] Needless to say, we can only indicate in a general way how fundamental research on this problem could be started.

If Buddhism wants to annihilate us, to decondition our human condition, to extinguish in us all *saṃsāric* existence, all remnants of creatureliness, it is because it presupposes that Man *is* not, that there is no *ātman*, so that the blowing out (*nirvāṇa*) of all spatiotemporal and experiential structures is the "true realization of our authentic 'nature.'" The destruction of all our constructions is the real human liberation, and yet this does not conflict with the central orthodox Buddhist attitude of universal compassion (*karuṇā*),[114] unlimited friendliness. You can embody a serene, joyful, and even pragmatically effective loving attitude only if you have realized the *śūnyatā* of all things.

If Christianity wants to divinize us, to make us share the divine nature and return through Christ to the Father, it is because it presupposes that the divine nature is the ultimate and most intimate constitution of a human being.[115] We are an offspring of God[116] and have to go back to the Father to realize fully what we are.[117] Yet this does not conflict with the distinction between God and us, nor with the Christian emphasis on death and resurrection, new birth and total repentance. The risen Christ, like the risen Christian, is certainly a new creature[118] but not another one (*aliud, non alius*). The person is the same.[119] In Scholastic terms: *gratia non destruit, sed supponit et perficit naturam*.[120] God does not become God, yet Man becomes what Man is not yet.

Similarly, if Humanism wants to humanize us by making us recognize and accept our human condition, and to help us resist the temptation of escaping into realms of unreality, it is because it presupposes that the future of Man is Man, and that our true dignity consists in affirming our humanness in spite of every allurement from above and below. We have to face our future with daring and dignity, and, even when confronted with the absurd or the meaningless, we must accept and affirm ourselves.[121] This attitude does not contravene the humanistic dogma that

---

114 In point of fact, *karuṇā* and *śūnyatā* are the two pillars of *Mahāyāna*, and many texts link them to each other.

115 See the well-known "Tu autem eras interior intimo meo et superior summo meo" of Augustine (*Confessions* III.6.11). See also Thomas Aquinas, *Sum. theol.*, I, q. 8, a. 1; I, q. 105, a. 5; Calvin, *Institutiones christianae religionis* III.7: "Quod si nostri non sumus, sed Domini, ergo ne vel ratio nostra, vel voluntas in consiliis nostris factisque dominetur [. . .]. Nostri non sumus: ergo quoad licet obliviscamur nosmetipsos ac nostra omnia. Rursum, Dei sumus: illi ergo vivamus et moriamur" (*Opera Calvini*, ed. Brunsvigae, 1864, vol. 2, col. 505–6); not to mention the mystics.

116 See Acts 17:28.

117 See Jn 17:22–26, et al.

118 See 2 Cor 5:17; Gal 6:15; Eph 4:24; Col 3:10; et al.

119 Interestingly enough, the Buddhist intuition of *nairātmyavāda* tallies in an astounding way with the Christian doctrine of the *perichōrēsis* (*circumincessio*).

120 See Thomas Aquinas, *Sum. theol.*, I, q. 1, a. 8 ad 2; I, q. 2, a. 2 ad 1; although Aquinas does not literally quote this famous principle.

121 Any humanism entails an affirmation of Man that transcends the very "Man" who affirms it.

denies any substantial instance superior to us, for the secularized "future" plays many of the roles of the monotheistic God; but humanism also requires a proper belief in humanity, which is a belief in the unseen. Humanism demands of us as heroic a posture as any traditional religion.

Nevertheless, despite all structural similarities between these worldviews, we cannot overlook their differing anthropologies, that is, the different conceptions of Man and ultimately of the reality underlying them. Nothing is more barren and dangerous than superficial agreements and merely tactical compromises. The injunction to humanize Man, which practically everyone would admit, means various and opposite things according to the different worldviews and religious traditions. The real encounter comes when we cease to analyze structural patterns and concentrate on the nature of the purpose itself. What is humanizing? We can do no more here than ask the question.

The Crossing of the Ways

If the study of religion means anything today, it has to address this problem. A whole new *methodic* is required, since we can no longer pose the problem in the limited and particularized way we have done so far, cutting the world into cultural compartments. Even modern humanism is, by and large, as provincial and limited to its own peculiar conception of "Man" and Reality as many of the more traditional cultures it criticizes. Nobody can decide a priori what it means to humanize our being, nor can this totally depend on a single anthropology. It requires not a methodology but a *methodic* of its own, which makes its way in and through the mutual interaction and possible cross-fertilization of different religions and cultures. A *dialogical dialogue* is necessary here.

This dialogical dialogue, which differs from a dialectical one, stands on the assumption that nobody has access to the universal horizon of human experience, and that only by not postulating the rules of the encounter from a single side can we proceed toward a deeper and more universal understanding of ourselves, and thus come closer to our own realization. At this point, to try to humanize humanity according to some preconceived scheme, even if convincing for some, would amount to repeating the same mistake so many religious traditions have made, in the conviction that they possessed the truth or had the duty, and so the right, to proclaim their message of salvation. No one can be excluded from the task of humanizing us; no human tradition should be silent in this common task.

We may add a final thought: the distinction between eclecticism and syncretism. The former is an uncritical mixture of religious traditions and an agreement among them, obtained by chopping off all possible discrepancies in favor of an amorphous common denominator. Syncretism allows for a possible assimilation of elements by virtue of which these elements cease to be foreign bodies, so that an organic growth within each tradition is possible, and the mutual fecundation of religious traditions becomes a genuine option.[122]

Avoiding eclecticisms, but keeping in mind possible interactions—although we should not minimize the existing philosophical, theological, or religious tensions between the traditions under consideration—we may envision corrections, warnings, and complementarities that may not only allay mutual suspicions and so often one-sided positions but also help cultivate a real human growth, and thus contribute positively to a concrete humanization of human life on Earth.

Let me indicate a few points for a further study. The central Buddhist concern is a timely reminder, both to Christianity and to every sort of humanism, that no amount of "revelation" or "reason" justifies manipulating humans under the guise of "the will of God" or the "demands of Reason" in order to steer humanity and the world to clearly defined goals. The ultimate goal is always so ineffable that it does not even exist. Buddhism is the thorough defense of the ultimate, absolutely ungraspable, mystery of existence. The mystery here being immanent.

The central Christian concern is a timely reminder, to Buddhism and to all humanisms, that no amount of self-effort and goodwill suffices to handle the human predicament adequately; we must remain constantly open to unexpected and unforeseeable eruptions of Reality itself, which Christians would call God or divine Providence. Christianity stands for the unselfish and authentic defense of the primordial rights of Reality, of which we are not the masters. The mystery here being transcendent.

Humanism, furtherly, is a timely reminder, to Buddhism and Christianity, not only that traditional religions have often forgotten their own sayings—like the "non-authority" of the Buddha,[123] who may even become the greatest obstacle to realizing one's own Buddha nature,[124] or like the Sabbath made for us and not vice versa,[125] and the freedom of the children of God,[126] made free by truth itself[127]—but also that the humanizing of "Man" cannot lose sight of the concrete person to be humanized. Pointing out the Way or proclaiming the Message will never suffice,

[122] See R. Panikkar, "Some Notes on Syncretism and Eclecticism Related to the Growth of Human Consciousness," in *Religious Syncretism in Antiquity: Essays in Conversation with Geo. Widengren*, ed. Birger A. Pearson (Missoula, MT: Scholars Press, 1975), 47–60.

[123] A recurrent theme of the Buddha's teachings is that they do not have authority of their own, but only inasmuch as the hearer experiences them as conveying a real message of liberation. See the Buddhist tradition: "Those who fantasize about the Buddha, who is beyond fancies and imperishable, are all slain by fancy and do not see the *Tathāgata*" (Candrakīrti, *Prasannapadā* XXII.15 [ed. La Vallee Poussin, trans. R. H. Robinson, 448]).

[124] This goes to the extreme of, "Kill the Buddha if you happen to meet him!" *Taishō Tripitaka* 47:500b (*apud* K. Ch'en, *Buddhism in China* [Princeton, NJ: Princeton University Press, 1964], 358).

[125] See Mk 2:27.

[126] See Rom 8:21, et al.

[127] See Jn 8:32.

if the conditions are not given and worked for. Secularity is the awareness of our full responsibility upon coming of age. The mystery here is at the intersection between immanence and transcendence.

Even at the risk of possible misunderstandings (if my words were interpreted only in one key), I will try to express what can be considered a true humanization within the framework of these three major human traditions. Humanizing Man means to make "Man" truly human, but the expression is treacherous and ambivalent, because this gerund—*humanizing*—is neither merely transitive nor merely intransitive. It is not as if someone else were humanizing us, or as if we ourselves could achieve what we are not yet. Humanizing "Man" means rather this plunge into reality and participation in the overall destiny of all that is, which takes place inside and outside each of us. It is a process by which each becomes truly a person, sometimes abandoning the image we have of ourselves, dying, disappearing, transcending ourselves; other times affirming our being when it is threatened by alien forces, but in every case entering into a deeper *ontonomic* relationship with Reality—whatever this may be or not be.

It means touching not only the shore of gentleness, power, and wisdom, but also the depths of despair, nothingness, and death. It means to be all that we are uniquely capable of; it cannot be compared to anything else. Each person is a unique knot in the universal net. It means to reach the heights of the Godhead, if this is the model we have of ourselves, provided that such a calling is not merely a wishful projection of lower unfulfilled desires. It means, for us, to touch the shore of nothingness, provided that we do not rest in that nonexisting place. It means to develop all the human potentialities, provided that these are not artificially concocted dreams. It means, finally, to know and accept the human predicament and, at the same time, to recognize that this very human predicament carries with it the constant overcoming of all that human beings are now.[128]

In this sense, today, the sincere and totally (because disinterestedly) committed *studium* of religion, with all its attendant risks, uncertainties, and joys, is perhaps one of the most authentic religious acts—at least for some of us.

---

[128] See Sermon 1 in Carl Jung's *The Seven Sermons to the Dead*, printed privately in 1916 and published as an Appendix to his autobiography *Erinnerungen, Träume, Gedanken*, ed. A. Jaffe (Olten-Freiburg: Walter, 1972), 389ff. Some excerpts: "Das Nichts oder die Fülle nennen wir das *Plērōma* [where the Greek Christian terminological bias is apparent]. Dort drin hört denken und sein auf, denn das ewige und unendliche hat keine eigenschaften" [*sic* with capitals].

13

Advaita and *Bhakti*

A Hindū-Christian Dialogue

priyo hi jñānino 'tyartham aham,
sa ca mama priyaḥ

I am much loved by the sage
and he is loved by me.

—*BG VII.17*

Introduction

A dialogue between Hinduism and Christianity very often gets stuck and cannot proceed further, with the consequent sense of frustration, because of fundamental misunderstandings based sometimes on mutual prejudices or lack of proper knowledge.* To mention only a few points: Hinduism is supposed neither to believe in a personal God nor to consider charity the first of religious duties. The concept of Person, which seems essential and indispensable for any exposition of Christian faith, is apparently unknown to the Hindū mind, and so on. From the other side, the more "realized" Hindū who mostly professes *advaita*[1] considers Christianity an inferior religion because it takes God to be essentially the "other," allowing no union or identification with Him. For the *advaitin* the

---

* Original text: "*Advaita e Bhakti:* Lettera da Vrindabran," *Humanitas* 10 (Brescia, 1965), 991–1001; then it appeared in *Myth, Faith, and Hermeneutics: Cross-Cultural Studies* (New York: Paulist, 1979), chapter 9.

[1] Advaita Vedānta, based mainly on Śaṇkarācārya's interpretation of the Upaniṣads and the Brahma Sutras, is one of the Hindū philosophical schools that predominate in many spiritual circles today. It understands itself as the culmination of all religions and philosophies insofar as it leads to and interprets the "ultimate experience" of a-duality, i.e., the essential nonseparability of the Self (*ātman*) and "God" (*Brahman*). Among the three classical "ways" of salvation in Hinduism—*karma* (works), *bhakti* (adoration and surrender), and *jñāna* (meditative knowledge)—this school represents the last. In fact, "realization" or "liberation" is said to be reached only by an intuitive consciousness. *Advaita* (as differentiated from Advaita Vedānta) would be the fundamental principle of a-dualism (*a-dvaita:* a-duality), devoid of its connections with the rest of the Vedantic philosophical garb.

concept of person would seem secondary, and so applying it to the Absolute is tantamount to idolatry.

These problems are certainly more than semantic—although fundamental terminological clarifications are urgently needed before a real dialogue can take place. The following letter hopes simply to show some implications of such a dialogue, which I have called an "intrareligious dialogue," as distinguished from an interreligious one. "Dialogue" is not just an external meeting with somebody who has other ideas than I have. Dialogue in the real sense arises precisely where I (or we) discover the same currents and problems within the religion of the "other" as I (or we) find in my (or our) own religious world. In this chapter I do not intend to talk about the Hindū's opinions or the Christian's ideas, but rather to enter straight into the problem at hand: love and identity, certainly one of the major issues in a Hindū-Christian dialogue. In this way, we can help each other face our own, sometimes hidden problems from a new perspective. For example, the authentic a-dualistic experience of the *advaitin* represents a challenge to the Christian's doctrine or experience of the Trinity and may very well lead us to discover important new aspects of the same mystery.[2]

In this case I have chosen the opposite example, namely the challenge that the notion that God is Love, with all its implications, represents to an *advaitin* who claims to be beyond all dualisms and therefore—since love seems to presuppose duality—also beyond love. This problem is primarily an internal matter for Hinduism, which in its main devotional trends is a religion of love (*bhakti*), and in its more contemplative and philosophical aspects a religion of knowledge (*jñāna*) (the latter claiming superiority over the former).

A Letter from Vṛāndāvan

In a long conversation in Vṛāndāvan, the birth place of Kṛṣṇa[3] and the town "consecrated" to *bhakti*, I had a heart-to-heart dialogue with a fellow pilgrim in which we examined the question of whether *bhakti* was justified in an *advaitin*. The following are some of the ideas suggested by our discussion.

Advaita

The common answer to the problem, which we quickly dealt with and dismissed, is that *bhakti* is only a first step to *jñāna*: until the ultimate intuition dawns, one can do no better than follow the path of devotion. This is a typical

---

[2] See R. Panikkar, *The Trinity and the Religious Experience of Man* (London: Darton, Longman & Todd; Maryknoll, NY: Orbis Books, 1973).

[3] Kṛṣṇa, the divine shepherd, is one of the main earthly manifestations of God (Viṣṇu). He is especially worshiped in Vrindaban (Vṛāndāvan), where he is said to have performed his play of love with Men.

advaitic answer; *bhakti* is no more than a preparation for *jñāna*, to be given up as soon as the latter is attained.

A second, equally traditional answer is that the true *jñānin*[4] does not believe in *bhakti* for himself, but fulfills its requirements for others, as Śaṇkara is said to have performed the funeral rites for his mother, or as the priest functions at ceremonies that are for the people. But this is not quite satisfactory, particularly for that type of *advaita* who does not wish to ignore the radical claim of love. Is there a place then for love in a true *advaitin*'s heart?

Here my partner in the dialogue told me of a *sādhu*[5] who had come to Vṛāndāvan because he had realized that the very structure of the only One is love, and that it is charged with a dynamic life; that love is indeed only another name for the experience of the Absolute. It is known that the *advaitic* experience is one of the void, but can it not also take the form of love? The same *sādhu* explained that he had given everything away, and told how overwhelmed he was with love and joy—so much so that once, when bathing in the Yamuna, he was even tempted to put an end to his life, letting it go, as it were, in the current of the river. Afterward he did not know why he had not done so; he felt it was because he was not ready for it, not mature enough. The contrast was obvious: while the *advaitin* has by his very experience overcome time and also death, the *bhakta* wants to throw his life away as an act of complete surrender.

A third point suggested itself here. If love is not to be an empty word, it implies a certain tension between the lover and the beloved, or at least a certain distance between them. In fact, *bhakti* etymologically means either separation (from *bhañj*) or dependence (from *bhaj*). But there is yet more for us to consider.

The apperception of Being as crystallized love seems to lead to the experience of its structure as universal love, an outpouring of love without regard for the objects on which it is lavished: in other words, an all-embracing love for everything that has even a spark of Being in it. But is love only an inherent harmony, or is there not in it still another element? Can it exist without a certain affective dynamism? Does it not demand a special I-you relationship in which the particular *you* cannot be exchanged for any other? And is there really room for such particularized and personal love in *advaita*?

It seems that the genuine experience of human love is not satisfied with involvement with the other as other in a general sense—in which the other is ultimately reduced to the self—but that it needs the other as a *particular* other, personal and unrepeatable. Every real love is unique: where then is the place for universality? Can *advaita* admit the particular? Has the love of a mother for her child, for instance, or that of a Man for his beloved, an

---

[4] *Jñānin* is a follower of the path of knowledge (*jñāna*).

[5] Hindū monk.

ultimate value? Can an *advaitin* feel such love? Will friendship find a place in heaven—that is, in God?

An *advaitin* can love everything: his affection, unconditioned by *nāma-rūpa* (name and form),[6] can embrace everything; for everything, insofar as it is, is the Self, and thus lovable. But is this love *real*? Can we apply the term "love" to something that makes an abstraction of all that I have, and that in a way eliminates my person—so that my ego possesses nothing that can attract the lover, be given as a gift, or earn the devotion of the beloved? What lover or beloved would be satisfied with a love without eyes and face? Or are these merely anthropomorphic images with no ultimate significance?

The classic *advaitic* answer is well known: one does not love someone—say friend, wife, or husband—for his or her own sake but for the sake of *ātman*.[7] Love is all there is; no lover or beloved—all distinction between them is blotted out. I feel that there is in this a deep truth, insofar as it answers the need to overcome dualism, but I am convinced that it is not the deepest truth of *advaita*, but rather a pitfall inherent in pure monism. I think that *advaita* would oppose such pure monism as it opposes all dualism. In what follows I shall try to remain faithful to an intuition of *advaita* that transcends these extremes of monism and dualism.

My doubts, however, were not resolved by any of these traditional answers, leading me to attempt a solution that is perhaps not fully in accord with the atmosphere of Vṛāndāvan's holy gardens. And yet it is closer to genuine *bhakti* than the words of Yudhiṣṭhira, who in the *Mahābhārata* is the very king of Dharma: "There can be no liberation for the Man who knows the bond of love [*snehena yukta*]."

And so we came to a fourth point, which alone, like the fourth quarter of *brahman*,[8] allows a full vision of the ultimate—and the ultimate mystery is what we are touching upon here.

If the structure of the ultimate is love, then it is loving Love or love of love, self-love; in other words, it is like an "eye" that sees itself, a "will" that loves itself, a "being" that pours itself out as "Being," a "source" that reproduces itself fully as an identical image, and that later emerges into Being as that which receives the source. The "image" is the Being. The source of Being, because it is the source, is not Being—but precisely its source. Furthermore, if this dynamism and tension are not to jeopardize the Absolute's total Oneness, the "mirrored" eye, the generated Being, the identical image does not stop the lavish flow of divine love but returns it again, loving with the same love, answering in the same measure, so that seen

---

6 *Nāma-rūpa* stands for the limitation of the relative existence. For *advaita*, the Ultimate is beyond any name and form, but for *bhakti*, both are manifestations of the Divine (especially as the name of God and His image).

7 See *BU* II.4.5.

8 According to *MandU* (esp. 3–7), there are four states in the Absolute, symbolized by the waking, dreaming, and the deep sleep state (these three being conditioned), whereas the fourth (*turīya*) is beyond any conditioning.

from the "outside," it looks as if nothing had happened in the "inner life" of the Absolute. Only one who shares in this dynamism can witness the unceasing flow of divine Life: a Love that gives itself up fully and is rescued, as it were, by the total answer of the beloved, returning the love of the Beloved by responding with love.

Now an *advaitin* is one who has realized the absolute a-duality of Being, Reality, the Ultimate, the Absolute, whatever the name we choose to indicate the Ineffable. There is no place for dualism, but there is none for monism either. Dualism cannot be ultimate, because where there are two, there is a relation between them that stands above and is more final than both. Monism cannot be ultimate either because it denies the problem's very assumption; in a pure monism there is no room even for factors like illusion, falsehood, time, a lower level of truth, and speech.[9] Here I am not concerned with expounding *advaita* but only with finding out whether it has a place for love.

Advaita *and Love*

Let me put it in this way: an *advaitin* is established in the supreme and unique I (*aham-brahman*). Yet this I, by the very fact of being the I, implies, brings forth a You as its necessary counterpart (*alter, non alius*, the partner—of the I—not another). In simpler terms, the I must somehow be reflected in a You, although this Thou is only the production of the I itself and not an external "other." In this You the I discovers itself, and really is (it, i.e., I). In other words: the You is the consciousness that the I not only has but is. In fact, this I knows himself, but his Knowledge is none other than the Knower. However, the Knowledge has come to be because the Knower has come out of himself, as it were, has "loved" that which by loving he knows to be his (own) knowledge, himself as known by himself. He could not know even himself were he not driven out, or did he not "despoil" himself, only to recover himself immediately in the "subject" (person), in which he has fully invested himself. This total gift of himself is Love. Now we are better equipped to deepen our problematic.

The *advaitin* installed in that I—in the Absolute, who we may say knows and loves Himself—recognizes and loves the sparks of being (which float out of nothing) for what they "are": "parts" or "objects" (though this is an improper use of the words) of that divine Knowledge and Love. He knows and loves "things" as (to use theistic terms) God knows and loves them, in that unique act by which He knows and loves Himself and in which He associates all that we call beings on earth, whatever nature they may possess. The *advaitin* not only sees everything in the One, he has an intuition of everything as a-dual, thus as not forming any kind of second vis-à-vis the only and unique One: *ekam eva advitīyam*, "one only

[9] See the *pāramārthika* (absolute reality) and *vyāvahārika* (world reality).

without a second"[10] because no *dvanda*, no pair, no duality can be ultimate. He loves everything in the same way as the unique and universal Love. In extension and degree, the true *advaitin* loves as does the Absolute.

Now a thing, whatever it may be, is insofar as it is known and loved by the absolute Knowledge and Love. As already said, things are nothing if not crystallizations of divine Love. A thing not only is insofar as it is loved; it is that very love. In itself it is nothing. If a thing were not sheer nothingness it could not be the pure "recipient" of that unique loving act of the Absolute I. Now, because this divine act constitutes that very thing, the integral thing—that is, the thing including its origin—is the whole I, the total and indivisible Love. Seen with respect to itself alone, that is, as the "thing" in "itself," it is a limited image of a boundless love, just as the whole sun is reflected, although not completely, in each piece of a broken mirror.

Now if this were to be expressed in theistic terms, it would be meaningless to say that God loves one thing more than another, not only because the "more" makes no sense with reference to God, but also because it is equally senseless with respect to the "things" themselves. If God loved a thing a little *more* than He actually does, that "thing"—as the crystallization of divine love—would cease to be what it is and instead be another "thing," the other thing with that *plus*.

Let us now consider the concrete question of the place of common human love in the heart of an *advaitin*. First of all, whimsical affection due to psychological or aesthetic causes must be eliminated; only that which has an ultimate ontological justification is admissible. In other words, we must either link human love with the very center of the Absolute, or admit that *bhakti* is not on the same footing as *jñāna*.

I love my mother, friend, wife, or son with a love that is not interchangeable. I do not love my beloved just because she is "mother" or "friend," but because it is *her*. No other mother would do: only *the* beloved can quench the thirst of the lover; there can be no substitute. Love does not admit indifference. Everything in the beloved is different and unique. Further, I do not love my mother or friend because it is my "mother" or "friend," but because of *her-self*, because of the *Self* that is in *her*. The *Upaniṣad* is right: it is for the sake of the *ātman*, the Self, but this *ātman* is neither her soul nor mine, nor different from us both.

Now the difficulty lies here. In the love of *advaitin* the problem does not even arise: he loves the other as other, the *you* as that particular you, experienced like an ultimate, with the consequent danger of idolatry. That is why in a dualistic context there is a certain antagonism between the love of God and the love of a creature, and dualistic religion stresses the necessity of loving the creature for God's sake. *Advaitic* love is incompatible with this dichotomy. If I love my beloved I cannot love him or her because of himself or herself, nor because of God. I must love her

---

[10] See *CU* VI.2.1.

with the identical love with which I love the Ultimate; to be more precise, that same current of Love that sweeps me into the love of the Absolute makes me love my beloved as that spark of the Absolute that she truly is. Even more: putting it in theistic terms, the love of the *advaitin* for his beloved is indeed the Love of God for both the beloved and the lover.

Person in the context of *advaita* is nothing but the concrete descent—or revelation—of (divine) love. The uniqueness of every person is based in this ever-different, and so unique, love relation. *Advaitic* love does not love the individual, but the personal, not the "property" of the beloved, but the divine gift bestowed upon her: that which the beloved does not possess, but is.

Advaitic *Love*

Let me try to describe this love. I love you, my beloved, without any "why" beyond or any "because" behind my love; I love you, simply, for in you I discover the Absolute—though not as an object, of course, but as the very subject loving in me. I love you with an inclusive and unique love, which is the current of universal love that passes through you, as it were, for in my love of you, universal love is kindled and finds its expression. I love you as you *are*—that is, insofar as you really are—the Absolute. I do not love you because of myself. This is important: any egoistic love is incompatible with *advaita*; any kind of concupiscence, be it desire of pleasure, fulfillment, self-assurance, comfort, or the like, is excluded. To love you for my own sake would amount to the worst kind of idolatry: egolatry. Any love that aims at enriching me, at complementing me, which, in a word, aims *at* me, may perhaps be a human and even a good love but it is in no sense *advaitic* love. The latter is neither for God's sake, as a foreign motivation for my love, nor—much less—for the *ego*'s sake.

The only love consistent with *advaita* is God's love—in both senses of the expression all in one: "my" love for Him and "His" love in me—passing through the creature I love. It is a passionate and true love that is sensitive to the finest, smallest details of true human love, yet it is passive because it is not ego-centered. From the outside it may even appear almost fatalistic. Every lover is taken up, wrapped in his love, overpowered by love. There is love in me and it happens to be directed to this particular person. It is a love that does not kindle in me my love for the Absolute, because it is that love itself that is not different from the Absolute. It is a personal and direct love that passes through me to the beloved, in a way, *making* the beloved *to be.* It is a creative love, because—in theistic terms—it is the very love of God toward a person that makes that person *to be*. An *advaitin* can love only if the Absolute loves; his love cannot be different.

This description may become a little more complete if we express this love in ontological terms. I love my beloved because my person is installed in the only I, and this I is Love and loves my beloved. In this sense, I "share" in the love of God for that person. God loves that person personally, that is, as she is, and so do I. She finds in my love the love of God, she "feels" somehow that through this love of mine she is loved. And now we can perhaps solve the difficulty we mentioned at the beginning: if this is so, and God loves every being, that personal touch inherent in every human love is fully preserved, because though the lover is an "associate" in God's universal love, he "shares" the constitutive relation of God's love to his beloved; or, in other words, there is an ontological neighborhood between the lover and the beloved. They are like two moments, or two poles in the infinite love of God. I love my beloved because I am that love of God that makes my beloved *to be*. There cannot be a more personal love.

No doubt I have been employing terms that can easily be construed as dualistic. I have spoken of the lover and the beloved as two people here on earth, and I have taken as example the love between a man and a woman. Yet I have also emphasized that these two subjects cannot be considered as if they were ultimate realities, two poles facing one another. The problem, then, is this: can I as I am, a human person, love you as you are, another person, or shall I have to give up this notion of personal relationship and simply try to develop a universal and indiscriminate love, because any kind of self-assertiveness is incompatible with *advaita*? Precisely here the purifying character of this highest type of love appears more clearly.

Advaitic love must be divine and cosmic, full of "personality" but devoid of individuality, selfishness, caprice, and concupiscence. It is the deepest and strongest love and also the most human because it reaches the core of the human being, its personality, its ontic relationship with God and with another being like itself. It is not a love of an individual's qualities, but of the heart of a person, love of the integral person: body, soul, and spirit. It is loving you really as you, a love that both discovers and effects the identity of lover and beloved. Real human love does not consist in gazing at one another but in looking in the same direction, in worshiping together in a unitive adoration. It is not authentic and ultimate unless it is a sacrament—a real symbol of the divine identity discovered in two pilgrim sparks fusing themselves in order to reach the single divine Fire.

At this point, we cannot proceed further without solving one of *advaita*'s main problems: the status of the person. It may well be that the concept of person needs revising and perhaps deepening, but we must resist attempting even an outline of this here. I wish to mention only one point relevant to our topic, namely, the implication of the Trinity. If God, the Father, is the ultimate I who calls—generates—the Son as His You, manifesting and reflecting Him, then the Spirit is not only the personified Love of the Father and the reciprocal self-gift of the Son, but the a-duality (*advaita*) of the Father and Son. In other words, *advaita* applied to the Trinity would mean that there are not three distinct beings (as if this would ever be possible ultimately!) but that the only I loves himself and discovers his own a-duality (which is the Spirit) in the (him)self that is the You (the Son). The

Trinity, on the other hand, applied to *advaita*, would show that a-dualism can have room for Love, understood precisely as the inner movement of this "One without a second" (*ekam eva advitīyam*).

The essence of the person is relationship; my person is nothing but a relation with the I. Properly speaking, the place of my personality is within the single You of the unique I. But my person is also related to others; it touches, so to speak, the shores of the reality of other people. My person is also related to my beloved whom I call *you*, and this I-you relationship makes us emerge from nothingness by the power of the life-giving Spirit who is Love. Thus we enter more and more into the You of ultimate I who is not different from God Himself. This is the ultimate level of human love and likewise the very condition of its possibility: when the Spirit responds through us to God. Here the personality reaches maturity, which is pure transparency.

Perhaps the last words of the book of Revelation may help express the same idea: "The Spirit and the Bride say, Come!"[11]—the Bride assuming and symbolizing the Universal transformed into and transparent to Love, which is precisely the Spirit. "Come" is the call to the Ultimate through Love, to *advaita* through *bhakti*, *Tat tvam asi*.[12] A *You* you are, Śvetaketu![13] We are insofar as we are the *You*, the *tvam* of the One.

---

[11] Rev 22:17.

[12] *CU* VI.8.7 ff.

[13] See R. Panikkar, *The Vedic Experience* (Berkeley: University of California Press, 1977), 747–53.

14

Bhakti–Karuṇā–Agapē

An Intercultural Challenge

Usually, introductions make things easier for the speaker.[1] Usually, introductions make things easier to the speaker. This time, however, he finds this to be quite difficult, because he has raised such high expectations that now you will have to accept to be just in front of a simple man, sharing with you his doubts, his anxieties, his love. My task was not to read a paper but to deliver a lecture. This means that I have been preparing myself, rather than preparing what to say. A paper is an organized system of words conveying some kind of meanings. A lecture, I think, has to "betray" the speaker, and I say "betray" because, in spite of all the screens he may have put up, he has to come out of his silence, fear, arrogance, ambition, or vanity.

I begin by stressing that what I would like to say—will remain unsaid. It will all depend on you, on your sympathy (*karuṇā*), whether I am going to succeed in conveying the issue in the title. I would like to stick to the intercultural challenge, in connection with a Buddhist-Chinese saying that, roughly translated, reads, "They are not words that allow man to understand." Before being able to understand the words, we must become "Men." In the old classical languages this word is not sexist: "Man" stands for the human being as such, and I like better to say "Man" rather than "human being." Most classical languages have not fallen into the process of defining all things and putting each of them in one compartment or another. When I want to enucleate my theological beliefs a little, I always say that, if you want to kill Christianity, make a "religion of the Book" of it. Christianity is an original Word, not a book. The word is a word when it is spoken by somebody to someone, saying something.

Now, to talk about love is as difficult and contradictory as it would be to talk about silence. Silence does not speak, but it lets the word emerge; as a saying teaches, "If your words are not more valuable than silence, shut up." Love does not speak either, but it spurs the words to appear. Words have a meaning only in relationship to something else. If I merely say, "I love you," that means nothing. If my heart overflows, and I look into your eyes, and you feel that there is something there,

---

[1] Original text *Bhakti–Karuṇā–Agapē: An Intercultural Challenge*, in M. Zlomislic, D. Goicoechea, S. K. Tebbutt, R. Kaushik, eds., *Bhakti–Karuṇā–Agapē with Raimon Panikkar* (New York: Global Academic Publishing, 2003), 39–53.

"I love you" is an original phrase that has never been said before. So, I ask you to have this kind of new innocence, to try to reenact, to understand the topic of this lecture. The real word, as I said, comes out of silence, and shoots with love, when it is a real word and not just a sign; otherwise, it is only information.

My topic will deal with the cross-cultural or intercultural challenge among three rich notions, crystallized in the three words—*bhakti*, *karuṇā*, *agapē*—that are in the title.

The three words are irreducible to one another; they are in a certain way incomparable. There is the temptation, into which I also do fall sometimes, to use "love" as a synonym for the three of them. But, by so doing, we impoverish human experience. That, in fact, reduces the three universes that breathe through these three words to one single notion. One needs two eyes to have a bifocal perception of the physical things. One needs three eyes to be in real contact with reality. The "third eye" is not just an invention of the Lamas of Tibet. The third eye, as some of you will know, was a most normal thing for the Victorines in the twelfth century, who spoke of the third eye without which reality is flat, monochrome, and lifeless.

In order to preserve these manifold dimensions, I developed the notion of "homeomorphic equivalence," which is a kind of third-order analogy. In this case, *agapē*, *bhakti*, and *karuṇā* are homeomorphically equivalent. They are not the same thing, as to their meaning and strength. On the other hand, to list "*karuṇā*, *bhakti*, *agapē*" is not like saying, "elephant, psyche, post office." They have something in common, but they are not the same thing, nor a "similar" thing like in a third-degree analogy. In their respective universes they play a role that is equivalent.

A simple example, before I get to my topic, is about Brahman and God. When you read the word "Brahman," do you translate it as "God"? That would be a very bad, faulty translation. On the other hand, you could not translate "Brahman" as "a piece of paper," or "God" as "a commander." Anyway, they are not the same. Brahman is neuter; God is masculine. God cares about the world; Brahman couldn't care less. The former is a creator; the latter doesn't need to create. So, they are not similar. They don't even perform the same function. They perform an equivalent function within the respective universes, each of which is felt to be unified by its own kind of worship, or whatever you will like to call it. *Agapē*, *bhakti*, *karuṇā* are homeomorphic equivalents. They are not simply three different aspects of one and the same thing.

Philosophically, we can talk about an underlying Platonism in the West. We can define the modern mind as "crypto-Kantian." Crypto-Kantianism conceives the "thing in itself" as being there, and at the same time it thinks of it as merely nominal. We say one thing, and another: I think the very thing is here, then I displace it and I say that it does not exist in itself. If you simply believe that all the paths lead to the mountain, then the mountain will collapse. The way you go is part of the reality and not just an abstract side of it. If you call it *karuṇā*, you say you mean love. Then you call it *bhakti*, and I say, "I know what you mean." No, a third eye is needed in order to respect things and allow them to be what they are.

These are not three different notions, but three different symbols belonging to three different universes. That is very hard to reenact now, since for four or five centuries the dominant world civilization has been a crypto-Kantianist one. That makes us believe that from one single standpoint we can embrace the whole, wide range of human spiritualities. That is frivolous, to say the least, and, phenomenologically speaking, it introduces a politically heavy word: colonialism.

Colonialism is not a bad thing. The colonialist peoples were highly respectable; they had the best intentions and the best—everything. Colonialism is a belief in monoculturalism, that is, that with one single culture we can do everything. And symbols have a greater "sticking power" than just concepts. If I say, "One king, one empire, one God," that sounds outdated. Now we say, "One world government, one World Bank, one world market, one United Nations organization," and we fall into the same trap. I am not promoting anarchy. It would rather mean more freedom and respect for the uniqueness of every single being. If the single being is unique, then it is incomparable. If it is incomparable, its very uniqueness is its own value.

In sum, there are three different universes. *Agapē* is mainly a monotheistic understanding—*mainly*. It basically is the experience that God loves us. The initiative comes from the Divine. You have the feeling that you are being loved, and that you are capable to react, to re-create that love, to hug the spiritual Bride. God loves you. He takes the initiative for you. You allow yourself to be loved. And by this allowance, you are purified. Then you respond in the most passionate ways to His love, which may have, or not, human figures and incarnations, but which leads the individual with affection. God loves us first, then we can understand how to "love your God with all your heart and all your soul and all your strength," without examining now what heart, soul, and strength mean. Without this monotheistic idea, be it explicit or implicit, *agapē* is not completely understandable.

Bhakti belongs to a different universe. To use Western words, we can say that we love God as parts of Him, since we are His sparks. We are sparks of the divine play, and we take part in it as partners. We don't need to say who loves first. You enter into the loving dance. You belong to one of the movements of Naṭarāja, and you respond accordingly. We love Him because He loves us, and the two are on the same level. The ignorant say that love and God are different, not knowing that they are the same. When they know that love and God are the same, they rush to God as love.

Karuṇā is a more cosmic attitude. It implies a universal sympathy. It is not individualizable and not personifiable either. *Karuṇā* is—let me translate it this way—the revelation of the loveliness of everything: it is up to you to discover the radiant, hidden plans that, perhaps because you are in a hurry or selfish or full of desire, you were not able to detect, to discover, therefore failing to fall in sympathy with everything.

Tempted as I am to make a more detailed analysis, and use a lot of Greek and Sanskrit words, and give a whole list and make classifications that would not classify everything, I will rather introduce us into the mystery conveyed by these three holy and sacred words. So I will avoid the temptation of more analysis, and instead go further in the general presentation of love as a formal concept embracing the main experiences behind the riches of these three religions, three universes within which you have to make all the required distinctions. *Bhakti* is not *prema*, *philia* is not *agapē*, etc. Within each universe there are a number of distinctions. The *bhakti* of one tradition in India is not the *bhakti* of another. I will use the word "love" in a formal way, which tries more or less to stand for the triple, threefold, and almost infinite division that our ancestors made when using these words.

We find a certain general aspect that I would like to underline when I speak of intercultural cross-fertilization, which is not multiculturalism. "Multiculturalism" is a word that is officially used in Canada. But, with all due respect, I would like to challenge this notion. Quebec is proud to be a multicultural society. Well, I don't think a society can be multicultural. "I am multicultural and you have only one single culture, you poor fellow. What can you ever know? I have the control over everything. We, the multicultural people, are above all anticultural people. We are multicultural because we soar above everything. We have made of this multiculture another culture that is perhaps even more empirical and more dangerous than all the other little ones that are satisfied only with their uniculture."

What we have today, however, is interculturality, meaning that no culture today stands alone. "No man is an island." We cannot be satisfied with the joy of a splendid isolation, with a wretched solitude. We need a cross-cultural fertilization. We need to learn from one another. We have to be open to the lessons of the others. It may well be that another culture cannot teach us anything. But it is imperative for us to learn from the other one. The burden is on the learning person, and the responsibility does not fall on the teacher. It is the disciple that makes the guru, and not the guru who chooses the disciple.

Interculturality means and lives through this cross-fertilization among cultures, which is imperative in hard times. But let me say that, in my opinion, there are still a lot of cultural condoms that prevent this mutual fecundation. And they can be summed up in the following attitude: "Well, I am better than you. I have a bigger part in truth than you. I am quite more developed." It is a sign of Western hubris in the political world today to think of three-quarters of the world population as underdeveloped. We wonder how these people have the guts to call the others "underdeveloped." When we wanted to correct this, we invented the phrase "on the way to development." "On the way." Ha, be happy, you are "on the way to development." You have all those computers and artificial intelligence, and you come to bankruptcy because the debt of the United States is three times the debt of all the other world nations together. But as for bank credit and nuclear weapons, we go on playing the game—"on the way to development." If the whole world became like the "developed" world, in seven years the planet would be completely barren. If the whole world consumed the amount of paper that the developed countries do, in two years no single tree would be left on earth.

But let's think of love. Love is not just the passing acceptance of a family. Love is passion. And passion can ultimately challenge you. Mutual fecundation is the conveyance of learning. We will now try to describe, briefly and in an elementary fashion, some of the features that occur in the three kinds of love, without, however, going into a deep analysis of any of them.

First of all, I think that the three traditions, or groups of traditions, as they are summarized by these three words, consider love as central and basic. It is not by accident that *agapē* stands or falls with Christianity. You take *karuṇā* from Buddhism, and Buddhism collapses. You eliminate *bhakti*, and Hinduism may still fix things, but they would get badly scribbled. So, the different kinds of love are essential. They are not accidental. They are not something that you can have or not. They are not there because you love this or that person, because that is better for your digestion. No, no, no! The central, basic love, sympathy, or whatever it is for the three traditions or groups of traditions opens three universes before us.

It is even more than that. Love is an ultimate reality, and that is a challenge. It is an intellectual challenge, although this is not the word I would like to use. But it is much more. If it is not ultimate, then love has no life, no meaning. In that case, the meaning would lie in something behind love, and that meaning would then be more ultimate than love.

If someone asks you, "Why do you love me?" and you cannot give an answer, then your love is finished. If I say, "I love you because you are young," then that love will not last. If I say, "I love you because you are rich," then the rest of you is not so valuable. If I say, "I love you because you are good," then what happens when I get angry? "I love you because . . ."; there must be no "because." "React to goodness, health, intelligence, helpfulness, etc., but love me." There is no "why." Love is the ultimate meaning.

The question about the meaning of love is a loveless question. It destroys love by the very fact that it asks for something beyond the ultimate. We sometimes lack intellectual humility. It is like asking your wife for anything. It is like sending stuff to the Buddha that he may do us a favor, when it might not be good for us, and he could have better things in store for us: "Brother, you cannot ask for that, because you don't know what you are asking. You are not aware of the limits of your question. If you do not know what you ask, you better keep silent." Love has no why. It is nothing beyond itself. It is irreducible to other values. It is irreducible to humility. It is meaninglessness, but sometimes we are scandalized by meaninglessness because we approach reality only with cold reason and a lifeless intellect. Young or sentimentalist people often ask, "Why?" But love has no why—that's why it cannot be grounded on something else. That's why it is free. There is no reason for love, because reality does not need to be teleological. Love is self-grounded. There is not any reason behind it. It is the ultimate force. You need a poet to say, "Love moves the sun and all the other stars."

Third feature. Love is a centrifugal force both in the universe and in the human being. It is a dynamic aspect of reality. Love is centrifugal: It goes, jumps, embraces, kisses, hates, goes out, does not let you be reduced to yourself. But love does not stop at you, does not move with you, it discovers something beyond—maybe your own true self. Love pushes you, drags you, pulls you. Maybe that is why Aristotle said that the Prime Mover was the *eromenon*. As the "erotically beloved," it attracts everything. Eros is something that loves and attracts.

There is a great temptation, in the East and in the West, to place love at a second level, because love does not allow for any reduction to the monolithic Being. In order to love, you need—I'm not going to say "to split," but you anyway need the complexity of reality. You need the other as other, and as non-other. A philosophical example will hopefully make clearer what I mean.

Fichte, Schelling, and undoubtedly Hegel and all Idealists discovered the power of the I. But from there to Marx is only a single step. Marx puts the "not" in front of it. They posit the I. He posits the non-I. But they all forget something that even philologists should know. In my opinion, it is a sign of the times that most languages have forgotten an extraordinarily rich revelation of human wisdom. And that is the dual.

The dual is neither singular nor plural. The dual is the grammatical experience of the Dao. The Tao is not the non-I, and it is not the I. The Tao is not the non-I (the thing or the *esse*, as they say), but it is part and parcel of the very I when the I is whole. The I can really say "I" when it discovers its own I immersed in the words, in the love of the Tao, and vice versa.

I can express this insight by using a different language. Love is not inferior to knowledge. The dichotomy between love and knowledge has been lethal for many a tradition. Lethal, because it reduced love to sentimentalism, to passion, to urge, to a certain type of intuition and liking and disliking, and the intellect to a cutting instrument. But, as Tagore says, "A man of intellect alone is like a knife without a handle. It wounds the hand of the person who uses it." Love and knowledge belong together, so that, if there is not knowledge, there is not love, and if there is no love, there is not knowledge. It does not mean that one is an ingredient of the other. They are constitutively and inherently the same human, basic experience. You are able to *be* inasmuch as you receive, and you are able to receive inasmuch as you are ready to *be*. If love is centrifugal, knowledge is centripetal. The two belong together. You cannot be exhausted in love, if your love is not full of intellect. And you cannot be exhausted in receiving, if you do not transmit what you have and have received.

The highest love is the highest knowledge, in all of these three positions. And the highest knowledge is the highest love. There is not either one of them without the other. This, not only at a psychological level: It is much more, it is a basic and radical reality. You cannot really experience either of them without the other. If you go to the *Upaniṣads* or wherever, you will find that to know is the same as to become what you know. Both are integral parts of the one and the same fundamental human act by which the human being is renewed, and by which every being is built up.

Love is a saving power, whatever we may mean by the word "salvation." It leads to *mukti*, to *mokṣa*, to *nirvāṇa*. It leads to heaven, to the beatific vision, to the fulfillment of one's life. Love has an intrinsic saving and liberating power. It gets rid of all fear and anxiety. Here again, the three traditions—in their corresponding ways—show us this power that saves us. This goes against the grain of our modern civilization. It is independent from our ways. We think that we can love by willpower. We think that we can get love by conviction. We thus make a nuisance of ourselves and give others a hard time. If love is not spontaneous, it is not love. If love is not for the sake of the other, it is not love.

One of the most important and healthy groups in Western society are nuns. But when I meet some of them, I always tell them, "You see, sisters, all you do for your sweet Jesus will not count to your benefit at all. Only the things you do, not for the sake of Jesus, but for the sake of this wretched fellow to whom you give a glass of water, or for a real friend to whom you give five minutes' conversation, or for that other one to whom you offer a smile, only *that* matters."

Spontaneity, not willpower. It does not happen through the "I." Capitalism does not enter here. If I had to use a more academic word for this gift, I would say "grace, *prasāda*, *rūah*," etc. Love has to be a gift. It has to be *given* you. When you are given that gift, you feel how much it is important to love. You cannot command it. It either comes or does not come. If you have a pure heart, it overflows without asking why, without saying, "For the sake of Jesus, for the sake of God, for the sake of whatever." It sometimes happens that, if I do a good thing for the sake of my career, my prestige, my ambition, I wind up with sad feelings. Unless my left hand does not know what the right hand has done, it was just propaganda. When love asks for this and that, then there is no love. Life, knowledge, and love go together. They are self-motivating. They have no why. They have no reason. They don't stand under the willpower, under our power and our will.

Today, the three universes are intermingling in the modern world. I would like to quote a passage of the Dalai Lama. In 1993, after those long-lasting, horrible events in Bombay,[2] the Dalai Lama delivered a message that was reported by the newspapers. He called upon an "indiscriminative, spontaneous, and unlimited compassion for all sentient beings. This is obviously not the usual love that one has for friends or family, which is alive with desire, attachment, and ignorance. The kind of love we should advocate is this wider love that you can have even for someone who has done you harm, your enemy." If I had not mentioned the author of these lines, probably many would have thought of a Christian saying, or a passage from the Gospels, or thought, "This is pure *bhakti*." "Even for your enemy." A love—he says—that is not alive with desire, attachment, and ignorance—that falls in with the classic distinction between the two kinds of love.

Now, this leads me to the contemporary challenge. I said that *agapē* implies the supremacy of the Divine, and that *bhakti* and *karuṇā* are cosmic attitudes, so to speak. In our present days we have an ingrained self-understanding of each of us as a separate individual. Individualism: that's why love has been degraded either to gratification, or to a psychological pattern, or to a sexual option, or to a second degree of the things that lead to our fulfillment, that make us feel better. That is neither *karuṇā* nor *agapē* nor *bhakti*. That may be selfishness, that may be a desire for self-fulfillment, or simply individualism. Against which, the Dalai Lama says that to love just "discriminately," with attachment and desire and ignorance, is not the kind of love which we need in order to live in peace and to live fully. It is not about individualistic love, which leads to anger. This is certainly not *agapē*, not *bhakti*, not *karuṇā*.

Now, is it not true that we, in our contemporary world, have a certain inborn resistance toward universal love? But how can I have an indiscriminative love? Would I not be inhuman if I did not feel that my child is different from any other child in the world, even though that other child is starving? Here, the "middle way" is needed. If I am incapable of loving in this universal way, my love for my child will just be a selfish attachment, which can give me some little pleasures, but certainly, afterward, much friction and many headaches. Many bad conflicts will arise, since the child is not going to live up to my standards, or what I would like him to be. To combine the total universal love with the concrete love: *that* is wisdom. Wisdom is the insight that lets me discover in the concrete, in my child, all the children of the world; in my wife, my husband, the entire manhood and womanhood of the world; in that flower, the infinite beauty of the whole creation; in that conversation, all the gusto of being.

If we do not live up to this kind of insight and experience, then any further step will be the same as the one before it. Then everything is a *telos*, then everything is

[2] A series of thirteen terrorist bomb explosions, making 250 victims.

final, definite. If everything is not irreducible and incomparable to anything else, we have lost the love in our lives, and we reduce ourselves to thinking machines.

One of our most important tasks, in philosophy, is to reintroduce love into the so-called external world. I don't want, now, to go into epistemology. I think epistemology is a wrong approach, but that would be a different issue. When love is seen as an intrinsic part of knowledge, then knowledge is put in its own place, because you feel that the union with what you know is never ended, never fulfilled. In fact, the very nature of reality is polarity, is love, is this very moment. If we reintegrate love with knowledge, we will overcome the epistemological gap between subject and object, which otherwise could not be overcome.

Love is Trinitarian: neither one nor two. It is the experience of the warp and woof of the very nature of reality. This, for me, is the cross-cultural challenge, letting us overcome our individualism. Then we can discover, through experience, the way love permeates us. We can discover that these loves and knowledge—to quote the *Gītā*—are precisely the two basic sides of this complex, fantastic, beautiful reality.

Glossary

(Unless otherwise specified, the terms in the glossary are Sanskrit.)

advaita: a-dualism (*a-dvaita*). Spiritual intuition that sees ultimate reality as neither monistic nor dualistic. The recognition that the merely quantitative problem of the one and the many in dialectical reasoning does not apply to the realm of ultimate reality. The latter, in fact, possesses polarities which cannot be divided into multiple separate units; not to be confused with monism.

advaitin: a follower of advaita, who professes a-duality of the ātman-brahman.

agapē (Gr.): love.

Agni: the sacrificial fire and the Divine Fire, one of the most important Gods or divine manifestations, the mediator or priest for Men and Gods.

agora (Gr.): public square for people to assemble in the cities of ancient Greece.

aham: first person nominative. *Aham* (as a principle of ontological existence or being) is generally distinguished from *ahaṃkāra* (as a psychological principle).

aiōn (Gr.): cosmic time, eternity; also a period of life.

aliud (Lat.): the other, neutral.

alius (Lat.): the other (other I).

anātman: absence of *ātman*, of the substantiality of an individual ontological Self.

anātmavāda: mainly Buddhist doctrine of the insubstantiality of the ā*tman* or Self.

Anthrōpos (Gr.): man, in a general sense.

āryasatyāni: the Noble Truths (traditionally four in number) that summarize the teachings of Buddha.

ātman: principle of life, breath, the body, the Self (from the root *an*, to breathe). Refers to the whole, undivided person and also to the innermost center of man, his incorruptible nucleus, which in the *Upaniṣad* is shown to be identical to Brahman. The Self or inner essence of the universe and man. Ontological center in Hinduism, which is negated in Buddhism.

āyus: vital force, vitality, life, temporal existence, the length of life granted to man. See Gr. *aiōn*, aeons.

Bhagavad-gītā: The "Song of the Glorious Lord," the "Song of the Sublime One," a famous ancient Indian didactic poem included in the *Mahābhārata* (often called the "New Testament of Hinduism"), the most well-known sacred book in India.

bhakti: devotion, submission, love for God, personal relationship with God, devotional mysticism. One of the paths of salvation through union with the divinity.

bodhisattva: the enlightened one. In particular, in Mahāyāna Buddhism, he who, having attained liberation on earth, makes a vow to help all other beings attain liberation before they enter *nirvāṇa*.

brahman: prayer, sacrifice, the inherent power in sacrifice; the Absolute, the ultimate reason underlying all things; in the *Upaniṣad* it is identified with the immanent Self (*ātman*). Also, one of the four priests who perform the sacrifice or the clergy in general.

buddhakāya: lit. "body of Buddha," universal solidarity, the behavior of the Buddha.

circumincessio (Lat.): compenetration of the three Persons of the Trinity. Corresponds to the greek *perichōrēsis*.

coincidentia oppositorum (Lat.): coincidence of the opposites.

compunctio cordis (Lat.): repentance, heartfelt sorrow, the essential attitude of monastic spirituality.

contemplatio (Lat.): contemplation of the world as the temple of God.

dharma: cosmic order, justice, duty, religious law, religious and social observances transmitted by tradition; religion as a collection of practices and laws. That which holds the world together. One of the four human purposes. (cfr. *puruṣāsartha*).

dharmakāya: mystical body of *dharma* in Mahayana Buddhism.

dhvani: connotation, allusion, poetic style.

diacronico: that which extends through time.

diatopico: that which extends through space.

duḥkha: disquieted, uneasy, distress, pain, suffering, anguish (lit. "having a poor axle hole," i.e. that which does not turn smoothly), a basic concept in Buddhism and Hinduism. Opposite of *sukha*.

Durgā: "difficult to access"; "the inaccessible." One of the most ancient names of the Divine Mother, consort of Śiva.

dvandva: pair of opposites, e.g., cold and heat, pleasure and pain.

ekam: one; generally the primordial oneness, the origin of all, later identified with Brahman.

epektasis (Gr.): dilatation, expansion, extension; man's trust in his divine destiny, according to St. Gregory of Nyssa. Hope.

epochē (Gr.): "suspension"; the suspending of all subjective judgements in the description of phenomena.

erōs (Lat.): love.

eschatology: from the Greek *eschaton*, which refers to the ultimate, both in relation to time (the last things that will happen, the end of this life), and in ontological importance (the ultimate reality).

exclusivism, inclusivism, pluralism: terms indicating an attitude toward non-Christian religions, which: a) considers the latter as being excluded from the salvation of Christ, b) absolutizes the salvation of Christ by granting a place to non-Christian religions, and c) recognizes that the different visions of the world are mutually irreducible.

fania [*phania*] (Gr.): direct manifestation, from *phanos*, lamp, light.

fides quaerens intellectum (Lat.): "faith seeking understanding."

Gītā: cfr. *Bhagavad-gītā*.

guru: See *ācārya*; usually refers to one who has attained fulfilment.

homeomorphism: theory used in comparative religion to discover functional equivalence in two or more religions.

hypostasis (Gr.): "that which stands beneath": substance, person. A key and controversial word in the first disputes regarding the Trinity, especially due to the ambiguity of its Latin tradition.

Īśa, Īśvara: the Lord, from the root *īś-*, to be lord, to guide, to possess. Although a generic term for Lord, in posterior religious systems it is more often used for Śiva than for Viṣṇu. In the Vedānta it is the manifested, qualified (*saguṇa*) aspect of Brahman.

jñāna: knowledge (from the root *jñā-*, to know), intuition, wisdom; frequently the highest intuitive comprehension, the attaining of *ātman* or *brahman*. *Jñāna* is the result of meditation or revelation. Cfr. *jñāna-mārga*.

kairos (Gr.): time, opportune moment, crucial point at which the destiny changes phase, epoch.

kalpa: a period of the world, a cosmic time of variable length.

kāma: the creative power of desire, personified as the God of love; one of the *puruṣārtha* or four life-goals of Hinduism.

karma, *karman*: lit. "act, deed, action," from the root *kṛ*, to act, to do; originally the sacred action, sacrifice, rite, later also moral act. The result of all actions and deeds according to the law of *karman* that regulates actions and their results in the universe. Later also connected with rebirth, it indicates the link between the actions carried out by a subject and his destiny in the cycle of deaths and rebirths.

karuṇā: comprehension and compassion; an important concept in Buddhism.

kenōsis (Gr.): annihilation, emptying of oneself, overcoming of one's *ego*.

kerygma (Gr.): message, proclamation (of the word of God), from the Greek *keryssō* (to proclaim), corresponding to the first level of the evangelical teaching.

kosmos (Gr.): order, the ordered universe, the wholeness of the world.

Kṛṣṇa: *avatāra* of Viṣṇu (lit. "the black one") and one of the most popular Gods. He does not appear in the *Veda*, but he is the revealer of the *Bhagavad-gītā*. He is the divine child and the shepherd God of Vṛndāvana, the incarnation of love and the playful God *par excellence*.

kṣatriya: member of the second caste (*varṇa*), which includes kings, warriors and aristocrats (·*brahmán*, ·*vaiśya*, ·*śūdra*).

kurukṣetra: the battlefield where the war of the *Mahābhārata* was fought and where Kṛṣṇa revealed the *Bhagavad-gītā* to Arjuna.

lama: head of Tibetan Buddhism.

logos (Gr.): word, thought, judgement, reason. In the New Testament Christ as the word of God (Jn 1).

mādhyamika: the school of the "middle way" in Mahāyāna Buddhism.

Mahābhārata: epic poem that tells the legendary story of the Indian people and expounds its prescriptive values.

mahāvākya: "great saying." Refers to great expressions of the *Upaniṣad* that express very concisely the content of the experience of the Absolute.

Mahāyāna: "great vehicle." Branch of Buddhism established in India two thousand years ago.

maithuna, *mithuna*: union, mating, copulation both in a sexual and metaphorical sense.

metanoia (Gr.): transformation, change of mentality or heart, conversion; going beyond (*meta*) the mental or rational (*nous*).

mikrotheos (Gr.): indicates divinity as a whole epitomized in man.

mokṣa: ultimate liberation from *saṃsāra*, the cycle of births and deaths, and from *karman*, ignorance and limitation: salvation. Homeomorphic equivalent of *sōteria*.

mukti: cfr. *mokṣa*.

mumukṣutva: desiderative form of the root *muc-* (See *mokṣa*); desire for salvation, and yearning for liberation, the necessary prerequisite for embarking on the path of liberation.

mūrti: solid form, body, hence incarnation, person, figure, statue, image. Mainly used for the sacred images of Gods. The *Veda* do not describe any cult of the image (*pūjā*), which is a development posterior to Hinduism.

mythos (Gr.): the horizon of presence which does not require further enquiry.

nāma-rūpa: "name and form," the phenomenic world that constitutes the *saṃsāra*.

Nāgārjuna: one of the most important philosophers of Mahāyāna Buddhism, founder of the Mādhyamika school.

nairātmyavāda: the theory of the denial of *ātman*, the self, the soul; radical unthinkability of the origin; see also *anātmavāda*.

nirvāṇa: lit. "the going out (of the flame)," extinction. The word does not refer to a condition, but indicates liberation from all dichotomy and conditioning, whether it be birth and death, time and space, being and non-being, ignorance and knowledge, or final extinction including time, space and being; the ultimate destination for Buddhism and Jainism.

noēma (Gr.): in the phenomenology of Husserl the unit of intellectual perception.

nomos (Gr.): custom, rule, law.

on (Gr.): participle of the verb "to be" (*einai*); being; that which is higher; entity; that which exists.

ontonomy: intrinsic connection of an entity in relation to the totality of Being, the constitutive order (*nomos*) of every being as Being (*on*), harmony that allows the interdependence of all things.

Pantokrator (Gr.): the Sovereign of all; designates Christ and also God.

pāramārthika: ultimate level, ultimate reality, true reality.

penthos (Gr.): repentance, sadness.

perichōrēsis (Gr.): notion of the early Church Trinitarian doctrine describing the interpenetration of divine persons. Corresponds to the Latin *circumincessio.*

phainomenon (Gr.): phenomenon, that which appears, that which shows itself.

pisteuma (Gr.): from *pisteuō*, to believe; that which the believer believes, the intentional sense of religious phenomena, the homeomorphic equivalent of *noēma*.

plērōma (Gr.): fullness, the full, complete.

polis (Gr.): the city-state of ancient Greece.

prajñā: understanding and awareness, consciousness, wisdom. See *gnōsis*, *jñāna*.

prasāda: divine grace, benevolence, serenity (though not Vedic).

pratītyasamutpāda: Buddhist doctrine of the "conditioned genesis" or "dependent origination," which claims that nothing exists for itself but carries within itself the conditions for its own existence, and that everything is mutually conditioned in the cycle of existence.

primum analogatum (Lat.): the point of reference for every analogy.

psychē (Gr.): soul, psyche, heart, animated being.

Puruṣa: the Person, the spirit, man. Both the primordial man of the cosmic dimension (*Ṛg-veda*) and the "inner man," the spiritual person existing within man (*Upaniṣad*). In the Sāṃkhya it is the spiritual principle of reality (See *prakṛti*).

Rāmāyaṇ: Indian epic poem.

res cogitans/res extensa (Lat.): thinking thing / extended thing, division of reality according to Descartes.

Ṛg-veda: the most ancient and important of the *Veda* texts.

sādhu: straight, leading straight to the goal, good, just. A good person, renunciant, monk or ascetic.

saeculum (Lat.): the human age, era, century; also spirit of the day.

Śaṃkara: eighth-century Hindu philosopher and teacher; one of the most famous exponents of non-dualist Vedānta.

saṃnyāsin: renunciant, ascetic; pertaining to the fourth stage or period of life (*āśrama*), to some the superior stage.

saṃsāra: the impermanent phenomenic world and the condition of identification with it, the temporal existence, the cycle of births and deaths, of conditioned existences; state of dependence and slavery.

sarvam duḥkham: "all is suffering," a classic Buddhist statement.

sensus plenior (Lat.): the fullest meaning (of a scripture).

Śiva: propitious, gracious, pleasant, benevolent. He who is of good omen; in the *Veda* it is Rudra who is known to the *Śvetāśvatara-upaniṣad* as Śiva, one of the most important Gods of Hindu tradition. He is the destroyer of the universe (See also *Brahmā*, *Viṣṇu*), and also the great *yogin* and model of ascetics. His consort is Pārvatī or Umā.

sōma (Gr.): body.

sōtēria (Gr.): salvation, liberation, redemption.

śravaṇa: "hearing, listening"; the ability to hear or to receive the teaching from the lips of the teachers. Listening in the *Veda* is the first of the three levels that the Vedānta considers necessary for attaining spiritual knowledge.

śūnya, śūnyatā: void, vacuity, nothingness, the structural condition of reality and all things; represents the ultimate reality in Buddhism (See *nirvāṇa*).

sūtrā: lit. "yarn, thread of a fabric." Short aphorism in a sacred text that generally cannot be understood without a comment (*bhāṣya*). The literature of the *sūtra* is part of the *smṛti* and is conceived to be easily memorized.

svadharma: intrinsic personal order, suited to one's own situation, caste, religion, etc.

Śvetaketu: son of Gautama; in the *Chāndogya-upaniṣad* a famous disciple of Uddalaka, to whom is imparted the highest teaching on the *ātman* and the *brahman*, which ends with: *tat tvam asi* ("that is you").

taṇhā (Pāli): thirst; thirst for existence; origin of all suffering, according to Buddhism. See *tṛṣṇā*.

tao or *dao* (Chin.): "way," a central concept in Chinese philosophy, especially Taoism.

Tathāgata: lit. "the one thus come, who has attained being, who has extinguished himself," an appellative of Buddha.

tat tvam asi: "that is you," an Upaniṣadic expression meaning that *ātman* is ultimately Brahman. One of the four Great Sayings (*mahāvākyāni*) of the *Upaniṣad*, as taught to Śvetaketu.

tempiternity: non-separation between time and eternity.

topos/topoi (Gr.): place/places.

triloka: the "triple world," totality of the universe, consisting in three realms: earth, atmosphere and sky, or earth, sky and the nether regions (later called hell); the inhabitants of the three worlds are Gods, men, and demons.

tṛṣṇā: thirst; See *taṇhā*.

turīya: the fourth foot of *brahman*, the last quarter; the state of pure transcendence, which is reached only through self-annihilation [*·vaiśvānara*, *·taijasa*, *·prajñā*].

tvam: you (personal pronoun, second person singular).

Upaniṣad: fundamental sacred teaching in the form of texts constituting the end of the *Veda*; part of the revelation (*śruti*) and basis of posterior Hindu thought.

vedānta: lit. "end of the *Veda*," i.e., the *Upaniṣad* as the climax of Vedic wisdom. In the sense of Uttaramī māṃsā or Vedāntavāda, a system of Indian philosophy (Advaita-vedānta, Dvaita-vedānta, etc.) based on the *Upaniṣad*, which teaches a spiritual interpretation of the *Veda*; one of the last schools of Hindu philosophical thought, of which the most renowned representatives include Śaṅkara, Rāmānuja and Madhva.

viator (Lat.): traveller, novice, aspirant, disciple.

Viṣṇu: important God in Hinduism, featured in the ancient *Veda*; his name means "the all-pervading one." Associated with the sun, he is famous for his three great strides with which he measured the three worlds. He later became the second component of the *trimūrti*, the preserver, and is mainly worshipped in his *avatāra* (See *Kṛṣṇa*, *Rāma*).

viṣṇuite: follower of Viṣṇuism, one of the three great religious orientations in Hinduism.

vyāvahārika: "relating to earthly matters, to mundane life," i.e. the earthly way of seeing, the practical perspective; the relative level.

yoni: female reproductive organ, womb, hence also home, place of rest; also the support or inner part of all things.

Index of Original Texts in This Volume

The Intrareligious Dialogue: Original text: *The Intrareligious Dialogue*. New York: Paulist Press, 1999.

Some Observations on Interreligious Dialogue: From a lecture delivered by Panikkar in Montserrat (Barcelona) in November 2004, according to the notes taken by Pierre-François de Béthune. Published in *DIM/MID International Bulletin* (Louvain-la-Neuve) no. 2 (2004): 17–21.

The Encounter of Religions: The Unavoidable Dialogue: Re-edition of *The Encounter of Religions: The Unavoidable Dialogue*, *Jñanadeepa* (Pune) 3, no. 2 (2000); inaugural article *Begegnung der Religionen. Das unvermeidliche Gespräch* of the new magazine *Dialog der Religionen* (Munich) 1991.

Human Dialogue within Religious Interindependence: Speech held at the Pio Manzù Research Centre, Rimini, Italy. Originally published in *Il fuoco nel cristallo* [Fire in the crystal] (Rimini), no. 21 (2001): 136–41.

For a Dialogue among Civilizations: Reworking of "Per un dialogo delle civiltà," a conference presentation at Città di Castello, Italy, August 1983. Translated from Italian by Daniella Engel.

Śūnyatā and Plērōma: *The Buddhist and Christian Response to the Human Predicament*: Original edition in J. M. Robinson (ed.), *Religion and the Humanizing of Man*, 67–86. Waterloo, Ontario: Council on the Study of Religion, 1972.

Advaita and Bhakti: A Hindū-Christian Dialogue: Original text: "*Advaita e Bakti*. Lettera da Vrindabran." *Humanitas* (Brescia) 10 (1965): 991–1001; later in Raimon Panikkar, *Myth, Faith, and Hermeneutics*, chapter 9. New York: Paulist Press, 1979.

Bhakti–Karuṇā–Agapē: An Intercultural Challenge: Original text *Bhakti–Karuṇā–Agapē. An Inter-Cultural Challenge*. In M. Zlomislic, D. Goicoechea, S. K. Tebbutt, R. Kaushik (eds.), *Bhakti–Karuṇā–Agapē with Raimon Panikkar*, 39–53. New York: Global Academic Publishing, 2003.

Index of Names

About the Author

An international authority on spirituality, the study of religions, and intercultural dialogue, Raimon Panikkar made intercultural and dialogical pluralism one of the hallmarks of his research, becoming a master "bridge builder," tireless in the promotion of dialogue between Western culture and the great Oriental Hindū and Buddhist traditions.

Born in 1918 in Barcelona of a Spanish Catholic mother and an Indian Hindū father, he was part of a plurality of traditions: Indian and European, Hindū and Christian, scientific and humanistic.

Panikkar held degrees in chemistry, philosophy, and theology, and was ordained a Catholic priest in 1946. He delivered courses and lectures in major European, Indian, and American universities.

A member of the International Institute of Philosophy (Paris), of the permanent Tribunal of the Peoples (Rome), and of the UNESCO Commission for intercultural dialogue, he also founded various philosophical journals and intercultural study centers. He held conferences in each of the five continents (including the renowned Gifford Lectures in 1988–1989 on "Trinity and Atheism").

Panikkar received international recognitions including honorary doctorates from the University of the Balearic Islands in 1997, the University of Tübingen in 2004, Urbino in 2005, and Girona in 2008, as well as prizes ranging from the "Premio Menéndez Pelayo de Humanidades" for his book *El concepto de naturaleza* in Madrid in 1946 to the "Premio Nonino 2001 a un maestro del nostro tempo" in Italy.

Panikkar lived in Tavertet in the Catalonian mountains, where he continued his contemplative experience and cultural activities from 1982 until his death on August 26, 2010. There he founded and presided over the intercultural study center Vivarium. Panikkar published more than fifty books in various languages and hundreds of articles on the philosophy of religion, theology, the philosophy of science, metaphysics, and Indology.

From the dialogue between religions to the peaceful cohabitation of peoples; from reflections on the future of the technological society to major work on political and social intelligence; from the recognition that all interreligious dialogue is based on an intrareligious dialogue to the promotion of open knowledge of other religions, of which he is a mediator; from his penetrating analysis of the crisis in spirituality to the practice of meditation and the rediscovery of his monastic identity; from the invitation of *colligite fragmenta* as a path toward the integration of reality to the proposal of a new innocence, Panikkar embodies a personal journey of fulfillment.

Among his most important publications with Orbis are: *The Trinity and the Religious Experience of Man* (1973); *Worship and Secular Man* (1973); *The Unknown Christ of Hinduism* (1981); *The Silence of God* (1989); *The Rhythm of Being* (1989); *Cosmotheandric Experience* (1993); and *Christophany* (2004).